美国文学学习辅导教程
（新升级版）
A Coursebook for the Study and Review of American Literature
（Newly Upgraded）

主　编：李正栓
Chief Compiler: Li Zhengshuan

编　者：李美萱　侯雨佳　刘凤月
Co-compilers: Li Meixuan　Hou Yujia　Liu Fengyue

图书在版编目（CIP）数据

美国文学学习辅导教程：新升级版：英文 / 李正栓主编 . —北京：商务印书馆，2023
ISBN 978-7-100-22735-3

Ⅰ.①美… Ⅱ.①李… Ⅲ.①英语—阅读教学—高等学校—教材 ②文学欣赏—美国 Ⅳ.① H319.4：I

中国国家版本馆 CIP 数据核字（2023）第 128911 号

权利保留，侵权必究。

美国文学学习辅导教程（新升级版）
李正栓 主编

商 务 印 书 馆 出 版
（北京王府井大街36号 邮政编码100710）
商 务 印 书 馆 发 行
北京新华印刷有限公司印刷
ISBN 978-7-100-22735-3

| 2024 年 1 月第 1 版 | 开本 710×1000 1/16 |
| 2024 年 1 月北京第 1 次印刷 | 印张 22¼ |

定价：59.80 元

内容提要

《美国文学学习辅导教程（新升级版）》共分为两编。上编为文学史基础知识部分，下编为经典文学作品选读部分。按照美国文学史发展阶段，上编针对每个发展阶段的时代特征、重要作家及其代表作品设计了多种题型的练习，主要有填空、单项选择、作家作品匹配、文学术语解释、简答论述等形式。下编涵盖了美国文学经典作品选段，选材详尽、全面，具有代表性，填空、选择、简评等题目的设计涵盖国内出版的众多美国文学教材的内容。此外，针对部分文学作品选段，设计了中西文学作品对比赏析练习，在提高学生美国文学欣赏能力的同时，弘扬中国文学的博大精深，将"课程思政"有机融入美国文学的学习中。本书有三个附录。附录一是美国文学主要作家作品简录，按历史年代顺序，总结各个时期的作家及其作品，供学生快速背诵。附录二是常用文学术语。这两个附录的设计是为了帮助学生对美国文学及作品有较全面的掌握。附录三是专门的常用美国文学术语。

本书作为一本实用参考书，适用于英语专业本科生、商务英语专业本科生、翻译专业本科生、自学考试英语专业本科生、报考英语语言文学专业研究生的广大考生以及广大美国文学爱好者。同时，本书也为广大美国文学教师进行教学和测试提供了必要参考。

前　言

　　我国高校英语专业高年级、高等教育自学考试英语专业本科段、英语专业函授本科均开设英美文学史及选读课，文学史与文学选读分别开设或合在一起，英国文学与美国文学分别开设或合在一起，视具体师资和学时而定。

　　2013年，教育部开始编制本科各专业教学质量国家标准，对课程进行严格要求。2018年，《普通高等学校本科专业类教学质量国家标准（外国语言文学类）》（以下简称《国标》）问世。2020年，《普通高等学校本科外国语言文学类专业教学指南》（以下简称《指南》）问世。这两个文件成为英语专业建设的重要依据。教育部认为，在树人过程中必须加强立德，培养具有中国情怀和国际视野的合格人才。2020年，教育部印发了《高等学校课程思政建设指导纲要》（以下简称《纲要》）。

　　《国标》将英语文学课程设置为英语专业核心课程，旨在提高学生对外国文学作品的主要内容和主题思想的理解和评论能力。《指南》指出，英语文学这个概念和范围扩大了传统的英美文学概念，但由于学时和师资有限，各学校仍以英国文学和美国文学构成英语专业重要的课程，更符合专业建设实际情况。多学固然好，学透更重要。在培养方案中，英国文学史和美国文学史作为必修课出现。《纲要》要求把"立德树人"根本任务落实到教学的方方面面，全面推进高校课程思政建设。讲授英国文学和美国文学的同时，还得加强课程思政建设，即把英美文学教学和中国文化教学与思考融通起来。

　　国家自2000年以来对英语专业教学大纲不断修订，表明了对英语专业教育的重视以及对英语专业人才要求的不断提高。教育部指示，要重视课程体系化，要重视课程质量，更要重视课程的德育培养作用。高校英语专业教学不仅要传授语言和文学等专业知识，更要承担起传承和传播中华文明和中华文化的神圣使命，将中西方意识形态和价值观念比较融入到教学中，使专业教育和德育教育同向同行，从而建立外语人才的文化自信和文化认同感，培养学生的国际视野、家国情怀和跨文化交际能力。

应当说，英美文学相关课程是我国高校英语院系的传统课程，是培养英语语言文学专业本科生及研究生基本功的必经途径，更是帮助外语人才树立正确的世界观、价值观和人生观，提升道德修养的重要阵地。近年来，全国各级各类出版社出版了大量优秀的有关教材，为学生学习和教师教学提供了诸多选择。但在日常教学中，经常有学生说英美文学课高深莫测，想要学懂实属不易，加之市面上可供练习的书相对较少，难以检验学习效果，更不能满足考前复习的需要。此外，我们在教学实践中发现，如果能在美国文学的学习过程中，加入同时代、同题材、同风格的中国文学相关内容，会增加学生文学学习的兴趣，更有助于培养学生对不同意识形态和价值观念的批判思维能力，在学好美国文学的同时，能更好地引导学生深刻领悟中国文化的博大精深。

我曾先后主编出版过数本英美文学练习书籍，受到学生和教师的厚爱，成为学生津津乐道的应试宝典，也成为教师考试命题的重要参考，被有的学校选入本科阶段必读书目和研究生入学考试参考书目。更令我欣慰的是，不少教师见到我后告诉我，他们是通过我编的练习考上了硕士，并为读博士打下了坚实的基础。近年来，英美文学教材又有新发展，在"新文科"建设背景下，在"课程思政"指导思想下，有必要编写一套最新的学习辅导教程，以适应新时代和新读者。

本书以外语教学与研究出版社出版的《美国文学史及选读》（第三版）和其他几本主要的美国文学教材为蓝本。为了使本书适应性强，能让使用不同教材的学生都能使用本书进行复习和巩固，我参考并吸收了多家出版社出版的美国文学教材的知识点，争取做到集各家之长，满足日常学习之需，全方位应对各类考试。有不少考上研究生的同学过分夸大了我主编的此类文学练习教材，说认真做书中的练习就能考上研究生。但我认为，还要学好本校教师为你选定的教材。学习教材之余大量地做我主编的书中的练习，效果的确非常好。

本书设计了各种各样的练习，主要有填空、单项选择、作家作品匹配、文学术语解释、简答论述等。全书共分五大板块：美国文学史练习、美国文学选段练习、参考答案、附录、参考文献。按照时间发展脉络，美国文学史练习板块由以下六大部分组成："Literature of Colonial America" "Literature of Reason and Revolution" "Literature of Romanticism" "Literature of Realism" "Twentieth-Century Literature I: Before WWII" "Twentieth-Century Literature II: After WWII"。

本书亮点之一就是美国文学选段练习部分单独成一板块，该板块直击考试重点，所选文学作品篇幅长短适中，代表性强，具有十分重要的预测作用。另外，本书题量丰富，实现了基本点、重点、难点的全覆盖。

本书后共有三个附录，比较有价值，能帮助学生高效地理解教材内容。它们分别是：美国文学主要作家作品简录、常用文学术语和常用美国文学术语。值得一提的是，本书对重点作家及作品做了整理和简录，紧跟时代要求，帮助学生精准定位重点与非重点。文学基础知识对增加和巩固考生的文学知识大有裨益。文学术语或文学批评知识仅供进一步的选读，略有难度，是为适应某些学校研究生命题而做的特殊安排。三个附录均参考了一些专家的成果（自1986年到2022年出版的主要教材），已在参考文献部分注明。我们在此代表广大读者向各位专家表示衷心的感谢。

本着实用、好用的原则，本书不单独介绍研究生阶段才学习的复杂、深奥的文学批评知识，而是将文学基础知识和文学术语合并，高度浓缩，呈现精华；因此本书条目更精简，内容更实际，并伴有实例，便于学生理解和记忆，对文学练习部分是有益的补充。

《美国文学学习辅导教程（新升级版）》共分两编。上编为文学史部分，下编为作品选读部分。这两编针对美国文学史上的重点作家及重点作品设计了各种各样的练习，例如填空、选择、辨认、配对、简答等形式。需说明的是，本次编写对书中美国文学史的时期划分更合理，共分为六个部分，符合大多数文学教材的编写体例。另外，附录中的作家作品中英文对照，非常方便学生快速学习。

《美国文学学习辅导教程（新升级版）》注重满足各种不同教学形式、教学层次以及自主学习的需要。希望广大的英语专业本科生、自学考试本科生、函授本科生及报考英语语言文学专业研究生的同学学习本书后有很大收获。

由于编者水平有限，错误或不当之处仍在所难免，望不吝指正。

李正栓

2024 年 1 月

目 录
CONTENTS

内容提要 ··· i
前言 ··· iii

上编　美国文学史练习
Part One　Exercises on the History of American Literature

Part I　　Literature of Colonial America ································ 3
Part II 　Literature of Reason and Revolution ························ 13
Part III　Literature of Romanticism ···································· 23
Part IV　Literature of Realism ··· 37
Part V 　Twentieth-Century Literature I: Before WWII ············· 55
Part VI　Twentieth-Century Literature II: After WWII ············· 88

下编　美国文学选段练习
Part Two　Exercises on Selected Readings of American Literature

Exercise 1 ··· 103
Exercise 2 ··· 103
Exercise 3 ··· 104
Exercise 4 ··· 104
Exercise 5 ··· 106
Exercise 6 ··· 107
Exercise 7 ··· 108
Exercise 8 ··· 110
Exercise 9 ··· 111
Exercise 10 ·· 112

Exercise 11	114
Exercise 12	114
Exercise 13	116
Exercise 14	116
Exercise 15	117
Exercise 16	118
Exercise 17	119
Exercise 18	120
Exercise 19	121
Exercise 20	121
Exercise 21	122
Exercise 22	122
Exercise 23	123
Exercise 24	124
Exercise 25	124
Exercise 26	125
Exercise 27	126
Exercise 28	127
Exercise 29	127
Exercise 30	128
Exercise 31	129
Exercise 32	130
Exercise 33	131
Exercise 34	132
Exercise 35	133
Exercise 36	134
Exercise 37	135
Exercise 38	136
Exercise 39	137
Exercise 40	139
Exercise 41	140
Exercise 42	141

Exercise 43 ·· 143

Exercise 44 ·· 144

上编参考答案
Key to Exercises of Part One

Part I	Literature of Colonial America ·································	147
Part II	Literature of Reason and Revolution ···························	160
Part III	Literature of Romanticism ·······································	163
Part IV	Literature of Realism ···	167
Part V	Twentieth-Century Literature I: Before WWII ················	177
Part VI	Twentieth-Century Literature II: After WWII ················	202

下编参考答案
Key to Exercises of Part Two

Exercise 1 ··· 223

Exercise 2 ··· 223

Exercise 3 ··· 223

Exercise 4 ··· 224

Exercise 5 ··· 224

Exercise 6 ··· 225

Exercise 7 ··· 225

Exercise 8 ··· 226

Exercise 9 ··· 226

Exercise 10 ··· 227

Exercise 11 ··· 228

Exercise 12 ··· 231

Exercise 13 ··· 235

Exercise 14 ··· 236

Exercise 15 ··· 237

Exercise 16 ··· 238

Exercise 17 ··· 239

Exercise 18 ··· 239

Exercise 19 ·· 240
Exercise 20 ·· 241
Exercise 21 ·· 241
Exercise 22 ·· 241
Exercise 23 ·· 242
Exercise 24 ·· 243
Exercise 25 ·· 244
Exercise 26 ·· 244
Exercise 27 ·· 246
Exercise 28 ·· 246
Exercise 29 ·· 246
Exercise 30 ·· 247
Exercise 31 ·· 248
Exercise 32 ·· 249
Exercise 33 ·· 250
Exercise 34 ·· 252
Exercise 35 ·· 252
Exercise 36 ·· 254
Exercise 37 ·· 255
Exercise 38 ·· 256
Exercise 39 ·· 257
Exercise 40 ·· 258
Exercise 41 ·· 259
Exercise 42 ·· 260
Exercise 43 ·· 261
Exercise 44 ·· 263

附录一 美国文学主要作家作品简录·· 265
附录二 常用文学术语·· 290
附录三 常用美国文学术语··· 324

参考文献·· 341

上编
美国文学史练习

Part One
Exercises on the History of American Literature

Part I

Literature of Colonial America

I. Fill in the Blanks.

1. At the beginning of the seventeenth century, _____ and _____ explorers explored the vast continental area that was to become the United States.
2. John Smith's vision helped lure the _____ and the _____ who were suppressed by the Church of England in the early 1600s.
3. The first American writer is _____, who was one of the governors of the colony.
4. Over the years the Puritans built a way of life that was in harmony with their somber religion. Their values included _____, _____, _____, and _____.
5. The Puritans regarded themselves as a _____ people, and it followed logically that anyone who challenged their way of life was opposing God's will and was not to be accepted.
6. Some of Anne Bradstreet's later poems were written for her _____ and revealed the process of her spiritual growth after her whole-hearted acceptance of _____ doctrine.
7. The poetry of _____ was also considered as a document of the struggles of a Puritan wife against the hardships of New England colonial life, and in some way is a statement to predicament of the women of the age.
8. The meaning of the poem _____ shows Edward Taylor's desires to be closer to God while doing everything pleasing to the Puritan religion.

9. In the poem *Huswifery*, Edward Taylor compared himself to the _____ used for spinning and weaving.
10. The _____, which makes the blanket, is compared to the creator— _____, which is the most influential comparison in the poem *Huswifery*.
11. The first distinctly American literature in English was written by _____.
12. The writers of the Southern and Middle Colonies made their greatest contributions to American literature in the eighteenth century, in the Age of _____ and _____.
13. _____ dominated much of the earliest American writing.
14. The Puritans wished to restore _____ to church services and the authority of the _____ to theology.
15. The Church of England was too close to _____ in doctrine, form of worship, and organization of authority.
16. John Cotton and Roger Williams represented the _____ mind.
17. _____ is the first true poet in the American colonies.
18. _____ became known as the "Tenth Muse" who appeared in America.
19. The English immigrants who formed the main stream of the American national history mainly settled in _____ and _____.
20. Among the members of the first permanent English settlement in North America, a man was called _____, whose reports of exploration have been honored as the first authentically American literature written in English.
21. John Smith's exploration enlightened the Pilgrims and the Puritans who viewed themselves as new saints with a spiritual mission to _____ and create a New Israel, _____, in the America that John Smith had described.
22. As the connotation of the word "puritan" itself implies, the Puritan was once called a "_____" by the opponents of the group in a sarcastic tone.

23. Because of their eagerness to completely break from the Church of England, Puritans were also known as "_____".
24. Edward Taylor was the most accomplished poetic craftsman of the early years. His work inherited the essence of the leading _____ poets of the _____ century.
25. Most of Edward Taylor's works deal with a shared theme about _____, with a host of poems based directly on the Psalms.
26. Edward Taylor was famous for his splendid poetic achievements. However, he did not publish any of his poems in his whole life. It was not until _____ that manuscripts of his poems were found, and a complete edition of his poems emerged in _____.

II. Choose the Best Answer for Each Question.

1. The first writings that we call American were written by the settlers in genres of the _____ and journals of these settlements, which were about their voyage to the new land, about adapting themselves to unfamiliar climates and crops, and about dealing with Indians.
   A. novels　　B. narratives　　C. novellas　　D. tales
2. The first permanent English settlement in North America was established at _____, _____ in 1607.
   A. Jamestown; Virginia　　　B. Johntown; Vermont
   C. Jamestown; West Virginia　D. Johntown; West Virginia
3. In _____, Anne Bradstreet expressed the true love between her husband and her.
   A. *To My Dear and Loving Husband*
   B. *Huswifery*
   C. *To My Dear and Beloved Husband*
   D. *Of the Vanity of All Worldly Creatures*
4. The rhyme scheme of the poem *To My Dear and Loving Husband*

was written in one single 12-line stanza of _____.

    A. pentameter   B. hexameter

    C. heroic couplets   D. heptameter

5. What is the figure of the speech in the sentence "If but a neck, soon should we be together"?

    A. simile   B. metaphor   C. synecdoche   D. metonymy

6. Most of Edward Taylor's works are about _____, with many poems based directly on the Psalms.

    A. love   B. human and nature

    C. religion   D. colony

7. The earliest settlers of the vast continental area that was to become the United States includes Dutch, Swedes, Germans, French, Spaniards, Italians, and Portuguese. Among them, _____ settled along the Hudson, Germans and Scotch-Irish in _____ and _____, and the _____ in Florida.

    A. Dutch; Pennsylvania; Europe; Swede

    B. Spanish; Europe; Mexico; Dutch

    C. Spanish; Mexico; New York; Italian

    D. Dutch; New York; Pennsylvania; Spanish

8. The Puritans had come to New England for the sake of _____.

    A. commercial venture   B. natural resource

    C. religious freedom   D. historical heritage

9. The Puritans made laws about _____ as well as _____.

    A. private morality; public behavior

    B. religious freedom; public safety

    C. private property; freedom

    D. public behavior; personal safety

10. If someone expects to totally grasp the colonial Puritan thoughts, he or she needs to learn about two important figures, _____.

    A. Roger Williams and Anne Bradstreet

    B. John Cotton and William Bradford

    C. John Cotton and Roger Williams

D. Roger Williams and Edward Taylor
11. From Anne Bradstreet's poetry, it is rather easy for us to see _____.
    A. Puritan ideology   B. religious freedom
    C. humility   D. spiritual
12. Her _____, without Anne Bradstreet's consent, brought the manuscript of her poems to England and arranged to have the book published under the title *The Tenth Muse Lately Sprung up in America*.
    A. brother-in-law   B. husband
    C. mother   D. sister
13. In 1607, one of the leaders of the Jamestown colony named Captain John Smith, sent a letter to the Virginia Company in London. Which of the following was one of his intentions?
    A. Renouncing the handling of the settlement.
    B. Safeguarding the rights of the planters.
    C. Declaring the value of the new land.
    D. Denouncing the misconduct of some leaders.
14. Which of the following cannot be summed up as the main points of the book *A Map of Virginia* written by Captain John Smith?
    A. To give a brief introduction and description of the country.
    B. To encourage the bold spirits needed to enlarge.
    C. To attract more people to move to the area that was to become the United States.
    D. To strengthen the English plantations in the new land.
15. Captain John Smith once wanted to seek a post as a guide to the Pilgrims, but they (the Virginia Company) did not admit the man. That was because _____.
    A. he had too much color and flamboyance for sober Puritan tastes
    B. he was totally aware of the exact truth
    C. they just wanted to make use of his publications and maps
    D. they were jealous of Smith's fame and talents
16. Who contributed more to the survival of the Jamestown colony

than anyone else?

A. Captain John Smith B. The Virginia Company
C. Ferdinand Magellan D. Cristoforo Colombo

17. Although the literature of Virginia and the South displayed less variety in the colonial time, New England had from the beginning a literature of ideas: theological, moral, historical, and _____.

A. political B. transcendental
C. supernatural D. naturalistic

18. At the very beginning, Massachusetts's original intention was to establish a theocracy—a society in which God would govern through the _____ which therefore became the supreme political body.

A. congress B. church C. parliament D. emperor

19. Because of _____, in practice theocracy often led to injustice and intolerance.

A. the wickedness of humankind
B. the severe natural environment
C. the imperfections of the human material
D. the corruption of the clergy

20. Puritans built attitudes towards life that was in line with their somber religion, one that stressed hard work, thrift, piety, and _____.

A. nobility B. integrity
C. sobriety D. self-emancipation

21. _____ was a prolific writer who composed more than 450 works during his life, an impressive output of religious writings which indicated that he was a model, as well as an advocate, of the Puritan ideal of hard work.

A. Anne Bradstreet B. Cotton Mather
C. Captain John Smith D. John Cotton

22. The Puritans made laws in order to restrain private morality as well as public behavior. Yet this _____ seemed to give rise to outbreaks of misbehavior, as if in reaction to the strictness.

A. very attempt to suppress all sin

B. accumulation of wealth

C. class differentiation

D. hatred of carnality and corruption

23. It is admitted that Puritan resistance to pleasure and the arts sometimes has been overestimated, but it is true that their lives were disciplined and dull. For example, Puritans tended to suspect _____ as symptoms of sin.

    A. joy and laughter   B. fraud and insult
    C. indulgence   D. money worship

24. The harshness of Puritan thought coincided with what Nathaniel Hawthorne called the "stern and black-browed Puritans." So, can you figure out what the image of God in Puritan religious teaching is?

    A. Philanthropic   B. Authoritative
    C. Fatherly   D. Wrathful

25. Which of the following do you think can be viewed as one of American earliest feminists and the first true poet in the American colonies?

    A. Amy Tan   B. Adeline Virginia Woolf
    C. Emily Dickinson   D. Anne Bradstreet

26. _____ is a religious poem written by Anne Bradstreet, which was taken seriously by the literary critics of the 20th century and considered to be an immortal work.

    A. *Contemplations*

    B. *The Tenth Muse Lately Sprung up in America*

    C. *To My Dear and Loving Husband*

    D. *A Letter to Her Husband, Absent upon Public Employment*

27. _____ was a female writer who undergone too much frustration during her life. As the first group of Puritan refugees to leave English shores between 1630 and 1642, her life showed us the bitter of never-ending struggle, from her difficult adaptation to the rigors

of the new land, to her dogged battle with illness.

   A. Anne Bradstreet   B. Charlotte Brontë
   C. Jane Austen   D. George Sand

28. The book by Anne Bradstreet once entitled *The Tenth Muse Lately Sprung up in America* was later published under the title _____, which is believed to be the first book written by a woman in the United States.

   A. *David's Lamentation for Saul and Jonathan*
   B. *Several Poems Compiled with Great Variety of Wit and Learning*
   C. *Of the Vanity of All Worldly Creatures*
   D. *To the Lighthouse*

29. Most of Anne Bradstreet's poems were tedious and imitative, but only the last _____ had a distinctive style.

   A. one   B. two   C. five   D. eight

30. *Several Poems Compiled with Great Variety of Wit and Learning* was the first book written by Anne Bradstreet, for which she became known as _____ who appeared in America.

   A. the "Queen of Love"   B. the "Tenth Muse"
   C. the "Statue of Liberty" D. the "Guardian Angel"

31. Anne Bradstreet once composed a great number of proactive poems which escaped from the constraint of moralism, such as _____.

   A. *The Flesh and the Spirit*   B. *Prometheus Unbound*
   C. *Elmer Gantry*   D. *Escape*

32. Which of the following poems revealed Anne Bradstreet's thought before she became a mother?

   A. *All Things Within This Fading World Hath End*
   B. *Upon the Burning of Our House*
   C. *With Troubled Heart and Trembling Hand I Write*
   D. *A Letter to Her Husband, Absent upon Public Employment*

33. Which of the following poems portrayed the inner complexity of the Puritan?

A. *With Troubled Heart and Trembling Hand I Write*
   B. *All Things Within This Fading World Hath End*
   C. *Upon the Burning of Our House*
   D. *A Letter to Her Husband, Absent upon Public Employment*
34. Which of the following poems is an elegy for Anne Bradstreet's dead grandchild?
   A. *With Troubled Heart and Trembling Hand I Write*
   B. *All Things Within This Fading World Hath End*
   C. *Upon the Burning of Our House*
   D. *A Letter to Her Husband, Absent upon Public Employment*
35. In Anne Bradstreet's poem *A Letter to Her Husband, Absent upon Public Employment* she wrote: "If but a neck, soon should we be together." What does she mean?
   A. "The neck" seemed to be something bridging head and heart.
   B. "The neck" was viewed as something blocking the union of head and heart.
   C. The author was not looking forward to the reunion with her husband.
   D. What the author said seemed to go against her inner mind.
36. In Line 8 of the poem *A Letter to Her Husband, Absent upon Public Employment*, what did Anne Bradstreet compare her husband to?
   A. The sun   B. The ocean   C. Her destiny   D. The star

III. Match-Making

	Column A		Column B
1.	Edward Taylor	a.	*Contemplations*
2.	John Smith	b.	*Huswifery*
3.	Anne Bradstreet	c.	*General History of Virginia*

IV. Define the Literary Terms.

1. American Enlightenment
2. American naturalism
3. American Puritanism

V. Answer the Following Questions Briefly.

1. What is the significance of American Puritanism in American literature?
2. Comment briefly on Charles Brockden Brown's contribution to American novel.
3. Give an introduction of the periods of American literature.

Part II

Literature of Reason and Revolution

I. Fill in the Blanks.

1. The establishment of a single nation from 13 original American states was persuaded by the arguments of statesmen and _____.
2. By the _____ century colonial America wasn't a group of scattered, struggling settlements any longer.
3. By the mid-eighteenth century, _____ was still a major center of thought.
4. The War for Independence lasted for _____ years from 1776 to _____.
5. The War for Independence succeeded finally establishing a _____ bourgeois _____ republic—the United States of America.
6. In the seventies of the 18th century, the bourgeois _____ greatly affected the spiritual life of the colonies.
7. American Enlightenment directly attacked the _____ traditions.
8. Secular education and literature rooted in American _____.
9. Jefferson's *Notes on the State of Virginia* (1785), and *Bartram's Travels* (1791) show the beginnings of _____.
10. Philip Freneau's power, style, sentiments and regular couplets are from _____ models.
11. *Poor Richard's Almanac* is an annual collection of _____.
12. America's first circulating library was set up by _____.
13. Benjamin Franklin founded a college that was to become the _____.

· 13 ·

14. His _____ brought Benjamin Franklin international praise.
15. Benjamin Franklin made great contributions to the theories of _____ and first used the terms "positive" and "negative" in electrical charges.
16. _____ was one of the first men to study and map the Gulf Stream.
17. The first colonial magazine edited by Franklin was _____.
18. Benjamin Franklin's best writing appeared in his _____.
19. In 1787, Benjamin Franklin was a delegate to the convention who wrote the _____.
20. The famous pamphlet _____ boldly advocated an idea similar to that of *Declaration of Independence* and brought the separatist agitation to a crisis.
21. In 1787, Thomas Paine secured foreign patents for his _____.
22. Thomas Paine described the advocacy of Rousseau's doctrines of freedom in his _____.
23. Thomas Paine's last important treatise is _____.
24. _____ was regarded as "Great Commoner of Mankind".
25. In 1776, _____, together with John Adams, Benjamin Franklin, Roger Sherman and Robert R. Livingston, drafted the *Declaration of Independence*.
26. In American literature, the 18th century was an Age of _____ and _____.
27. Philip Freneau became close friends with the future fourth president of the United States _____.
28. Philip Freneau gained his first popular success in New York as a _____ of the British.
29. In 1791, Philip Freneau founded the _____ in Philadelphia with Thomas Jefferson's support.
30. Philip Freneau has been called the "_____".
31. Philip Freneau is perhaps the most outstanding writer of the _____ period.

II. Choose the Best Answer for Each Question.

1. The word "state" was beginning to take the place of "colony" in the people's thinking, which indicated the _____ trend.
   A. literary   B. political   C. cultural   D. economic

2. Philadelphia, New York, and the state of Virginia became sources of _____ and _____ talent.
   A. political; literary   B. scientific; economic
   C. cultural; political   D. economic; political

3. The British attempted to ensure American's dependence on the mother country politically and economically in the following ways except _____.
   A. requiring Americans to ship raw materials abroad
   B. requiring Americans to import finished goods at prices higher than the cost of making them in this country
   C. ruling the colonies from overseas and taxing the colonies without giving them representation in Parliament
   D. blocking American trade and economic contact with other countries

4. Benjamin Franklin's initial purpose of writing the book *The Autobiography* was to _____.
   A. record his achievements   B. guide his son
   C. alert reader   D. contribute to literary creation

5. Which is the task of representatives of the Enlightenment?
   A. Disseminating knowledge among the people.
   B. Advocating federative ideas.
   C. Fighting for the freedom.
   D. Believing the religious obscurantism.

6. In American literature, the Enlighteners were opposed to the following except _____.
   A. the colonial order   B. religious obscurantism
   C. the Puritan tradition   D. the secular literature

7. Benjamin Franklin has multiple identities except _____.
   A. a scientist	B. a master of diplomacy
   C. a humanitarian	D. a poet
8. According to the *Spectator Papers* (1711-1712) of the English essayists Addison and Steele, _____ created his writing.
   A. Thomas Jefferson	B. Benjamin Franklin
   C. Thomas Paine	D. Philip Freneau
9. Benjamin Franklin's weekly newspaper, the _____ (later the *Saturday Evening Post*) was the greatest publication in America at that time.
   A. *Pennsylvania Gazette*	B. *Collected Works*
   C. *Poor Richard's Almanac*	D. *The General Magazine*
10. The reason why *Poor Richard's Almanac* was the most popular book of its kind is its _____.
    A. political ideas	B. incisive language
    C. shrewd humor	D. positive attitude
11. Which book spread Benjamin Franklin's reputation?
    A. *Pennsylvania Gazette*	B. *Collected Works*
    C. *Poor Richard's Almanac*	D. *The General Magazine*
12. America's first circulating library was established in _____.
    A. Boston	B. Philadelphia
    C. Pennsylvania	D. New York
13. Benjamin Franklin was elected to learned societies in _____ and _____.
    A. Boston; England	B. England; France
    C. England; America	D. New York; England
14. Benjamin Franklin was the epitome of the _____.
    A. American Enlightenment	B. Sugar Act
    C. Chartist Movement	D. romanticist
15. Which book is perhaps the most quoted of all Benjamin Franklin's writings?
    A. *Pennsylvania Gazette*	B. *Collected Works*

C. *Poor Richard's Almanac*   D. *The General Magazine*

16. In his leisure time, Thomas Paine preferred reading the study of _____ and the _____.
    A. philosophy; poetry   B. politics; economics
    C. new science; literature D. social philosophy; new science

17. _____ was the pioneer which considered that the government's role was to protect life, liberty and property.
    A. Benjamin Franklin   B. Thomas Paine
    C. Thomas Jefferson   D. Philip Freneau

18. In 1772, Thomas Paine wrote his first pamphlet _____.
    A. *The Age of Reason*
    B. *Common Sense*
    C. *American Crisis*
    D. *The Case of the Officers of the Excise*

19. _____ recognized Thomas Paine's peculiar talent and recommended him as "an ingenious worthy young man".
    A. Philip Freneau   B. John Bunyan
    C. Benjamin Franklin   D. Thomas Jefferson

20. Benjamin Franklin shaped his writing after the _____ of the English essayists Joseph Addison and Richard Steele.
    A. *Spectator Papers*   B. *Walden*
    C. *Nature*   D. *The Sacred Wood*

21. The first pamphlet published in America to urge immediate independence from Britain is _____.
    A. *Rights of Man*   B. *Common Sense*
    C. *The American Crisis*. D. *Declaration of Independence*

22. Thomas Paine was regarded as an important figure in _____ and _____.
    A. America; England   B. London; France
    C. Paris; America   D. Paris; London

23. "These are the times that try men's souls", these words were once read to George Washington's troops and did much to shore

up the spirits of the revolutionary soldiers. Who is the author of these words?

 A. Benjamin Franklin   B. Thomas Jefferson

 C. Thomas Paine   D. George Washington

24. Thomas Paine's *Rights of Man* (Part I, 1791; Part II, 1792) recommend _____.

 A. overthrowing of the British monarchy

 B. advocating federative ideas

 C. taking part in the Revolution

 D. believing the religious obscurantism

25. Thomas Paine's deistic treatise which advocates a rationalistic view of religion is _____.

 A. *The Age of Reason*

 B. *Common Sense*

 C. *The Case of the Officers of the Excise*

 D. *The American Crisis*

26. Thomas Paine's pamphlets on _____ and _____ made a difference in social reform and progress.

 A. philosophy; literature   B. politics; social philosophy

 C. new science; freedom   D. freedom; reason

27. It was _____ who famously declared: "Where liberty is, there is my country."

 A. Thomas Jefferson   B. Benjamin Franklin

 C. Thomas Paine   D. Alexander Hamilton

28. It was not until January 1776 that a widely heard public voice demanded complete separation from England. The voice was that of _____, whose pamphlet *Common Sense*, with its heated language, increased the growing demand for separation.

 A. Thomas Paine   B. Thomas Jefferson

 C. George Washington   D. Patrick Henry

29. Thomas Jefferson served for _____ terms as American president.

A. one　　　　B. two　　　　C. three　　　　D. four

30. Thomas Jefferson's democratic theories of education was embodied in _____.
    A. the University of Virginia
    B. Mount Holyoke Female Seminary
    C. the University of Pennsylvania
    D. Hartford Female Seminary

31. Thomas Jefferson's attitude, that is, a firm belief in progress, and the pursuit of happiness, was typical of the period we now call _____.
    A. Age of Evolution   B. Age of Reason
    C. Age of Romanticism   D. Age of Regionalism

32. _____ became the first Rector of the University of Virginia.
    A. Philip Freneau   B. Thomas Paine
    C. Benjamin Franklin   D. Thomas Jefferson

33. Which statement about Philip Freneau is not true?
    A. He was a satirist.   B. He was a pamphleteer.
    C. He was a poet.   D. He was a novelist.

34. The first work independently completed by Philip Freneau was _____.
    A. *The House of Night*   B. *The Beauties of Santa Cruz*
    C. *The Power of Fancy*   D. *The British Prison-Ship*

35. F. L. Pattee called _____ "the first distinctly romantic note heard in America".
    A. *The House of Night*   B. *The Wild Honey Suckle*
    C. *The British Prison-Ship*   D. *The Indian Burying Ground*

36. As a poet, _____ indicates American literary independence.
    A. Philip Freneau   B. John Bunyan
    C. Benjamin Franklin   D. Thomas Jefferson

37. _____ was neoclassical by training and taste yet romantic in essential spirit.
    A. Thomas Paine   B. Thomas Jefferson

C. Philip Freneau	D. Benjamin Franklin
38. Among Freneau's poems, _____ is regarded the best.
    A. *The House of Night*	B. *Miscellaneous Works*
    C. *The British Prison-Ship*	D. *The Wild Honey Suckle*
39. The poem "The Indian Burying Ground" was published in 1788 in his collection of essays and poems _____.
    A. *Daily Advertiser*	B. *Miscellaneous Works*
    C. *National Gazette*	D. *The Beauties of Santa Cruz*
40. The emergence of _____, a more intellectualized and liberalized religion, in the 18th-century America came directly from the Enlightenment.
    A. utilitarianism	B. Deism
    C. rationalism	D. romanticism
41. Literature in the period of American _____ was predominantly public and utilitarian.
    A. rationalism	B. Revolution
    C. realism	D. romanticism
42. _____ carries the voice not of an individual but of a whole people. It is more than writing of the Revolutionary period; it defines the meaning of the American Revolution.
    A. *Common Sense*
    B. *The American Crisis*
    C. *Declaration of Independence*
    D. *Defence of the English People*
43. In the Reason and Revolution Period, Americans were influenced by the European movement called the _____ Movement.
    A. Chartist	B. Romanticist
    C. Enlightenment	D. Modernist
44. At the initial period, the spread of ideas of the American Enlightenment was largely due to _____.
    A. journalism	B. pamphlets
    C. political poems	D. satirical novels

45. _____ seemed to represent the Age of Reason and Revolution in his paradoxical faith in both social order and in natural rights, in love of stability and devotion to revolutionary change.
   A. Thomas Paine   B. Thomas Jefferson
   C. George Washington   D. Benjamin Franklin
46. In Philadelphia, _____ edited *Pennsylvania Magazine*, and contributed to *Pennsylvania Journal*.
   A. Thomas Paine   B. Thomas Jefferson
   C. George Washington   D. Benjamin Franklin
47. _____ boldly advocated a *Declaration of Independence*.
   A. *Common Sense*   B. *The American Crisis*
   C. *Rights of Man*   D. *Defence of the English People*
48. For the pamphlet _____, Thomas Paine was charged with treason and fled to France, where he was made a citizen.
   A. *Common Sense*   B. *The American Crisis*
   C. *Rights of Man*   D. *Defence of the English People*
49. _____ was noteworthy first because of the nature of his poems. They were truly American and very patriotic. In this respect, he reflected the spirit of his age.
   A. Thomas Paine   B. Thomas Jefferson
   C. Philip Freneau   D. Benjamin Franklin
50. Most American literature in the 18th century was _____.
   A. political   B. pastoral   C. satirical   D. Romantic

III. Match-Making

   Column A   Column B
1. Benjamin Franklin   a. *Declaration of Independence*
2. Thomas Paine   b. *The Wild Honey Suckle*
3. Thomas Jefferson   c. *The American Crisis*

4. Philip Freneau   d.   *The Autobiography*

IV. Define the Literary Terms.

1. *Declaration of Independence*
2. Autobiography

V. Answer the Following Questions Briefly.

1. Why does *The Autobiography* become a classic?
2. Give a brief analysis of *The American Crisis*.

Part III

Literature of Romanticism

I. Fill in the Blanks.

1. Before 1860 the United States had begun to change into an _____ society.
2. Through the first half of the nineteenth century, _____ communal societies flourished.
3. With the development of _____, a host of notable women began to fight for their rights and for social reform.
4. Mount Holyoke Female Seminary in Massachusetts was the first college-level institution for _____.
5. The American transcendentalists formed a club called the _____ Club.
6. The Transcendental Club often met at Ralph Waldo _____'s Concord home.
7. A number of ideas of American writers inherited from the Romantic traditions of _____.
8. _____ was the first American writer of imaginative literature.
9. American politics, art, and philosophy until the Civil War were rich in _____ values.
10. Transcendentalists advocate cultural rejuvenation and oppose the _____ of American society.
11. There were two representatives extremely advocating the doctrines of transcendentalism. One was Ralph Waldo Emerson who believed man is a part of _____, and the other was Henry Da-

vid Thoreau who observed _____ in the "unspotted innocence" of nature.

12. With the development of _____, American artists began to write patriotic songs, to paint vast panoramas of American scenes and to design monumental buildings.
13. In the 1820s, the _____ of landscape painters appeared.
14. In the nineteenth century, the gardens of rich Americans even were decorated with _____ which indicated the successful invasion of nature into works of man.
15. By the 1850s _____ had been paid great interest.
16. In the nineteenth century, statesmen started to take advantage of the emotional force of their _____ to control American politics.
17. Romantic writers attached great importance to the _____ of emotion.
18. In 1828 _____ published *An American Dictionary of the English Language*.
19. In 1755, Samuel _____ published his remarkable dictionary named *Dictionary of the English Language*.
20. Washington Irving was the first great _____ of American romanticism.
21. The first American belletrist was _____.
22. Washington Irving also wrote two biographies. One is *The Life of Oliver Goldsmith*, and the other is *The Life of* _____.
23. _____ created the expression "the almighty dollar".
24. James Fenimore Cooper was considered as the first important American _____.
25. *The Spy* (1821) tells a tale during _____.
26. James Fenimore Cooper wrote the first official history of the _____ in 1839.
27. James Fenimore Cooper's _____ stories gave him an enduring reputation.
28. William Cullen Bryant's first poem appeared in _____.

29. William Cullen Bryant's work _____ was called the "most perfect brief poem in the language" by Matthew Arnold.
30. William Cullen Bryant's translated *The Iliad* and *The Odyssey* into English _____ in his latter works.
31. Ralph Waldo Emerson's first book is _____.
32. Lots of Ralph Waldo Emerson's works were deeply affected by the Scottish writer _____.
33. Transcendentalism was brought to New England by _____.
34. The scene "old employees of the shipping office rocked on the chairs in town, where there had been a hustle and bustle of life" appeared in the introductory chapter to _____.
35. Nathaniel Hawthorne's college friends included Henry Wadsworth Longfellow and _____ the fourteenth President of the United States.
36. Nathaniel Hawthorne's special talent was to create strongly _____ stories touching the deepest roots of man's moral nature.
37. Hester Prynne is the heroine in Nathaniel Hawthorne's novel *The _____ Letter*.
38. Nathaniel Hawthorne was called "the largest brain with the largest heart" in American literature by his friend _____.
39. Washington Irving had successfully domesticated European subject matter while Longfellow domesticated _____.
40. _____ became the only American to be honored with a bust in the Poet's Corner of Westminster Abbey after his death.
41. Besides lyrics and longer poems Henry Wadsworth Longfellow wrote dramatic works, among which *Michael _____* is the most conspicuous.
42. Henry Wadsworth Longfellow and James Russell _____ are the only two American poets commemorated in the Poet's Corner of Westminster Abbey.
43. The American who was praised as a pioneer in poetic and fictional techniques in Europe was _____.

44. Generally speaking, Edgar Allan Poe has been regarded as the father of the _____.
45. Edgar Allan Poe's poem *The* _____ is perhaps the best example of onomatopoeia in the English language.
46. Edgar Allan Poe's poem *The* _____ was published in 1845 as the title poem of a collection.
47. Henry David Thoreau was the truest disciple of _____.
48. Henry David Thoreau is considered as a significant contributor to New England _____.
49. Although Henry David Thoreau was not highly praised during his lifetime, he is now recognized one of the most famous American writers of the _____.
50. At an early age, Herman Melville was encouraged by _____'s novels.
51. Herman Melville's masterpiece _____ failed to be popular in his time. However, it laid the foundation for his modern fame.
52. *Moby Dick* was regarded as the first American _____.
53. The English author named Sir Walter _____ was, in a way, responsible for the Romantic description of landscape in American literature and the development of American Indian romance. His Waverley novels were models for American historical romances.
54. Published in 1823, "The _____" was the first of *The Leatherstocking Tales*, in their order of publication time, and probably the first true romance of the frontier in American literature.
55. In *The Pioneers*, _____ Bumppo represents the ideal American, living a virtuous and free life in God's world.
56. Herman Melville stopped writing novels as well as stories and turned to poetry in his late years. _____ is his most famous poetic work.

II. Choose the Best Answer for Each Question.

1. In the first half of the nineteenth century, _____ became America's largest city as well as the economic and cultural capital of the nation.
   A. Boston   B. New York
   C. Philadelphia   D. Virginia

2. _____'s *The Sketch Book* (1819-1820) is the first work by an American writer that won financial success on both sides of the Atlantic.
   A. Philip Freneau   B. John Bunyan
   C. Washington Irving   D. Thomas Jefferson

3. A new romanticism appeared in England in the last years of the _____ century and spread to America early in the _____ century.
   A. sixteenth; seventeenth   B. seventeenth; eighteenth
   C. sixteenth; eighteenth   D. eighteenth; nineteenth

4. The ideas of transcendentalists were from all the following except _____.
   A. German idealistic philosophy
   B. the revelations of Oriental mysticism
   C. neo-Platonism
   D. the realistic literature of Europe

5. Transcendentalism prevailed in New England from the _____ to the Civil War.
   A. 1820s   B. 1830s   C. 1840s   D. 1850s

6. _____ was the most leading spirit of the Transcendental Club.
   A. Henry David Thoreau   B. Ralph Waldo Emerson
   C. Nathaniel Hawthorne   D. Walt Whitman

7. Transcendentalists recognized _____ as the "highest power of the soul".
   A. intuition   B. logic
   C. data of the senses   D. thinking

8. Transcendentalism appealed to those who disdained the harsh God of the Puritan ancestors, and it appealed to those who scorned the pale deity of New England _____.
   A. transcendentalism   B. humanism
   C. naturalism   D. Unitarianism
9. In the nineteenth century, American principal literary forms were all the following except _____.
   A. manifestos   B. novels   C. short stories   D. poems
10. Which work doesn't obviously reflect the desire for escaping from society and returning to nature?
    A. *The Sketch Book*   B. *Walden*
    C. *Huckleberry Finn*   D. *The Leatherstocking Tales*
11. The Schoolroom Poets were a group of 19th-century American poets from _____.
    A. New England   B. Virginia
    C. Massachusetts   D. New York
12. With the growth of cultural nationalism, composers adapted European _____ forms to American legends and lore.
    A. literary   B. poetic   C. operatic   D. prosy
13. The works of following writers except _____ pay attention to the demonic and the mystery of evil.
    A. Edgar Allan Poe   B. Herman Melville
    C. Nathaniel Hawthorne   D. Washington Irving
14. A greater literary interest in American language and its common people was aroused by _____.
    A. nationalism   B. realism
    C. transcendentalism   D. romanticism
15. The first great prose stylist of American romanticism was _____.
    A. James Fenimore Cooper   B. William Cullen Bryant
    C. Ralph Waldo Emerson   D. Washington Irving
16. The first modern short stories and the first great American juvenile literature appeared in the _____.

A. *The Sketch Book*   B. *Bracebridge Hall*
C. *A History of New York*   D. *Tales of a Traveler*

17. In the early 19th century, statesmen such as _____, came to dominate American politics not with their prose but with the emotional force of their oratory.
    A. Daniel Webster   B. Daniel Defoe
    C. Philip Freneau   D. Thomas Paine

18. The first writer who wrote history and biography as literary entertainment in modern times was _____.
    A. Washington Irving   B. William Cullen Bryant
    C. Ralph Waldo Emerson   D. James Fenimore Cooper

19. The only American writer of his generation that could criticize the British in a humorous way was _____.
    A. Thomas Jefferson   B. William Cullen Bryant
    C. Washington Irving   D. Ralph Waldo Emerson

20. _____ is an exuberant parody of a current serious history of the early Dutch settlers and has become a humorous classic.
    A. *The Sketch Book*   B. *The Deerslayer*
    C. *A History of New York*   D. *The Last of the Mohicans*

21. Washington Irving's _____ achieved an international success.
    A. *The Sketch Book*   B. *Rip Van Winkle*
    C. *A History of New York*   D. *The Alhambra*

22. Washington Irving wrote the excellent social comedy *Charles the Second*, or *The Merry Monarch* with _____.
    A. Edgar Allan Poe   B. Herman Melville
    C. John Howard Payne   D. Washington Irving

23. Washington Irving wrote a number of important works in Spain on diplomatic business except _____.
    A. *A Tour on the Prairies* (1835)
    B. *Voyages and Discoveries of the Companions of Columbus* (1831)
    C. *A History of the Life and Voyages of Christopher Columbus* (1828)
    D. *A Chronicle of the Conquest of Granada* (1829)

24. _____ was called a father of American literature and "The American Goldsmith".
    A. Edgar Allan Poe   B. Herman Melville
    C. John Howard Payne   D. Washington Irving
25. The main theme of *Rip Van Winkle* is _____ and preservation of tradition.
    A. radical changes   B. harmonious living conditions
    C. change with continuity   D. beautiful natural sceneries
26. _____ tells a story about espionage against the British during the Revolutionary War.
    A. *The Sketch Book*   B. *The Spy*
    C. *A History of New York*   D. *The Pilot*
27. James Fenimore Cooper had two kinds of the most popular works: the sea adventure tale and the frontier saga. Of all his sea romances, the best is _____.
    A. *The Sketch Book*   B. *The Spy*
    C. *The Prairie*   D. *The Pilot*
28. Allan Nevins called the five novels "the nearest approach yet to an American epic". These five novels include *The Deerslayer*, *The Last of the Mohicans* and the other three except _____.
    A. *The Prairie*   B. *The Spy*
    C. *The Pioneers*   D. *The Pathfinder*
29. _____'s claim to greatness in American literature lies in the fact that he created a myth about the formative period of the American nation.
    A. James Fenimore Cooper   B. William Cullen Bryant
    C. Nathaniel Hawthorne   D. Henry Wadsworth Longfellow
30. The American was aware of his past and the European was aware of America owing to _____.
    A. James Fenimore Cooper   B. William Cullen Bryant
    C. Washington Irving   D. Ralph Waldo Emerson
31. As a poet, _____ also had a fame as one of the great editors of

American journalism.

A. James Fenimore Cooper B. William Cullen Bryant
C. Washington Irving D. Ralph Waldo Emerson

32. William Cullen Bryant's climax of work is probably _____.

A. *The Prairie* B. *The Spy*
C. *To a Waterfowl* D. *The Pathfinder*

33. The first American who gained the stature of a major poet is _____.

A. James Fenimore Cooper B. William Cullen Bryant
C. Washington Irving D. Ralph Waldo Emerson

34. In William Cullen Bryant's view, the death of a man simply represents the returning to the _____.

A. nature B. God C. destiny D. life

35. *The American Scholar* and _____ made Ralph Waldo Emerson famous.

A. *Representative Men* B. *English Traits*
C. *The Divinity School Address* D. *The American Scholar*

36. Ralph Waldo Emerson's most famous work is _____ which was first published in 1841.

A. *Self-Reliance* B. *Nature*
C. *Representative Men* D. *English Traits*

37. In the introductory chapter of _____, Nathaniel Hawthorne showed his close attention to the dark side of Puritanism, the harshness and the persecutions.

A. *Ethan Brand* B. *The Custom House*
C. *The Great Stone Face* D. *Young Goodman Brown*

38. Nathaniel Hawthorne's experience of group life supplied the material to his later novel _____.

A. *The Blithedale Romance*
B. *The Ambitious Guest*
C. *The Scarlet Letter*
D. *The Marble Faun*

39. From Henry David Thoreau's jail experience came his famous essay, _____, which states Henry David Thoreau's belief that no man should violate his conscience at the command of a government.
   A. *Walden*　　　　　　　　　　B. *Nature*
   C. *Civil Disobedience*　　　　　D. *Common Sense*

40. The finest example of Nathaniel Hawthorne's symbolism is the recreation of Puritan Boston in _____.
   A. *The Scarlet Letter*　　　　　B. *Young Goodman Brown*
   C. *The Marble Faun*　　　　　　D. *The Ambitious Guest*

41. The following characters appear in the novel *The Scarlet Letter* except _____.
   A. Hester Prynne　　　　　　　　B. Arthur Dimmesdale
   C. Roger Chillingworth　　　　　D. Uncas

42. *The House of the Seven Gables* is a famous mystery-haunted novel written by _____.
   A. Nathaniel Hawthorne　　　　　B. Washington Irving
   C. Mark Twain　　　　　　　　　D. Herman Melville

43. Like Edgar Allan Poe, _____ often used grotesque or fantastic events, but his work is broader in range and has more depth of thought.
   A. Ralph Waldo Emerson　　　　　B. William Cullen Bryant
   C. Nathaniel Hawthorne　　　　　D. Henry Wadsworth Longfellow

44. To _____ and Herman Melville, the telling of a tale is a way of inquiring into the meaning of life.
   A. Ralph Waldo Emerson　　　　　B. William Cullen Bryant
   C. Nathaniel Hawthorne　　　　　D. Henry Wadsworth Longfellow

45. The prose romance *Outre-Mer* (1833-1835) imitated the work _____.
   A. *The Scarlet Letter*　　　　　B. *The Ambitious Guest*
   C. *The Sketch Book*　　　　　　D. *Hyperion*

46. _____ was Henry Wadsworth Longfellow's first collection of po-

ems.

   A. *The Courtship of Miles Standish*
   B. *Divine Comedy*
   C. *Voices of the Night*
   D. *Ballads and Other Poems*

47. With the appearance of _____ in 1855, which is about American Indians, Henry Wadsworth Longfellow's poetical reputation was established.
   A. *Evangeline*   B. *The Courtship of Miles Standish*
   C. *Song of Hiawatha*   D. *Michael Angelo*

48. _____'s writings belong to the milder aspects of the Romantic Movement.
   A. Ralph Waldo Emerson   B. William Cullen Bryant
   C. Nathaniel Hawthorne   D. Henry Wadsworth Longfellow

49. _____'s *The Courtship of Miles Standish*, published in 1858, is a popular poem, remarkable for its humor and vivid depiction of American scenery.
   A. James Fenimore Cooper   B. William Cullen Bryant
   C. Nathaniel Hawthorne   D. Henry Wadsworth Longfellow

50. Henry Wadsworth Longfellow's best translation work is _____.
   A. Nathaniel Hawthorne's *The Scarlet Letter*
   B. Washington Irving's *Sketch Book*
   C. Dante Alighieri's *Divine Comedy*
   D. Ralph Waldo Emerson's *The American Scholar*

51. Edgar Allan Poe's first collection of short stories is _____.
   A. *The Raven*
   B. *To Helen*
   C. *Messenger*
   D. *Tales of the Grotesque and Arabesque*

52. Edgar Allan Poe's last poem is _____, which is in memory of his wife, Virginia Clemm.
   A. *The Raven*   B. *To Helen*

C. *Messenger* D. *Annabel Lee*

53. No other American poet ever surpassed _____'s ability in the use of English as a medium of pure musical and rhythmic beauty.
    A. Walt Whitman   B. William Cullen Bryant
    C. Nathaniel Hawthorne   D. Edgar Allan Poe

54. The best of Edgar Allan Poe's poems is _____.
    A. *To Helen*
    B. *The Raven*
    C. *Annabel Lee*
    D. *Tales of the Grotesque and Arabesque*

55. The sound of _____'s words casts a magic spell over the readers. His tone is awesome, sad and melancholy.
    A. Walt Whitman   B. William Cullen Bryant
    C. Edgar Allan Poe   D. Nathaniel Hawthorne

56. _____ was the first American writer to form the technique of the short story and to create the genre of detective story.
    A. Edgar Allan Poe   B. Henry Wadsworth Longfellow
    C. Washington Irving   D. Ralph Waldo Emerson

57. The most significant matter for Henry David Thoreau is _____ and independence of mind.
    A. self-reliance B. confidence C. freedom D. harmonious

58. _____ is regarded as one of the foremost American writers on account of his clear prose style and his prescient views on nature and politics.
    A. Edgar Allan Poe   B. Henry Wadsworth Longfellow
    C. Henry David Thoreau   D. Ralph Waldo Emerson

59. The book *Walden* compresses the time into a single calendar year and uses passages of four seasons to represent _____.
    A. natural changes   B. human development
    C. people's challenges   D. social progress

60. To avoid the influence of _____ and frantic schedules, Henry David Thoreau went to Walden Pond.

A. material things   B. society
C. challenges   D. people

61. Herman Melville's great talent was discovered in the _____.
    A. 1910s   B. 1920s   C. 1930s   D. 1940s

62. If one wants to know the 19th century American mind and America itself, he should read the book _____.
    A. *Benito Cereno*   B. *Moby Dick*
    C. *Billy Budd*   D. *Mardi*

63. _____ is set in the 17th century. It is an elaboration of a fact which the author took out of the life of the Puritan past.
    A. *Moby Dick*   B. *The Scarlet Letter*
    C. *Nature*   D. *Walden*

64. Although _____ is ambiguous and his tales are often capable of more than one interpretation, he is certainly at his best when writing about evil.
    A. Ralph Waldo Emerson   B. William Cullen Bryant
    C. Nathaniel Hawthorne   D. Henry David Thoreau

65. _____'s aesthetics brought about a revolution in American literature in general and in American poetry in particular.
    A. Ralph Waldo Emerson   B. William Cullen Bryant
    C. Nathaniel Hawthorne   D. Henry David Thoreau

III. Match-Making

Group One

	Column A		Column B
1.	Washington Irving	a.	*The Scarlet Letter*
2.	James Fenimore Cooper	b.	*To a Waterfowl*
3.	William Cullen Bryant	c.	*Moby Dick*
4.	Ralph Waldo Emerson	d.	*Walden*
5.	Nathaniel Hawthorne	e.	*Voices of Night*

6. Henry Wadsworth Longfellow   f. *The Raven*
7. Edgar Allan Poe   h. *The American Scholar*
8. Henry David Thoreau   i. *The Sketch Book*
9. Herman Melville   j. *The Last of the Mohicans*

Group Two

Column A   Column B
1. Herman Melville   a. *Nature*
2. Henry Wadsworth Longfellow   b. *The House of the Seven Gables*
3. Edgar Allan Poe   c. *Civil Disobedience*
4. Washington Irving   d. *The Pioneers*
5. Henry David Thoreau   e. *The Life of Washington*
6. James Fenimore Cooper   f. *Michael Angelo*
7. Nathaniel Hawthorne   h. *Thanatopsis*
8. Ralph Waldo Emerson   i. *Typee*
9. William Cullen Bryant   j. *Tales of a Traveler*

IV. Define the Literary Terms.

1. Transcendentalism
2. Romanticism
3. Symbolism

V. Answer the Following Questions Briefly.

1. What are the manifestations of romanticism in America?
2. What's Washington Irving's main contribution to American literature?
3. Give an analysis of Edgar Allan Poe's poem *Annabel Lee*.

Part IV

Literature of Realism

I. Fill in the Blanks.

1. In _____ the United States abolished slavery in order to achieve racial equality.
2. The age of steel and steam, electricity and oil was between the end of _____ and the beginning of _____.
3. The dominant culture force of America in the latter half of the nineteenth century was _____.
4. In 1824, _____ founded the Hartford Female Seminary.
5. On June 5, 1851, the novel *Uncle Tom's Cabin* appeared serially in the magazine _____.
6. Harriet Beecher Stowe's work _____ achieved an overnight success.
7. The first genuine epic poem of America was Walt Whitman's work _____.
8. The poetic style used by Walt Whitman is now named _____.
9. The works of Shakespeare and _____ arouse Walt Whitman's interest in literature.
10. The central ideas of Walt Whitman's poetry are democracy, equality, and _____.
11. Walt Whitman is recognized as father of _____ and singer of the Great Public.
12. A number of Emily Dickinson's poems seem to be _____ in form.

13. Samuel Langhorne Clemens is better known by the pen name _____.
14. _____ gained an international fame as humorist-frontier philosopher.
15. Mark Twain set out to make arrangements for his work _____ in 1906.
16. _____ called Mark Twain "the true father of our national literature".
17. Mark Twain had a dramatic effect in _____ American literature.
18. _____ was the founder of realism in literature.
19. Mark Twain's work *The Mysterious* _____ tells of the visits of an angel to the village of Eseldorf in Austria in 1590.
20. The result of Mark Twain's European trip was a series of newspaper articles, later published as a book called _____ *Abroad*.
21. One of Samuel Langhorne Clemens's best books *Life on the* _____ is built around his experiences as a steamboat pilot.
22. Mark Twain made _____ an acknowledged, acceptable literary medium in the literary history of the country.
23. _____ was a writer who was expert in humor and satire.
24. Henry James turned into a British citizen in order to show his approval of England in _____.
25. Henry James's _____ (1878) brought him international reputation for the first time.
26. Henry James took advantage of the modern _____ technique to research people's psychological world.
27. Kate Chopin was famous as a _____ writer.
28. *The Story of an Hour* is a _____ novel.
29. Most of O. Henry's novel plots come from real experiences of his own and other people. He was very friendly and talkative and especially loved to collect creation materials by chatting with _____, _____, even tramps and thieves.
30. O. Henry's short novels tend to expose social reality and reflect the

life of the people at the bottom of society, and many of his stories tell about the lives of poor people in _____ and other places.

31. There is a popular American short story writer who loves to arrange unexpected endings at the end of the novel. For example, he suddenly makes the protagonist's mood change surprisingly or makes the protagonist's fate suddenly reversed. This kind of ending is highly dramatic and is called _____ style ending.

32. As we all know, O. Henry's best volume is _____, which mainly describes the lives of regular people in New York.

33. O. Henry's _____ is a very moving story of a young couple who sell their best possessions in order to get money for a Christmas present for each other.

34. _____, which traces the material rise of the heroine and the tragic decline of her lover, was Theodore Herman Albert Dreiser's first novel.

35. The book _____ was Theodore Herman Albert Dreiser's first true commercial success. He began his career as a full-time writer after that.

36. _____, _____, and _____ marked that Theodore Herman Albert Dreiser finished his shift from the sympathy of pathetic protagonists to the power of those extraordinary individuals who acted as dominant roles in business and society. The three works make up the "Trilogy of Dreiser".

37. The notion that men who possess higher sexual energy tend to be financially successful is carried over into the rather weak autobiographical novel written by Theodore Herman Albert Dreiser, _____.

38. _____ is widely recognized as Theodore Herman Albert Dreiser's greatest and most successful novel.

39. As time passes, _____ has been recognized as a profound and prescient critic of debased American values and as a powerful novelist.

40. In Theodore Herman Albert Dreiser's books, protagonists and char-

acters are all from the _____ level of the society.

41. Novels and polemical works as _____, _____, *The War of the Classes,* and *Revolution* faithfully recorded Jack Griffith London's sincere intellectual and personal participation in the socialist movement.

42. In Jack Griffith London's most popular novels _____ and _____, his competing, deeply felt commitment to the fundamental reality of the law of survival and the will to power is dramatized.

43. In Jack Griffith London's autobiographical novel _____ he portrayed a perfect image of a superman, and the book is widely known as a central document for London scholars.

44. In 1916, Sherwood Anderson published his first book _____. Before that, Carl Sandburg and Floyd Dell had encouraged him a lot.

45. _____ is Sherwood Anderson's masterpiece, which launched his career and established his status in the history of American literature.

46. Sherwood Anderson's later works are slightly inferior to those of his peak period. However, his best later works belonged to _____, published in three volumes: *The Triumph of the Egg* (1921), *Horses and Men* (1923) and *Death in the Woods* and other stories.

II. Choose the Best Answer for Each Question.

1. The manifestations of the greatly expanded power of the federal government during the Civil War are the following except _____.
   A. the first conscription laws were passed
   B. a national currency was issued
   C. the Fourteenth Amendment to the Constitution was adopted
   D. the first federal income taxes were levied

2. The _____ Amendment to the Constitution abolished slavery within the United States.

A. Twelfth   B. Thirteenth   C. Fourteenth   D. Fifteenth
3. The American first transcontinental railroad finished in 1869 linked _____ and _____.
   A. the Atlantic; the Pacific   B. the Pacific; the Arctic
   C. the Atlantic; the Arctic   D. the Pacific; the Gulf of Mexico
4. American dominant industry was _____ from the end of the Civil War to the beginning of World War I.
   A. crude oil   B. manufacturing
   C. steel making   D. alternating electrical current
5. The influences of the development of business and industry were all that except _____.
   A. it widened the gap between the rich and the poor
   B. it led to reform movements and labor unions
   C. debt-ridden farmers and immigrant workers were full of compliant
   D. it made Chicago the nation's second largest city
6. In 1891, _____ (founded in 1883) became the first American magazine over half a million circulation.
   A. *Pennsylvania Magazine*   B. *The General Magazine*
   C. *The North American Review*   D. *The Ladies Home Journal*
7. With New England's cultural dominance wakening, _____ became the nation's literary center.
   A. Boston   B. New York   C. New England   D. Chicago
8. _____ believed the author's right to present an idealized and poetic portrait of life, to avoid representations of "squalid misery."
   A. Edgar Allan Poe   B. Henry Wadsworth Longfellow
   C. James Fenimore Cooper   D. Ralph Waldo Emerson
9. _____ was the first American writer of local color who was widely popular in the 1860s.
   A. Bret Harte   B. Henry Wadsworth Longfellow
   C. Harriet Beecher Stowe   D. Ralph Waldo Emerson
10. William Dean Howells had shown his realistic theories ex-

cept _____.

A. *A Modern Instance*

B. *A Hazard of New Fortunes*

C. *The Rise of Silas Lapham*

D. *The Man That Was a Thing*

11. Mark Twain's most famous work of American realism and one of the great books of world literature is _____.

    A. *A Modern Instance*

    B. *A Hazard of New Fortunes*

    C. *Huckleberry Finn*

    D. *Life on the Mississippi*

12. _____ appealed for the approach of the more "smiling aspects of life" as the more "American" in the 1880s.

    A. Bret Harte   B. Walt Whitman

    C. William Dean Howells   D. Ralph Waldo Emerson

13. The works of Jack London, Henry Adams and Theodore Dreiser are filled with the pessimism and deterministic ideas of _____.

    A. naturalism   B. romanticism

    C. realism   D. transcendentalism

14. The original title of *Uncle Tom's Cabin* was _____.

    A. *A Modern Instance*

    B. *The Man That Was a Thing*

    C. *The Rise of Silas Lapham*

    D. *A Hazard of New Fortunes*

15. *Uncle Tom's Cabin* achieved a great success overnight and has been published in approximately _____ languages since then.

    A. twenty   B. thirty   C. forty   D. fifty

16. The publication of the novel _____ stirred a great nation to its depths and hurried on a great war.

    A. *My Bondage and My Freedom*

    B. *Stanzas on Freedom*

    C. *Voices of Freedom*

D. *Uncle Tom's Cabin*
17. The symbol of the development of capitalism in America was that _____.
    A. it became a rural, agrarian and isolated republic
    B. the industrialized North defeated the agrarian south
    C. the inhabitants were idealistic, confident, self-reliant and faithful in God
    D. America had transformed into an industrialized and commercial society
18. The significant local colorists include the following except _____.
    A. Hamlin Garland   B. Walt Whitman
    C. Harriet Beecher Stowe   D. Kate Chopin
19. The definition of Local Colorism as having "such quality of texture and background that it could not have been written in any other place or by anyone else than a native" was made by _____.
    A. Walt Whitman   B. Hamlin Garland
    C. Emily Dickinson   D. Harriet Beecher Stowe
20. Ideas of the Eastern religions or German transcendentalists used in Walt Whitman's poetry originated from reading the works of _____.
    A. Henry Wadsworth Longfellow
    B. Hamlin Garland
    C. Ralph Waldo Emerson
    D. Harriet Beecher Stowe
21. _____ advanced Emily Dickinson's literary and cultural taste and affected her ideas on religion.
    A. Benjamin Newton   B. Hamlin Garland
    C. Harriet Beecher Stowe   D. Charles Wadsworth
22. As Emily Dickinson's teacher, _____ supplied her with intellectual challenge and contact with the outside world.
    A. Benjamin Newton   B. Hamlin Garland
    C. Charles Wadsworth   D. Mark Twain
23. Emily Dickinson's most excellent creation of poems can date back

to the _____.

A. early 1860s   B. late 1860s   C. early 1870s   D. late 1870s

24. _____ was considered as "the nun of Amherst".

   A. Walt Whitman   B. Mark Twain
   C. Emily Dickinson   D. Harriet Beecher Stowe

25. The significant topics included in Emily Dickinson's poems were _____ and _____.

   A. nature; human   B. death; eternal life
   C. nature; life   D. human; death

26. Mark Twain wrote his most outstanding works in a large mansion in Hartford except _____.

   A. *The Gilded Age*
   B. *The Adventures of Tom Sawyer*
   C. *Jumping Frog*
   D. *Life on the Mississippi*

27. With the increasing success, Mark Twain's intellectual _____ and _____ of human nature also gradually grew.

   A. pessimism; despair   B. attention; sympathy
   C. pessimism; sympathy D. curiosity; attention

28. _____ was considered as "the true father of our national literature".

   A. Walt Whitman   B. Mark Twain
   C. Emily Dickinson   D. Harriet Beecher Stowe

29. _____ regarded Mark Twain as "the first truly American writer".

   A. Hamlin Garland   B. H. L. Mencken
   C. William Faulkner   D. Ernest Hemingway

30. _____'s later works unmistakably showed his change from an optimist and humorist to an almost despairing determinist.

   A. James Fenimore Cooper   B. William Dean Howells
   C. Hamlin Garland   D. Mark Twain

31. Ernest Hemingway made statements about Mark Twain, "all modern American literature comes from one book— _____."

A. *The Mysterious Stranger*
B. *The Man That Corrupted Hadleyburg*
C. *Roughing It*
D. *The Adventures of Huckleberry Finn*

32. Henry James's first novel was _____.
    A. *Daisy Miller*   B. *Roderick Hudson*
    C. *Watch and Ward*   D. *The Bostonians*

33. While Mark Twain and William Dean Howells satirized European manners at times, _____ was an admirer.
    A. O. Henry   B. Henry James
    C. Walt Whitman   D. Jack London

34. Walt Whitman published his poem "I Hear America Singing" in the _____ edition of *Leaves of Grass*.
    A. first   B. second   C. third   D. fourth

35. As a productive writer, Henry James was recognized as a "literary master" in _____.
    A. England   B. Europe   C. New York   D. America

36. _____ was the forerunner of psychological realism.
    A. Kate Chopin   B. Mark Twain
    C. Henry James   D. Walt Whitman

37. Kate Chopin's two major short story collections were *Bayou Folk* and _____.
    A. *A Night in Acadie*   B. *The Story of an Hour*
    C. *Desiree's Baby*   D. *The Storm*

38. _____ is now regarded as a forerunner of feminist authors of the 20th century.
    A. Emily Brontë   B. Elizabeth Browning
    C. Emily Dickinson   D. Kate Chopin

39. *The Story of an Hour* is a boutique among short stories of _____.
    A. Kate Chopin   B. Mark Twain
    C. Henry James   D. Walt Whitman

40. The publication of the first edition of *Leaves of Grass* was

in _____.
A. 1845 B. 1850 C. 1855 D. 1860

41. Generally speaking, the most popular and the best poem to commemorate Lincoln's death is _____.
    A. *Song of Myself*   B. *I Hear America Singing*
    C. *Cavalry Crossing a Ford*   D. *O Captain! My Captain!*

42. William Sidney Porter is the real name of the literary giant _____, who specializes in short stories.
    A. Gustave Flaubert
    B. Henri René Albert Guy de Maupassant
    C. O. Henry
    D. Anton Pavlovich Chekhov

43. Which of the following famous American writers had never received a good education?
    A. O. Henry   B. John Griffith London
    C. Robert Penn Warren   D. Benjamin Franklin

44. O. Henry's story creation ability was indeed inspired by people around him. For example, his maiden aunt often entertained him by reading stories to him, and teachers and a group of peers sometimes started a _____ game.
    A. story-telling   B. role-playing
    C. children's play performing D. composition competition

45. The title of one of O. Henry's books, *The Four Million* contains some thoughts of the author. Do you know what this title implies?
    A. The author holds the view that all the people of New York City are worth writing about, and not simply the upper "Four Hundred."
    B. New York is a large city with four million people; however, it can't accommodate the dream of an ordinary person.
    C. It is known to all that New York is the first city in America, and the author is proud of the strength and prosperity of his country.
    D. The author believes that the lives of four million ordinary people

are too boring. Only the lives of four hundred people in the upper class are worth describing.

46. O. Henry has a special sympathy for the poor people. He showed his hatred towards the rich who oppressed and exploited them. This attitude is especially reflected in one of his novels _____.
    A. *The Gift of the Magi*
    B. *An Unfinished Story*
    C. *The Cop and the Anthem*
    D. *The Last Leaf*

47. There is a lot of evidence that O. Henry's works were influenced by _____'s style. The resemblance between the two writers was remarkable, such as clear story structure and keen observation of details.
    A. Ernest Hemingway
    B. Stefan Zweig
    C. Gustave Flaubert
    D. Maupassant

48. Which of the following Chinese novels has a protagonist similar to Soapy in *The Cop and the Anthem*?
    A. *Rickshaw Boy*
    B. *Kong Yiji*
    C. *Diary of a Madman*
    D. *Four Generations in One House*

49. Theodore Herman Albert Dreiser had some precious qualities, for example, his moral earnestness and his endurance to persist in the face of failure, disappointment, and despair. Do you know from whom he inherited these qualities?
    A. His mother
    B. His father
    C. His teacher
    D. His ancestors

50. Which of the following American writers once worked as an itinerant journalist for the *Chicago Globe*, and then slowly finished the transition from a reporter to a famous writer?
    A. Mark Twain
    B. Romain Rolland
    C. O. Henry
    D. Theodore Herman Albert Dreiser

51. For what reason was Theodore Herman Albert Dreiser's first novel, *Sister Carrie*, shelved by the publisher?
    A. Because it is not in line with the core values at that time and against the wishes of the rulers.

B. Because it broke the American dream and made people lose their newly established confidence in life.
   C. Because it depicts social transgressions by characters who feel no remorse and largely escape punishment, and because it uses "strong" language and names of living persons.
   D. Because it was strongly denounced by literary critics, for it is not conducive to the growth of teenagers.
52. Which of the following does not belong to the "Trilogy of Dreiser"?
   A. *The Financier*   B. *An Unfinished Story*
   C. *The Titan*   D. *The Stoic*
53. What is the central theme of *An American Tragedy* written by Theodore Herman Albert Dreiser?
   A. Concerns and confusions about the future of the United States.
   B. The identification of potency with money.
   C. Regret and sympathy for the Beat Generation.
   D. Personal dissatisfaction with the Lost Generation.
54. During the last two decades of his life, Theodore Herman Albert Dreiser entirely discarded fiction creation and began to be absorbed in _____.
   A. political activism and polemical writing
   B. current affairs review writing
   C. literary criticism writing
   D. government documents writing
55. Which of the following does not belong to the negative evaluation of Theodore Herman Albert Dreiser's works by critics at that time?
   A. His writing is viewed as a gathering of chaotic structure and terrible plots.
   B. His writing is often regarded as crude and awkward.
   C. He is controversial, and his personal behavior is immoral.
   D. He is a poor thinker and a dangerous political radical.
56. Literary circles generally believe that Theodore Herman Albert Dreiser won the respect and love of readers mainly because of

his _____.

A. humorous language style and delicate description which hit the mind directly

B. exciting plot arrangement and unexpected ending

C. thought-provoking central thought and social significance

D. powerful narrative based on a large quantity of material and detailed illustrations

57. In the later phase of Theodore Herman Albert Dreiser's writing career, he tended to balance his more pessimistic views with _____.

A. belief in the possibilities of the world peace

B. belief in the possibilities of the American dream

C. belief in the possibilities of social justice

D. belief in the realization of personal ideal

58. What happened at the end of the 19th century that made Jack London decide to improve his educational level to change his condition and that of others?

A. He joined in the parade organized by the unemployed but was jailed for vagrancy.

B. He wrote a book to express support for the unemployed.

C. He was caught by the police when stealing from pedestrians in the street.

D. He picked a quarrel and made trouble when he was drunk.

59. What led Jack Griffith London to be influenced by the hopeful socialism of Marx on the one hand and the rather darker views of Nietzsche and Darwinism on the other?

A. Knowledge   B. Temperament

C. Social atmosphere D. Logic

60. Sherwood Anderson's works pay much attention to _____, with emphasis on lower-class people.

A. the psychological and emotional aspect of American small-town life

B. life and work experience of nobodies from all walks of life

C. heavy blow brought by the war to the industrial development of America

D. the material and ethical aspect of American small-town life

61. Sherwood Anderson's works uncover the important transnational period in American history, that is, from a rural to a predominantly _____ society.

A. industrial   B. Romantic   C. modernized   D. idealistic

62. *Winesburg, Ohio* was a remarkable success, which was a collection of tales of the "_____" characters he had known during Sherwood Anderson's youth in Ohio.

A. grotesque   B. pathetic   C. humorous   D. treacherous

63. Despite his limited writing scope, Sherwood Anderson's _____ provided new perspectives for the literature of the 20th century.

A. sensitive depictions of poverty and eccentricity and his deceptively simple style

B. concise depictions of poverty and gentility and his deceptively fantastic style

C. profound analysis of human nature and society

D. sober understanding of human's life span

64. Which of the following writers is the first to write in colloquial style since Mark Twain?

A. Ernest Hemingway   B. Sherwood Anderson
C. William Faulkner   D. Robert Frost

65. Which of the following is not the writing characteristic of Sherwood Anderson's short stories?

A. He arranged a lot of ups and downs in the whole work which always affected the reader's heart, and he was very talented at creating a terrible atmosphere.

B. He made fantastic use of the point of view of outsider characters as a way to criticize conventional society.

C. His sensitive depictions of poverty and eccentricity and his deceptively simple style, with its matter-of-fact Midwestern sentences.

D. He gave the craft of the short story a decided push toward stories presenting a slice of life or a significant moment as opposed to panorama and summary.

66. Sherwood Anderson advocated simplicity and directness of style, which of the following writers has never been influenced by him?
   A. Francis Scott Key Fitzgerald   B. Ernest Hemingway
   C. William Faulkner   D. Edward Estlin Cummings

67. Which of the following writers respectfully called Sherwood Anderson "the father of my generation of American writers" and "the tradition of American writing which our successors will carry on"?
   A. Ernest Hemingway   B. Mark Twain
   C. William Faulkner   D. Robert Frost

68. In *Winesburg, Ohio*, why does the little boy have a look of fear on his face when he sees the loving teacher, Wing Biddlebaum, who is about to touch his head?
   A. People in the town mistake him for a pedophile who has committed a series of savage sexual assaults on young children.
   B. As an orphan, the little boy is afraid that he will be trafficked to somewhere to do manual labor by his teacher.
   C. It is rumored that his teacher often whipped the students who didn't finish their homework.
   D. There are rumors that the teacher is a psycho killer. He has killed several boys in the past few months.

69. In *Paper Pills*, Sherwood Anderson describes Doctor Reefy who has a peculiar habit of stuffing pieces of paper into his pockets until they become round hard paper balls. What do the round hard paper balls symbolize?
   A. The round hard paper balls are symbolic of difficulty with human communication.
   B. The round hard paper balls are symbolic of the dark side of hu-

man nature.

C. The round hard paper balls are symbolic of friendship between bosom friends.

D. The round hard paper balls are symbolic of a dream that can never be realized.

70. In *Winesburg, Ohio*, after watching a prolonged and ineffectual conflict between the baker and the cat, mother puts her head on her hands and weeps. Try to interpret the reason why mother weeps.

    A. She is so controlling that her son doesn't develop as she expects.
    B. She suddenly realizes her terrible relationship with her son and her complete failure as a mother.
    C. The mother thinks that she is a member of the nobility, but the cruel reality dashes her dream.
    D. She has an almost abnormal love for her son, and she forbids him to leave her.

71. In *Departure* written by Sherwood Anderson, George Willard leaves Winesburg. What does his departure mean to him and people in the small towns?

    A. The town of Winesburg is only an illusion and his life there has become but a background on which to paint the dreams of his childhood.
    B. The town of Winesburg has disappeared and his life there has become but a background on which to paint the dreams of his manhood.
    C. The town of Winesburg is just the scene in George Willard's dream, which has nothing to do with reality.
    D. Capitalist society will eventually be replaced by socialism, and there is no absolute ideal kingdom.

III. Match-Making

Column A
1. Harriet Beecher Stowe
2. Walt Whitman
3. Emily Dickinson
4. Mark Twain
5. Henry James
6. Kate Chopin
7. O. Henry
8. Theodore Herman Albert Dreiser
9. Sherwood Anderson
10. Jack London

Column B
a. *An Unfinished Story*
b. *Winesburg, Ohio*
c. *Sister Carrie*
d. *The Call of the Wild*
e. *Uncle Tom's Cabin*
f. *The Portrait of a Lady*
g. *The Adventures of Tom Sawyer*
h. *The Awakening*
i. *Leaves of Grass*
j. *Wild Nights—Wild Nights!*

IV. Define the Literary Terms.

1. Free verse
2. O. Henry-style ending

V. Answer the Following Questions Briefly.

1. What are the literary characteristics of the Realistic Age?
2. How much do you know about realism?
3. What is the relationship between realism and local color in America?
4. Please briefly define realistic literature and try to conclude its characteristics.
5. Briefly summarize the storyline of *The Call of the Wild*.

6. Is *The Call of the Wild* a simple dog's story? Make a brief comment on the novel.
7. How is the idea of "survival of the fittest" displayed in *The Call of the Wild*?
8. Why did the author use "he" to refer to a dog in *The Call of the Wild*?
9. Make a brief comment on *Winesburg, Ohio*.
10. Comment briefly on the contribution Sherwood Anderson made to American literature.

Part V

Twentieth-Century Literature I: Before WWII

I. Fill in the Blanks.

1. In the years preceding World War I, _____ and _____ remained vital forces in American literature.
2. The best-selling American books in the first decades of the twentieth century were _____.
3. Early in the twentieth century, a rising number of "little magazines" brought numerous avant-garde writers to the attention of a limited but sophisticated audience, among them, the most influential was _____.
4. The _____ stands as a great dividing line between the 19th century and the contemporary American literature.
5. In the decade of _____ American literature achieved a new diversity and reached its greatest heights.
6. The most significant American poem of the 20th century was _____.
7. In 1920, Sinclair Lewis published his memorable denunciation of American small-town provincialism in _____.
8. "_____", a burst of literary achievement in the 1920s by Negro playwrights, poets, and novelists, who presented new awareness into the American experience, paved the way for the emergence of numerous black writers after mid-century.
9. The _____ of the 1930s greatly weakened the American nation's self-confidence.

10. John Steinbeck described the sweat-drenched lives of factory workers and migrant farmers in some memorable novels, among them, the best known is _____.
11. The writers of the fifties used a prose style modeled on the works of Ernest Hemingway and _____, narrative techniques derived from _____, and psychological insights taken from the writing of _____ and his followers.
12. Wallace Stevens's work is mainly inspired by the belief that "_____", that is, true ideas, correspond with an innate order in nature and the universe.
13. It was not until 1923, Wallace Stevens, at the age of 44, was finally persuaded to publish a book of poems, _____, which was part of a revolution in American poetry.
14. Wallace Stevens was regarded as a poet of the _____ group. He was gifted in using metaphors and symbols, meanwhile, he experimented a lot with styles, sound, and rules of rhymes.
15. Wallace Stevens's brilliant masterpiece *The Snow Man* published in 1921 was written in the modern era but revealed more of a _____ style, which appeared during the Romantic era.
16. _____ is a collection of Wallace Stevens's occasional lectures on poetry.
17. For the publication of his *Collected Poems*, _____ received the National Book Award and the Pulitzer Prize.
18. After his death, Wallace Stevens's previously uncollected works appeared in the title of _____.
19. "_____", Edwin Arlington Robinson's hometown, serves as the title of an early collection of his poetry, and the background for a group of vivid character sketches in verse.
20. _____ had a similar experience to Herman Melville. Sometime around 1904, one of his books came to the attention of President Theodore Roosevelt, who offered a job for Robinson in the customhouse in New York.

21. Like Robert Frost, _____ was also renowned for mastering the use of a dry, sometimes biting, New England humor.
22. _____ is a classical theme in Edwin Arlington Robinson's poems.
23. "_____" is included in *Richard Cory*, a narrative poem first published in 1897. In the poem, Robinson just composed a surprising ending, like that of O. Henry's short story.
24. _____ was a short-lived writer who possessed a quadruple identity as a novelist, poet, artist, and journalist in the history of American literature.
25. As an observer of psychological and social reality, Stephen Crane's writing style is driven by _____, _____ and _____.
26. In *Black Riders Came from the Sea* written by Stephen Crane, Black riders first appear exactly as real heroes, however, the poet uncovers the real hero in the last word of the last line— _____.
27. In _____, Stephen Crane reveals such a point of view: This world is now godless, and such a thing as a Savior is nothing but a religious fantasy.
28. In _____, Stephen Crane coveys such a perspective: nature is cruel and indifferent for the dangerous condition of survivors. However, friendships and mutual assistance among people can sometimes bring a slim chance of survival.
29. Stephen Crane's novel _____ relates the story of a good woman's downfall and destruction in a slum environment.
30. War in the novel _____ by Stephen Crane is a plain slaughter-house. There is nothing like valor or heroism on the battlefield, and if there is anything, it is the fear of death, cowardice, the natural instinct of man to run from danger.
31. Robert Frost's first book, _____, brought him to the attention of influential critics, among them the American expatriate Ezra Pound, who praised Frost as _____.
32. Robert Frost was a serious poet, the background of his poems is

_____ and his poems always focus on _____.

33. In *The Road Not Taken* written by Robert Frost, the "yellow wood" may symbolize _____.

34. In *The Road Not Taken,* the poets employed each "_____" to symbolize a possibility in life; the "_____" is the embodiment of every individual in the human world.

35. The poem of Robert Frost, *The Road Not Taken,* is very regularly structured with 4 classic 5-line stanzas, with the rhyme scheme "abaab" and in _____ tone or style.

36. In *Stopping by Woods on a Snowy Evening*, Robert Frost implied that while enjoying the tranquil scenery, he was tempted by a mysterious seduction to _____.

37. Among Robert Frost's poems, _____ is one of the few which generates a sense of horror.

38. In Robert Frost's poems, *Design*, the flower, spider, and the moth are respectively the embodiment of _____, _____, and _____.

39. *After Apple-Picking* is a well-known poem written by _____.

40. One of Robert Frost's longest poems, _____ is one of his most witty and wise anecdotal discussions about the values of life and character.

41. Poems written by Carl Sandburg eulogize, from the standpoint of a _____, the lives of outcasts, the contributions of immigrants and common people to urban culture, and the occupations of those who have survived or been sacrificed in the rise of industrial civilization.

42. Of poems written by Carl Sandburg, _____ shows impressive consistency of tone, and _____ uses the techniques of symbolism.

43. _____ carried forward Walt Whitman's long line but mitigated its rhetorical impact and intensity, and composed what are often in effect prose paragraphs.

44. Carl Sandburg was proud late in his career to "favor _____ poems for _____ people." His most ambitious attempt to accomplish that aim was _____.

45. Carl Sandburg's significant work in prose is a monumental and celebratory biography of _____, culminating in _____, a four-volume work that won the Pulitzer Prize in 1940.

46. Critics widely consider Carl Sandburg to be a hearty follower of _____, and pieces of evidence show that Sandburg took advantage of _____'s epigrammatic style.

47. The short poem *Fog* written by _____ is quite similar to Japanese Haiku in structure because this poem was done in 1916 when American Imagist poets led by _____ were experimenting to imitate the form of Japanese Haiku.

48. In the poem *Grass*, the grass may have several symbolic meanings. It could represent _____ after the death on the battlefield.

49. _____ was an American poet closely associated with both modernism and Imagism, moreover, he had a dual role as a poet and a doctor.

50. _____ was one of William Carlos Williams's most experimental books. When it was published, Williams was sharply criticized by many of his peers.

51. William Carlos Williams published one of his seminal books of poetry, _____, which contained a lot of classic poems including "The Red Wheelbarrow" and "To Elsie".

52. William Carlos Williams's modernist epic collage of place, _____, mixes long poem and prose, records a lot of local history materials, and is considered as one of the representative works of modern American philosophy poetry.

53. William Carlos Williams summarized his poetic method in the phrase "_____". _____ is the representative expression of his creed.

54. Ezra Pound once gave some advice and encouragement to _____,

who candidly acknowledged the value of Pound's assistance in the final revision of _____.

55. _____ and _____ were the early leaders in restoring to poetry the use of literary reference as an imaginative instrument.

56. A large part of Ezra Pound's work consists of "_____" in modern English of poems from earlier literatures, chiefly Greek, Latin, Italian, Provencal, and _____. Among these poems, his _____ is a masterpiece.

57. _____ was politically controversial and notorious for what he did during WWII. The final obstacle for the reader is the violence of his distrust of capitalism and his allegiance to the Utopian concept of "social credit."

58. _____ written by Ezra Pound, a satire of the materialistic forces involved in World War I, is a masterpiece.

59. In the long list of Ezra Pound's achievements, _____, a series of poems which he wrote from the 1920s throughout his life, is the most outstanding.

60. _____ once said: "Great literature is simply language charged with meaning to the utmost possible degree."

61. In constructing Imagism, a controversial American poet named Ezra Pound took a lot of inspiration from _____ poetry.

62. _____ was the first American writer to be awarded the Nobel Prize in Literature, and the prize-winning work is _____.

63. The first published book of Sinclair Lewis, _____, is about adventure stories written for children. The first serious novel of Lewis, _____, depicts a romantic adventure of a gentleman.

64. _____ depicts the most affluent and successful upper class of American society. The film based on the book received great success at the time. In 2005, *Time* magazine named it one of the "100 Best Movies" of the past 80 years.

65. _____ is a satirical novel concerning American culture and society, which criticizes the empty middle-class life and the social pres-

sure brought about by conformity.
66. The disadvantages and advantages of Sinclair Lewis's novels both vividly represent the characteristics of modern American literature. Critics call him "_____".
67. In 1920, Sinclair Lewis made his memorable denunciation of American small-town provincialism in _____.
68. In 1920, Eugene Gladstone O'Neill won his first Pulitzer Prize for _____. In 1922, he won his second Pulitzer Prize for _____. He won his last two Pulitzer Prize for _____ and _____.
69. _____ was the first American playwright to receive the Nobel Prize in Literature.
70. _____ is widely recognized as the most heralded work of Eugene Gladstone O'Neill.
71. In 1916, Eugene Gladstone O'Neill's first play _____ was put on by the Provincetown Players, which was significant not only for him but for American drama.
72. _____, a founding father of modernist poetry, took notice of Eliot's poetic genius and offered him some help.
73. *The Waste Land* won _____ more fame and reputation and made him the symbol of 20th-century modernism.
74. The immortal long poem, _____, is widely acclaimed as a revolutionary manifesto to break up with English poetic tradition.
75. Thomas Stearns Eliot wrote seven plays, the best of which is _____, a verse play on an ancient historical subject, written in 1935.
76. Thomas Stearns Eliot's last important work is _____, a profound meditation on time and timelessness, written in four parts.
77. "_____", one of the essays in *The Sacred Wood*, is the earliest statement of Thomas Stearns Eliot's aesthetics, which provided a useful instrument for modern criticism.
78. Thomas Stearns Eliot's second volume of criticism _____ (1914) was much admired for its critical method.

79. _____, the virgin piece of Francis Scott Key Fitzgerald, which reflects exactly the flavor and interests of a new generation, was a great success and soon became the bestseller at that time.

80. _____ is a novel that presented Francis Scott Key Fitzgerald's view on modern life of both psychological and physical malaise which characterized the times by meaninglessness and purposelessness.

81. _____ is the final novel of Francis Scott Key Fitzgerald, which was unfinished for his sudden death.

82. _____ was recruited by the Red Cross for World War I. Unfortunately, he was soon charged with treason. This experience provided the raw material for his first literary work, _____.

83. In Edward Estlin Cummings's works, science, industry, and machines are often the object of condemnation. Instead, _____, _____, _____, and _____, are the frequent themes of his poems.

84. Some of Edward Estlin Cummings's poems are virtually unreadable because of his experimental skills—Cummings deliberately presented them as "_____" to please the reader's eye with all the beauty contained in a pattern.

85. William Faulkner started his tentative writing with a collection of poetry _____.

86. A famous American writer _____ encouraged William Faulkner to develop his own style, to focus on prose, and to take advantage of his own southern background.

87. _____ firmly established William Faulkner's reputation as a powerful representative novelist of the Deep South.

88. William Faulkner's first novel of the sage, _____, is a book about the homecoming of the dying soldier and the disillusionment of the Lost Generation.

89. _____, the first book of the Yoknapatawpha series composed by William Faulkner, reveals his fuller development as a writer and founds his own themes and setting for writing.

90. _____ is William Faulkner's most favorite and most difficult novel and it helps Faulkner to win the world fame.
91. _____ composed by William Faulkner is an original stream of consciousness short novel composed of 59 _____.
92. William Faulkner was awarded the Pulitzer Prize for fiction by two of his works, _____, and his last novel _____.
93. In the "Yoknapatawpha saga," which took William Faulkner 33 years to complete, Yoknapatawpha County is a fictional name for _____ County in northern Mississippi. Its capital, Jefferson, refers to _____ where the author lived.
94. Writers like Ernest Hemingway and William Faulkner tried to represent the absurdity theme in traditional novelistic devices, while the writers in the 1960s regarded the conventional novel as "Literature of _____".
95. Quentin is a character in William Faulkner's novel _____.
96. Joe Christmas is a character in William Faulkner's novel _____.
97. _____ was said to touch William Faulkner in writing, and her well-known novels are *The Heart Is a Lonely Hunter* and *The Ballad of the Sad Café*.
98. The book _____ establishes Ernest Hemingway as a representative of writers who dealt with the Lost Generation.
99. _____ together with *The Great Gatsby* are known collectively as the landmark of the revival of American novels.
100. _____ caught the mood of the post-war generation and brought international fame to Ernest Hemingway.
101. _____ is the longest and the most ambitious work of Ernest Hemingway, describing the Spanish Civil War and the title comes from _____'s *Meditation*.
102. In the short novel _____, John Steinbeck portrayed the tragic friendship between two migrant workers.
103. In the work _____, John Steinbeck describes the fate of the lowly whose instinctive responses to life lead only to destruction.

104. _____ is generally regarded as John Steinbeck's masterpiece.
105. In 1935, John Steinbeck published _____, a collection of short stories which vividly described the life of poor Mexican-Americans with affection and humor.
106. John Steinbeck's post-war novel _____ reflects his bitter feelings against those greedy, rapacious elements of society which made the war possible.

II. Choose the Best Answer for Each Question.

1. The United States began the twentieth century with a population of less than 76,000,000, and the rural approximately accounts for _____ of the total.
   A. one-third   B. two-fifths   C. two-thirds   D. four-fifths
2. Early in the 20th century, _____ published works that would change the nature of American poetry. However, these works did not cause a sensation among the general audience.
   A. Ezra Pound   B. Thomas Stearns Eliot
   C. Robert Frost   D. both A and B
3. Which of the following is not the cause that made possible the publishing of a vast number of inexpensive paperbacks?
   A. The increase of wealth and education.
   B. The expansion of mass distribution book clubs.
   C. The technological advances in printing.
   D. The further expansion of colonialism.
4. *Poetry: A Magazine of Verse*, founded in Chicago by Harriet Monroe in 1912 contains the poems of many famous American poets, such as Ezra Pound and T.S. Eliot. These works _____.
   A. forced changes in the conventional relationships between poets and their audiences
   B. required readers to be armed with modernist sympathies and ad-

vanced intellectual understanding

C. caused fierce competition in the publishing market

D. both A and B

5. Writers of the first post-war era self-consciously acknowledged that they were a _____, devoid of faith and alienated from a civilization.

A. Lost Generation　　　　B. Beat Generation

C. Angry Generation　　　D. Painful Generation

6. The publication in 1922 of _____'s *The Waste Land*, helped to establish a modern tradition of literature rich in learning and allusive thought.

A. Thomas Stearns Eliot　　　　B. George Eliot

C. Francis Scott Key Fitzgerald　D. Ezra Pound

7. Francis Scott Key Fitzgerald summarized the experiences and attitudes of the 1920s in his masterpiece novel _____.

A. *This Side of Paradise*　　B. *The Great Gatsby*

C. *The Last Tycoon*　　　　D. *Tender Is the Night*

8. After the First World War, a group of new American dramatists emerged. Being hostile to the outworn and timid theatrical convention, they created works of tragedy, stark realism, and _____.

A. harmony between man and nature

B. social protest

C. money worship

D. national unity

9. The American "Thirties" lasted from the Crash, through the ensuing Great Depression, until the outbreak of the Second World War in 1939. This was a period of _____.

A. poverty and bleakness　　　B. important social movements

C. a new social consciousness　D. all of the above

10. In the 1960s and 1970s America's prose writers turned increasingly to _____.

A. experimental techniques and absurd humor

B. mocking examination of the irrational and the disordered

C. both A and B

D. appreciating examination of the sober-minded

11. An American woman writer named _____ who had settled down in Paris since 1903, gathered the young expatriates to her literary salon, and gave them a name the Lost Generation.

    A. Gertrude Stein   B. Adeline Virginia Woolf
    C. Emily Brontë   D. Anne Brontë

12. Wallace Stevens's passion for perfection is evident in his _____.

    A. disciplined thought
    B. intense and brilliant craftsmanship
    C. meticulous propriety of his language
    D. all of the above

13. For many readers, it seemed that Wallace Stevens had carried originality to the point of mere eccentricity, and he was called _____.

    A. a "dandy"   B. a "virtuoso of the insane"
    C. a writer of "near nonsense"   D. all of the above

14. _____ tends to be an eternal theme in Wallace Stevens's later poetry.

    A. The problem of the interrelation between the ideal and the real
    B. The problem of the contradiction between the ideal and the real
    C. The problem of the interrelation between chastity and the purity
    D. The problem of the contradiction between innocence and the evil

15. Which of the following statements about Wallace Stevens is appropriate?

    A. Most of his important poems were composed during the Great Depression and the two World Wars.
    B. He showed little concern about the sufferings and frustrations of the time.
    C. He believed that, as a poet, what he should and could do was to help his people to become more happily aware of the beauty, pleasure, excitement and meaning in the sordidness of reality.

D. All of the above.

16. _____ was prominent in two fields of activity which did not seem compatible with one another: he was a very successful businessman and a very remarkable contemporary poet at the same time.
    A. Wallace Stevens   B. William Faulkner
    C. Ernest Hemingway   D. Ezra Pound

17. Many of Wallace Stevens's remarkable poems derive their emotional power from reasoned revelation. This philosophical intention is supported by the titles Wallace Stevens gave to his volumes such as _____.
    A. *Harmonium*   B. *Ideas of Order*
    C. *Parts of a World*   D. all of the above

18. Which of the following poems was not written by Wallace Stevens?
    A. *Anecdote of the Jar*   B. *Departmental*
    C. *Peter Quince at the Clavier* D. *The Emperor of Ice-Cream*

19. *Richard Cory* and *Miniver Cheevy* are excellent examples of Edwin Arlington Robinson's _____ attitude.
    A. pathetic   B. realistic   C. ironic   D. optimistic

20. The poem *Ben Jonson Entertains a Man from Stratford* was written by Edwin Arlington Robinson. It is a brilliant commentary on _____'s character.
    A. Shakespeare   B. Ben Jonson
    C. Percy Bysshe Shelley   D. Samuel Johnson

21. In his trilogy *Merlin* (1917), *Lancelot* (1920), and *Tristram* (1927), Edwin Arlington Robinson wrote the most extensive poems based on _____ since Alfred Tennyson.
    A. the Arthurian legends   B. the Biblical stories
    C. the Greek mythologies   D. Indian legends

22. Which of the following statements about Edwin Arlington Robinson and his works is incorrect?
    A. He created out of the model of his hometown, a naturalistic

world, Tilbury town, where life seems futile and meaningless.

B. Robinson was skillful in staying content with the old way and calmly expressing his individual view of life and hence succeeded in evaluating the current society.

C. Robinson was good at non-poetic language for non-poetic subjects.

D. He was gifted in writing in dialect, and he made the effort to use plain language.

23. Which of the following statements about Edwin Arlington Robinson and his works is correct?

A. His poems are characterized by a striking ironic tone, and he was not keen on the innovative or experimental writing of poems of the time.

B. Traditional factors such as beat, rhyme, rhythm, meter, foot, etc. can be still seen in his poems.

C. In his poems, the sense of humor is too often juxtaposed with a pervading sense of alienation or futility.

D. All of the above.

24. *Miniver Cheevy* is a dramatic lyric poem centering on a twentieth-century misfit. The title sounds rather similar to "mini achieves," which is a vivid sketch of an ambitious and cynical young man who believes that _____.

A. anyway, he will become a millionaire one day

B. everyone around him is not as capable as him. They are all fools

C. he would be successful in any other age but the present one

D. as long as he wants, there is nothing he can't do

25. Which of the following comments on *The Black Riders and Other Lines* is correct?

A. It is the first collection of poems composed by Stephen Crane.

B. It was composed in a very experimental form and with many astonishing elements.

C. It seems to be too unconventional to be universally recognized.

D. All of the above.
26. Which of the following comments on Stephen Crane is correct?
    A. His writings endow "a sudden direction and a fresh impulse" with the whole aesthetic movement of the nineties.
    B. Crane added his sensitivity into the sounds of words, the rhythms of language and a highly original use of symbol, color and metaphor to express the different grades of epistemological uncertainty.
    C. Crane's poetry, written in free verse with delicate rhyme, is thought to be a pioneer to Imagist Movement.
    D. Both A and B.
27. Which of the following comments on Stephen Crane is incorrect?
    A. Crane was obsessed by war, death and violence.
    B. In his works we can observe his firm-minded irony and his essential vision.
    C. As a precursor of naturalistic writers, Crane dissects the position of man, who has been segregated not only from society but also from God and nature.
    D. In a word, Crane was a great, ambitious, creative but penniless literary giant.
28. What does "come from the sea" imply in *Black Riders Came from the Sea* written by Stephen Crane?
    A. The distance and adventurous spirit.
    B. The broad horizon and mind.
    C. The cruelty and power of nature.
    D. None of the above is true.
29. Stephen Crane's best short stories include *The Open Boat*, *The Blue Hotel*, and _____, all reinforcing the basic Stephen Crane motif of environment and heredity overwhelming man.
    A. *Dreiser Looks at Russia*   B. *An Experiment in Misery*
    C. *Tragic America*   D. *The Red Badge of Courage*
30. Which writer has a naturalist tendency?

A. Stephen Crane B. Edwin Arlington Robinson
C. Theodore Dreiser D. All of the above

31. In the pre-war period, such writers as _____, pointed out the contradictions between what American preached and they practiced.

    A. Mark Twain B. Jack London
    C. Stephen Crane D. all of the above

32. Which of the following is not true about Robert Frost?

    A. By the end of his life he had become a national bard.
    B. He received honorary degrees from forty-four colleges and universities and won five Pulitzer Prizes.
    C. The United States Senate passed resolutions honoring his birthdays.
    D. When he was eighty-seven, he read his poetry at the inauguration of President John F. Kennedy.

33. Which of the following is true about Robert Frost?

    A. Even though he followed the principle of "the old-fashioned way to be new", Robert Frost had never rejected the revolutionary poetic principles of his contemporaries.
    B. As a poet of nature he had obvious affinities with realistic writers, notably William Wordsworth and Ralph Waldo Emerson. He saw society as a storehouse of analogy and symbol.
    C. He had little faith in religious dogma or speculative thought.
    D. His concern with nature reflected deep moral uncertainties, and his poetry, for all its apparent complexity, often probed some superficial ideas.

34. What are the main differences between Robert Frost's works and those composed by his contemporaries in the early 20th century?

    A. Frost did not break with the older poetic tradition, nor did he make many experiments with form.
    B. He learned from tradition and made the colloquial New England speech into a poetic expression.

C. His poems are filled with more energy and wisdom, loaded with more pleasure, reflecting life and truth.

D. All of the above.

35. What are the characteristics of Robert Frost's poems in rhythm?

    A. He only wrote in a completely metrical form and totally rejected free verse.

    B. He only wrote in free verse and totally rejected metrical forms.

    C. Sometimes he wrote in a form that borrows freely from both—a form that might be called semi-free and semi-conventional.

    D. None of the above is correct.

36. It would be a mistake to imagine that Robert Frost is easy to understand just because he is easy to read. On the contrary, the profound ideas are often delivered by _____.

    A. plain language and simple form

    B. flowery language and sophisticated form

    C. sincere emotion and humble tone

    D. rich imagination and exquisite wording

37. *The Road Not Taken* written by Robert Frost elucidates such an admonishment: _____.

    A. People come to the world to suffer and they will never get a little bit of happiness.

    B. In order to possess something worthwhile, someone has to give up something which seems as lovely and valuable as the chosen one.

    C. As long as there is reasonable planning, people can get everything they want.

    D. It is not human themselves that could dominate their fate, but nature or God.

38. The repetition of the last two lines in the poem, *The Road Not Taken*, indicates _____.

    A. the speaker's sense of responsibility or simply his helplessness in front of nature

B. the speaker's sense of anxiety or simply his terror in front of nature

C. the speaker's sense of fearlessness or simply his confidence in front of nature

D. none of the above is true

39. The poem *Design* written by Robert Frost gives us such enlightenment: _____.

    A. People always live in endless reincarnation, and there is no way to get rid of it.

    B. No one in this world is completely safe; each may exist as the other's prey.

    C. The world is very beautiful. Human beings can coexist with their enemies.

    D. All life experiences are designed by God, without exception.

40. In the Thirties, poets like Archibald MacLeish and _____ wrote compassionately about common people, workers, and farmers.

    A. Emily Dickinson   B. Ezra Pound
    C. Robert Frost   D. Langston Hughes

41. Which of the following was not written by Robert Frost?

    A. *Tilbury Town*   B. *A Witness Tree*
    C. *Steeple Bush*   D. *In the Clearing*

42. Robert Frost is famous for his lyric poems. Which of the following lyric poems was not written by Robert Frost?

    A. *Birches*

    B. *Stopping by Woods on a Snowy Evening*

    C. *After Apple-Picking*

    D. *Richard Cory*

43. The following three poets opened the way to Modern poetry except _____.

    A. Ezra Pound   B. Thomas Stearns Eliot
    C. Edward Estlin Cummings   D. Robert Frost

44. Among the following writers, _____ and Jack London commit-

ted suicide.

A. Ernest Hemingway B. Robert Frost
C. William Wordsworth D. Harriet Beecher Stowe

45. _____ was absolutely committed to the notion that a poet lives in two worlds—the world of reality and the world of imagination—and builds bridges between them.

A. Edwin Arlington Robinson B. Wallace Stevens
C. Robert Frost D. Carl Sandburg

46. Like his contemporary, Robert Frost, Carl Sandburg lived to enjoy enormous popular acclaim, but unlike Frost, Sandburg never _____.

A. gained the broad approval of the literary establishment
B. was cautious and intelligent as the former
C. wrote poems in free or blank verse
D. received the heartfelt support of the majority of authors

47. The poems that made Sandburg well-known appeared in the following four volumes except _____.

A. *Chicago Poems* B. *Cornhuskers*
C. *Smoke and Steel* D. *Leaves of Grass*

48. With the precedent of Walt Whitman behind them, poems written by Carl Sandburg depict a comprehensive panorama of American life, embracing _____.

A. prairie
B. eastern, and western landscapes
C. vignettes of the modern city
D. all of the above

49. Carl Sandburg's language draws on the colorful diction of immigrants and the lingo of urban dwellers. However, _____ in his verse.

A. he reveals the yearning for the upper class and derogation towards the poor
B. subtleties of imagery or rhythm overrides unadorned directness

of statement

C. unadorned directness of statement overrides subtleties of imagery or rhythm

D. none of the above is correct

50. Carl Sandburg insisted on innovation in American poetry by _____.

    A. originating new ways of expression

    B. shifting the subject matter from rural landscapes to modern industrial city life

    C. trying to praise modern mechanical culture and adopt colloquial diction

    D. all of the above

51. The poems that made Carl Sandburg famous appeared in four volumes. They are the following except _____.

    A. *Chicago Poems*   B. *Cornhuskers*
    C. *Smoke and Steel*   D. *Design*

52. As a poet, Carl Sandburg was associated with the Imagists and wrote well-known Imagist poems such as _____.

    A. *Fog*   B. *Lost*
    C. *Monotone*   D. all of the above

53. Carl Sandburg had also taken interest in folk songs which he tried to collect and sing during his travels. These folk songs appeared eventually in print in his well-known _____.

    A. *Good Morning, America*   B. *The People, Yes*
    C. *In Reckless Ecstasy*   D. *The American Songbag*

54. Most of the important 20th-century American poets were related to the Imagist Movement, including _____.

    A. Ezra Pound   B. Wallace Stevens
    C. Carl Sandburg   D. all of the above

55. It is not fair to say that _____ did not see the evils of modern life. But it is also true that he wrote chiefly "to help the sick and give the people hope". Therefore, he was optimistic.

A. Thomas Stearns Eliot B. Wallace Stevens
C. Francis Scott Key Fitzgerald D. Carl Sandburg

56. _____ was a socialist. His voice was a hearty voice from the masses of the people he had close contact with all his life.
    A. Thomas Stearns Eliot B. Wallace Stevens
    C. Francis Scott Key Fitzgerald D. Carl Sandburg

57. Which of the following can be considered as William Carlos Williams's contribution to the development of American literature?
    A. He has been recognized as a forefather of open verses. His unique style injected new blood into the modern American poets.
    B. He had an especially significant influence on many of the American literary movements of the 1950s.
    C. He made some attempts in developing and constructing the new poetics and was known as one of the greatest poets in the history of American modern poetry.
    D. All of the above.

58. Which of the following awards has William Carlos Williams never won?
    A. The National Book Award B. Bowling Root Poetry Prize
    C. United States Poet Laureate D. The Pulitzer Prize for poetry

59. Which of the following statements about Ezra Pound is correct?
    A. Pound advocated the use of myth and personae in poetry. His poetry is dense with personal, literary, and historical allusions.
    B. Pound was a leading spokesman of the "Imagist Movement", and he was one of the most influential American poets and critics, often called "the artist's poet".
    C. Pound's translation Cathay, a collection of ancient Chinese poems, was widely recognized.
    D. Pound functioned as a bridge between Chinese and western cultural communication.

60. "The apparition of these faces in the crowd; Petals on a wet, black

bough." This is the shortest poem written by _____.

    A. Thomas Stearns Eliot   B. Robert Frost

    C. Ezra Pound   D. Edward Estlin Cummings

61. Deeply influenced by Confucian ideas, _____ showed great interest in Chinese literature and translated the poetry of Li Po into English.

    A. Ezra Pound   B. Robert Frost

    C. Thomas Stearns Eliot   D. Edward Estlin Cummings

62. Ezra Pound's long poem _____ contained more than one hundred poems loosely connected.

    A. *The Waste Land*   B. *The Cantos*

    C. *Don Juan*   D. *Queen Mab*

63. Which of the following can be considered as "the most sensational event in twentieth-century American publishing history"?

    A. The great success of *Main Street.*

    B. The great success of *Babbitt.*

    C. Sinclair Lewis became the first American writer to win the Nobel Prize in Literature.

    D. Sinclair Lewis was the only one who dare to criticize the current social situation.

64. Which of the following works of Sinclair Lewis was awarded the Pulitzer Prize and was once adapted as a Hollywood film in 1931?

    A. *Arrowsmith*   B. *Dodsworth*

    C. *Babbitt*   D. *Kingsblood Royal*

65. Which of the following statements about the three stages of Sinclair Lewis's literary career is correct?

    A. The first stage (1910-1919) can be called the training period. Most of the works in this period totally break with the old conventions.

    B. The second stage (1920-1930) can be called the flowering period. However, during this time, his status in American literature had not yet been established.

C. The third stage (1931-1951) stretched over the rest of his life. In this period, he never reached to the level when he was the author of *Main Street*.

D. None of the above is true.

66. Which of the following statements about Sinclair Lewis and his works is incorrect?

    A. His literary creation infused new energy to American literature, which is his main contribution to America.

    B. As the spokesman of the American lower class, he showed his aversion to the elegant and optimistic romanticism in the 19th century.

    C. The novels of Lewis mostly employ irony to expose the evils and contradictions in American bourgeois society.

    D. His pen attacks all kinds of social ills. His novel is treated as a prism in American literature.

67. How many Pulitzer Prizes has Eugene Gladstone O'Neill won?

    A. One   B. Four   C. Three   D. Five

68. _____ was regarded as the greatest American playwright in the history of American literature.

    A. Eugene Gladstone O'Neill   B. Robert Frost
    C. Adeline Virginia Woolf   D. Thomas Stearns Eliot

69. Which of the following statements about Eugene Gladstone O'Neill is correct?

    A. He is among the first Americans to use daily speeches and dialect in his plays, and to concentrate on characters on the fringes of society.

    B. He is unanimously regarded as the father of modern American drama and well deserved the title of "American Shakespeare".

    C. He is not the only American playwright to have won the Nobel Prize in Literature.

    D. Both A and B.

70. In the 1920s, Eugene O'Neill established an international reputation

with such plays as _____.

A. *The Emperor Jones* B. *Anna Christie*

C. *The Hairy Ape* D. all of the above

71. The magic of _____'s power lies in his never ceasing attempt to improve his art in step with the spirit of the times. He began writing in a naturalistic vein, then, he moved on and became obsessed with devices such as symbolism and Expressionism. During the 1940s, he turned back to what he had started with. Thus, his career came full circle.

    A. Tennessee Williams B. Arthur Miller

    C. Clifford Odets D. Eugene O'Neill

72. Which of the following statements about Thomas Stearns Eliot is incorrect?

    A. Eliot was more English than American, for he spent more time in England, however, he didn't identify with English cultural values.

    B. Eliot was regarded as a founding father of the 20th-century modernist poetry.

    C. Eliot was the most influential critic of his time and an excellent playwright.

    D. In 1948 Eliot became a Nobel Prize winner for literature.

73. In 1920, Thomas Stearns Eliot published his _____, containing, among other essays, "Tradition and the Individual Talent", the earliest statement of his aesthetics.

    A. *Four Quartets* B. *The Sacred Wood*

    C. *Murder in the Cathedral* D. *Ash Wednesday*

74. Thomas Stearns Eliot's later poetry took a positive turn toward faith in life. This was demonstrated by _____, a poem of mystical conflict between faith and doubt.

    A. *Four Quartets* B. *The Sacred Wood*

    C. *Murder in the Cathedral* D. *Ash Wednesday*

75. In his work _____, Thomas Stearns Eliot satirized the straw men, the Guy Fawkes men, whose world would end "not with a

bang, but a whimper."

    A. *Four Quartets*   B. *The Sacred Wood*

    C. *Murder in the Cathedral*   D. *The Hollow Men*

76. In 1927, _____ was confirmed in Anglican Church and became a British subject. So, both countries claim his works as part of their own literature.

    A. Thomas Stearns Eliot   B. Wallace Stevens

    C. Robert Frost   D. Carl Sandburg

77. _____'s later poetry took a positive turn toward faith in life, in strong contrast with the desperation of *The Waste Land*.

    A. Thomas Stearns Eliot   B. Wallace Stevens

    C. Francis Scott Key Fitzgerald   D. Carl Sandburg

78. In satirical counterpoint, _____'s Sweeney poems had symbolized the rising tide of anticultural infidelity and human baseness.

    A. Thomas Stearns Eliot   B. Francis Scott Key Fitzgerald

    C. Ernest Hemingway   D. Carl Sandburg

79. Francis Scott Key Fitzgerald has usually been given the credit to coin the term the "_____" to describe that era.

    A. Gilded Age   B. Realism Age

    C. Decayed Age   D. Jazz Age

80. Francis Scott Key Fitzgerald's greatest contribution to American literature, even the whole world literature, is that _____.

    A. he is usually credited with coining a term to describe that era

    B. he found intuitively, in his own experience, the manifestation of the intense agony of the nation and created a myth of American life

    C. T.S. Eliot who read his *The Great Gatsby* three times thought highly of it as "the first step that American fiction has taken since Henry James"

    D. his favorite work, *The Great Gatsby* was a sensitive and symbolic expression of themes of modern life concerned with the satirical portrayal of the American Dream, inductive outside while corrupted inside

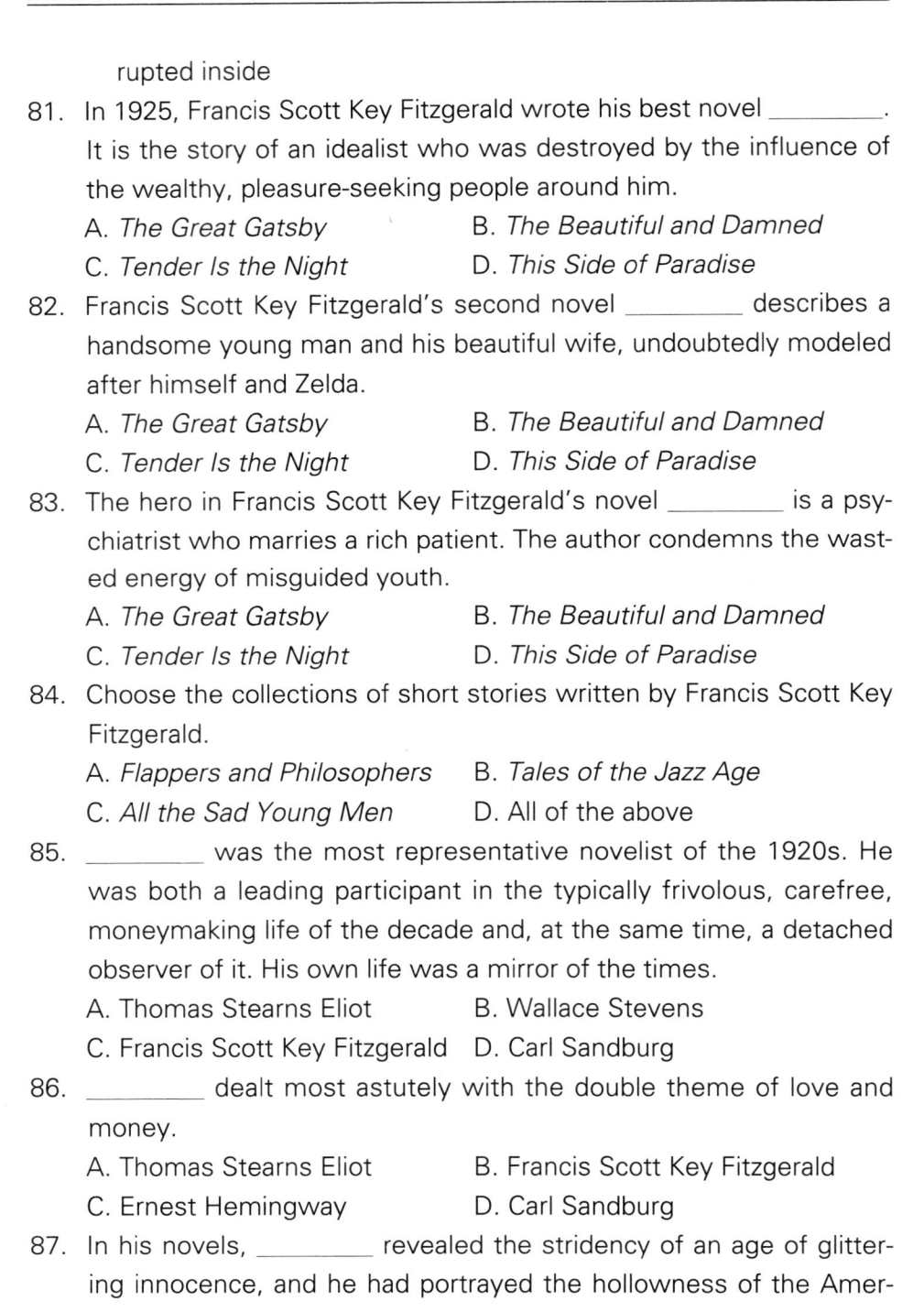

81. In 1925, Francis Scott Key Fitzgerald wrote his best novel _____. It is the story of an idealist who was destroyed by the influence of the wealthy, pleasure-seeking people around him.
    A. *The Great Gatsby*
    B. *The Beautiful and Damned*
    C. *Tender Is the Night*
    D. *This Side of Paradise*

82. Francis Scott Key Fitzgerald's second novel _____ describes a handsome young man and his beautiful wife, undoubtedly modeled after himself and Zelda.
    A. *The Great Gatsby*
    B. *The Beautiful and Damned*
    C. *Tender Is the Night*
    D. *This Side of Paradise*

83. The hero in Francis Scott Key Fitzgerald's novel _____ is a psychiatrist who marries a rich patient. The author condemns the wasted energy of misguided youth.
    A. *The Great Gatsby*
    B. *The Beautiful and Damned*
    C. *Tender Is the Night*
    D. *This Side of Paradise*

84. Choose the collections of short stories written by Francis Scott Key Fitzgerald.
    A. *Flappers and Philosophers*
    B. *Tales of the Jazz Age*
    C. *All the Sad Young Men*
    D. All of the above

85. _____ was the most representative novelist of the 1920s. He was both a leading participant in the typically frivolous, carefree, moneymaking life of the decade and, at the same time, a detached observer of it. His own life was a mirror of the times.
    A. Thomas Stearns Eliot
    B. Wallace Stevens
    C. Francis Scott Key Fitzgerald
    D. Carl Sandburg

86. _____ dealt most astutely with the double theme of love and money.
    A. Thomas Stearns Eliot
    B. Francis Scott Key Fitzgerald
    C. Ernest Hemingway
    D. Carl Sandburg

87. In his novels, _____ revealed the stridency of an age of glittering innocence, and he had portrayed the hollowness of the Amer-

ican worship of riches and the unending American dream of love, splendor and fulfilled desires.

A. Thomas Stearns Eliot   B. Francis Scott Key Fitzgerald
C. Ernest Hemingway   D. Carl Sandburg

88. Edward Estlin Cummings was one of the most outstanding poets of the 20th Century. However, he remained a controversial figure for _____.

A. he was clearly hostile to women and was protested by feminists
B. he wrote a lot of works criticizing the shortcomings of the times, which annoyed many critics
C. his aggrieved experience in a French detention camp for three months
D. the dexterous novelty of his versification and his daring experimentation

89. Edward Estlin Cummings was famous for the experiments. The bold attempts can be manifested in that _____.

A. he deliberately ignored the conventional capitalization of the proper names "god" and "america" and even refused to capitalize the word "i"
B. he violated the regular grammar by freely splitting or combining words, using purposeful under-punctuation, and breaking phrases by cadence to the advantage of the melody
C. he often employed words and phrases symbolically or simply as an image to display something meaningful in mind but probably illogical in appearance
D. all of the above

90. William Faulkner was the _____ American writer to win the Nobel Prize in Literature for "his powerful and artistically unique contribution to the modern American novel."

A. third   B. fifth   C. fourth   D. sixth

91. William Faulkner's Yoknapatawpha novels mainly have something to do with the three Sagas in Yoknapatawpha Coun-

ty: _____, _____, and _____.

A. the Sartoris family; the Compson family; the Snopes family

B. the Sartoris family; the Smith family; the Snopes family

C. the Compson family; the Snopes family; the Smith family

D. the Sartoris family; the Compson family; the Smith family

92. Which of the following comments about William Faulkner is incorrect?

    A. Faulkner was one of the most influential writers in the history of American literature and was the representative of the stream of consciousness.

    B. He made a strong and incomparable art contribution to the American novel.

    C. He was the new symbol that the power of the innovation of European modernist novel transferred to the American continent.

    D. American poet laureate Robert Frost once said, "He told us how to create literature in these materials, his power is so strong."

93. The term "Southern Renaissance" refers to the prosperity of southern American novels in the 1920s. Who had made the greatest contribution to this grand occasion?

    A. Ernest Hemingway   B. William Faulkner
    C. John Steinbeck   D. Carl Sandburg

94. There are three main subjects in William Faulkner's writing: _____, _____, and _____.

    A. history and the problem of race

    B. folk humor of the old South

    C. horror, violence and abnormal

    D. all of the above

95. Which of the following descriptions about *The Sound and the Fury* composed by William Faulkner is wrong?

    A. The novel has achieved great critical success and a prominent place among the greatest of American novels.

    B. It plays a role in William Faulkner's receiving the Pulitzer Prize in

Literature.

C. This novel is widely popular due to William Faulkner's technique of construction, which means his ability to recreate thinking patterns.

D. It is an essential development in the stream-of-consciousness narrative technique.

96. Thomas Sutpen is a character in William Faulkner's novel _____.
    A. *Absalom, Absalom!* B. *Light in August*
    C. *Go Down, Moses* D. *The Sound and the Fury*

97. _____ wrote about the society in the South by inventing families which represented different social forces: the old decaying upper class; the rising, ambitious, unscrupulous class of the "poor Whites"; and the Negroes who labored for both of them.
    A. William Faulkner B. Francis Scott Key Fitzgerald
    C. Ernest Hemingway D. Gertrude Steinbeck

98. In William Faulkner's *The Sound and the Fury*, he used a technique called _____, in which the whole story was told through the thoughts of one character.
    A. stream of consciousness B. Imagism
    C. symbolism D. naturalism

99. William Faulkner's novel _____ describes the decay and downfall of an old southern aristocratic family, symbolizing the old social order, told from four different points of view.
    A. *The Sound and the Fury* B. *Startoris*
    C. *The Unvanquished* D. *The Town*

100. William Faulkner's novel _____ is about a poor white family's journey through fire and flood to bury the mother in her hometown, Yoknapatawpha.
     A. *Intruder in the Dust* B. *As I Lay Dying*
     C. *Absalom, Absalom!* D. *Light in August*

101. Publication of _____ in 1952 caused people a great shock, and at the same time brought Ernest Hemingway the Nobel Prize in Literature in 1954.

A. *The Old Man and the Sea*   B. *A Farewell to Arms*
C. *For Whom the Bell Tolls*   D. *The Snows of Kilimanjaro*

102. _____ was endowed with the spiritual monument of American nation and the founder of narrative/literary journalism.

   A. William Faulkner   B. Francis Scott Key Fitzgerald
   C. Ernest Hemingway   D. Gertrude Steinbeck

103. As Ernest Hemingway said, "If a writer knows enough about what he is writing, he may omit things that he knows. The dignity of movement of an iceberg is due to only one-ninth of it being above water. So, I always try to write on the principle." The principle above refers to _____.

   A. William Faulkner   B. theory of omission
   C. iceberg theory   D. both B and C

104. *In Dubious Battle* was _____'s most clearly "Proletarian" novel of class struggle.

   A. Thomas Stearns Eliot   B. Francis Scott Key Fitzgerald
   C. Ernest Hemingway   D. John Steinbeck

105. _____'s treatment of the social problems of his time, particularly the plight of the dispossessed farmer, earned him a Pulitzer Prize in 1940 and, in 1962, a Nobel Prize in Literature.

   A. Thomas Stearns Eliot   B. Francis Scott Key Fitzgerald
   C. Ernest Hemingway   D. John Steinbeck

106. _____ wrote sympathetically about poor, oppressed California farmers, migrants, laborers, and the unemployed, making their lives and sorrows very understandable to his readers.

   A. Thomas Stearns Eliot   B. Francis Scott Key Fitzgerald
   C. Ernest Hemingway   D. John Steinbeck

107. _____ nearly always wrote the dialogue of his books just as it should sound, using the strange spelling to denote the regional accent, and inserting many words of slang and dialect.

   A. William Faulkner   B. Francis Scott Key Fitzgerald
   C. Ernest Hemingway   D. John Steinbeck

108. During the Depression years, _____'s fiction combined warm humor, regionalism, and violence with a realistic technique that produced a unique kind of social protest.
   A. William Faulkner   B. Francis Scott Key Fitzgerald
   C. Ernest Hemingway   D. John Steinbeck

III. Match-Making

Group One
Column A   Column B
1. Wallace Stevens   a. *The Cantos*
2. Edwin Arlington Robinson   b. *Black Riders Came From the Sea*
3. Stephen Crane   c. *Richard Cory*
4. Robert Frost   d. *The Red Wheelbarrow*
5. Carl Sandburg   e. *The People, Yes*
6. William Carlos Williams   f. *A Boy's Will*
7. Ezra Pound   g. *The Snow Man*
8. John Ernst Steinbeck   h. *The Grapes of Wrath*

Group Two
Column A   Column B
1. Sinclair Lewis   a. *Bound East for Cardiff*
2. Eugene Gladstone O'Neill   b. *Babbitt*
3. Thomas Stearns Eliot   c. *The Enormous Room*
4. Francis Scott Fitzgerald   d. *This Side of Paradise*
5. Edward Estlin Cummings   e. *The Waste Land*
6. Hilda Doolittle   f. *The Sound and the Fury*
7. William Faulkner   g. *The Sun Also Rises*
8. Ernest Hemingway   h. *The Flowering of the Rod*

IV. Define the Literary Terms.

1. Harlem Renaissance
2. Hemingway heroes
3. Imagism
4. Southern Renaissance
5. Stream of consciousness
6. The Beat Generation
7. The Jazz Age
8. The Lost Generation
9. The Waste Land Painters

V. Answer the Following Questions Briefly.

1. Give an analysis of Ezra Pound's *In the Station of the Metro*.
2. Give an analysis of Edwin Arlington Robinson's *Richard Cory*.
3. Give an analysis of Robert Frost's *The Road Not Taken*.
4. Give an analysis of Robert Frost's *Fire and Ice*.
5. Give an appreciation of Robert Frost's *Departmental*.
6. Give an appreciation of Robert Frost's *Design*.
7. Give an analysis of Wallace Stevens's *Anecdote of the Jar*.
8. Give a brief summary of *The Waste Land*, the masterpiece of Thomas Stearns Eliot.
9. Give an analysis of Thomas Stearns Eliot's *The Love Song of J. Alfred Prufrock*.
10. Give a story summary and an analysis of chapter 3 of *The Great Gatsby*.
11. Give an analysis of John Steinbeck's *The Grapes of Wrath*.
12. Give an analysis of William Faulkner's *The Sound and the Fury*.
13. Summarize American poetic revolution of the 20th century.
14. What is Thomas Stearns Eliot's style of poetry? What is his main

contribution to literature?
15. What is Ezra Pound's main contribution to American literature?
16. How do you understand the Jazz Age in America under Francis Scott Key Fitzgerald's pen?
17. Discuss William Faulkner's style, theme and point of view.
18. What's Ernest Hemingway's contribution to American literature?

Part VI

Twentieth-Century Literature II: After WWII

I. Fill in the Blanks.

1. Since the Emancipation, large numbers of African American gathered in _____ of New York City, including all their artists and intellectuals over, which made the district the hub of black life.
2. Richard Wright was the initiator of African American literary tradition of violent self-assertion, whose work _____ was considered as a watershed in the tradition of the African American novel. After its publication, Toni Morrison's _____ became another milestone in African American literature.
3. N. Scott Momaday's Pulitzer Prize winning novel _____ led to the breakthrough of Native American literature into the American mainstream.
4. _____ was the representative writer of Jewish novel with his works in essence affirmatively humanistic. Another Jewish novelist _____, was well known for one novel, *The Catcher in the Rye*.
5. Jack Kerouac's _____ is often considered a defining work of the postwar Beat Generation that was inspired by jazz, poetry, and drug experiences.
6. James Mercer Langston Hughes reached the summit of his achievements when he was honored with the informal title of "_____".
7. In his poem *The Negro Speaks of Rivers*, James Mercer Langston

Hughes expresses his passionate love for world civilization, and the letter "I" is the symbol of _____.

8. Elizabeth Bishop's poetry is always a reflection of her life. Her poetry, including her first book of verse, _____ and *Questions of Travel*, is filled with descriptions of her travels.

9. Unlike her friend Robert Lowell, who wrote in the "confessional" style, Elizabeth Bishop used subtle rhythms, unlikely rhymes, and the _____'s technique of implication and suggestion to depict the precise images of the physical world.

10. As "one of the most important American poets" of the twentieth century, Elizabeth Bishop was considered a "_____".

11. _____ is one of Elizabeth Bishop's most famous poems, which gives a true-to-life description of a caught fish, big, old and ugly, covered with scratches.

12. Along with Eugene O'Neill and Arthur Miller, Tennessee Williams is considered among the three foremost playwrights in 20th century American drama. He rose from obscurity and achieved great success by his play _____ debuted on Broadway.

13. Ralph Ellison was so impressed by T.S. Eliot's _____ that he decided to turn from music to literature. And his work _____ earned him the National Book Award for Fiction, which was his ticket into the American literary establishment.

14. _____, as an international literary hero, made a landmark contribution to American black literature and American literature and broke new ground for the future of African American literary and the development of its literary theory.

15. Ralph Ellison's novel, _____ questions the nature of reality and meaning of social responsibility and explores the limits of human possibility.

16. Saul Bellow, born into a family of Russia Jewish immigrants in Canada, was a major novelist of his generation. He received the _____ Prize in Literature for "the combination of the human

understanding and subtle analysis of contemporary culture in his work."

17. There are usually _____ endings in Saul Bellow's novels, as he thought that "no noble assumptions, man should have at least sufficient power to overcome humiliation and to complete his own life."

18. Arthur Miller's play _____ earned him a great success, winning a Tony Award for Best Author, the New York Drama Circle Critics' Award, and the Pulitzer Prize for Drama, which was the first play to win all three of these major awards.

19. _____'s masterpiece *Life Studies* marked the beginning of a new school of "_____".

20. Jerome David Salinger, as an American novelist and short story writer, was propelled onto the national stage by his work _____.

21. Along with William S. Burroughs and Allen Ginsberg, _____ was seen as the leading figure and spokesman of the Beat Generation.

22. In addition to Faulkner, Mary Flannery O'Connor was regarded as the most outstanding writer in the _____ American literature.

23. _____ was regarded as a major poet of the Beat Generation. Influenced chiefly by Walt Whitman and William Blake, he strove to write in a style of _____ verse, and preferred the usage of common words and varieties of long lines following the speech and _____ patterns.

24. Jack Kerouac's experimental writing style is known as "_____".

25. Edward Albee's _____ marks the beginning of American absurdist drama.

26. _____, who won the Nobel Prize in 1993, has been the central figure in putting fiction by and about African American women at the forefront of the late twentieth-century literary canon.

27. Ken Kesey, as a counterculture figure, considered himself a link between the _____ of the 1950s and the hippies of the 1960s.

28. _____, who is a master of American postmodern literature, is

recognized by the American literary world as the most mysterious hermit.

29. Joseph Heller's _____-22 is one of the most famous novels dealing with the subject of absurdity in typical "obscure" techniques.

30. Kurt Vonnegut's _____-Five focuses particularly on the absurdity of life and man's modern diseases of schizophrenia.

31. Ken _____'s masterpiece, *One Flew over the Cuckoo's Nest* amplifies, in its comic exaggeration, the plight of man being dehumanized.

32. *Gravity's Rainbow* by Thomas _____ has won the National Book Award.

33. Jack Kerouac's experimental writing style is known as "_____ prose", which enabled him to enjoy a freedom from accepted rules and limitations in writing.

34. One distinct group of poets in the postwar period is the _____ School, whose poetry seems to share common features such as ruthless, excruciating self-analysis of one's own background and heritage, one's own most private desires and fantasies etc., and the urgent "I'll-tell-it-all-to-you" impulse.

35. In the postwar period, avant-_____, postmodernism, and metafiction have been largely synonymous with "experimental".

36. Edward Albee's _____ marks the beginning of American absurdist drama.

II. Choose the Best Answer for Each Question.

1. Which of the following cannot be included in excellent writers in the Harlem Renaissance?
   A. Richard Wright   B. Ralph Ellison
   C. Alice Walker   D. Amy Tan

2. _____ was praised as the founding author of "The Native American Renaissance" in end-1960s.
   A. Richard Wright
   B. Alice Walker
   C. James Mercer Langston Hughes
   D. N. Scott Momaday
3. Pearl Buck, C. Y. Lee, Maxine Hong Kingston, Amy Tan and so on were all the representatives of Asian American Writers. Among the masterpieces of these writers, Amy Tan's _____ turned out to be a kind of watershed.
   A. *The Bonesetter's Daughter*   B. *The Joy Luck Club*
   C. *The Moon Lady*   D. *The Kitchen God's Wife*
4. Which of the following writers can be viewed as the most prominent American novelist of the absurd in the postwar?
   A. Joseph Heller   B. J. D. Salinger
   C. Kurt Vonnegut   D. Saul Bellow
5. Which of the following cannot be classified as American novels of the absurd?
   A. *Slaughterhouse-Five*
   B. *One Flew Over the Cuckoo's Nest*
   C. *The Sun Also Rises*
   D. *Catch-22*
6. Which of the following statements about James Mercer Langston Hughes's career as a writer is incorrect?
   A. In 1921, Hughes published his first poem *The Negro Speaks of Rivers*.
   B. Hughes used to gain the recognition and help of his senior, Vachel Lindsay, a very popular poet of the time.
   C. His other collections include *Dear Lovely Death*, *The Negro Mother*, *Dream Keeper*, *The New Song*, *Shakespeare in Harlem*, and *Ask Your Mama*.
   D. He was the first prominent Black writer in American literary his-

tory, and he was also a master in novel writing and composer of plays for dumb shows.

7. Which of the following is not the characteristic of James Mercer Langston Hughes's works?
   A. Obvious mood swings
   B. Subjects of Black life and racial themes
   C. Short lines and simple stanza patterns
   D. Strong rhythms of jazz and strict rhyme schemes derived from blues songs

8. In his poem, *Dreams*, James Mercer Langston Hughes makes use of two metaphors: First when life is regarded as a lively bird, dream is compared to the wings which enable a bird to fly; when life is considered as a piece of warm rich land, dream is the _____ which enlivens everything on earth.
   A. tender light of the moon   B. warm sunshine
   C. timely rainfall   D. darkness of the edge of dawn

9. Which of the following statements about Theodore Huebner Roethke is incorrect?
   A. He was good at depicting the specific details of life and displaying the momentary aspiration of people.
   B. In his poems, metaphysical tension expresses itself in varied metaphors and fractured syntax.
   C. Unlike most poets of his time, he was always optimistic in discussing such themes as life and death.
   D. He wrote poems using simple words and easy structure. His early poems were written in an unconventional style, while his later poems used some modern experimental skills.

10. Which of the following is not Theodore Huebner Roethke's work?
    A. *Open House*   B. *The Negro Mother*
    C. *The Lost Son*   D. *Praise to the End!*

11. Elizabeth Bishop, an American poet and short-story writer, received the Pulitzer Prize for the combined volume _____ and the Na-

tional Book Award for *The Complete Poems*.

    A. *North & South* and *A Cold Spring*

    B. *A Cold Spring* and *Geography III*

    C. *North & South* and *Questions of Travel*

    D. *East & West* and *A Cold Spring*

12. Who is considered as "Miller's contemporary"?

    A. Eugene O'Neill   B. Arthur Miller

    C. Tennessee Williams   D. George Bernard Shaw

13. Which of the following plays made Tennessee Williams one of American best playwrights and earned him a Drama Critics' Award and his first Pulitzer Prize?

    A. *The Glass Menagerie*   B. *A Streetcar Named Desire*

    C. *Camino Real*   D. *Sweet Bird of Youth*

14. Ralph Ellison was best known for his novel _____.

    A. *Juneteenth*   B. *Going to the Territory*

    C. *Invisible Man*   D. *Flying Home: And Other Stories*

15. Saul Bellow's _____ depicts the life and experiences of a middle-aged Jewish intellectual, showing his involvements with two wives and other women, with his children, with a friend who betrays him, and with his occupations of teaching and writing.

    A. *Herzog*

    B. *Seize the Day*

    C. *The Adventures of Augie March*

    D. *Mr. Sammler's Planet*

16. Influenced by the modern literature, Saul Bellow merges realism, _____ and romanticism into his literary creation.

    A. naturalism   B. modernism

    C. existentialism   D. neo-realism

17. _____ is widely considered to be one of the greatest plays of the 20th century, which is even called by some critics the American *King Lear*.

    A. *A Streetcar Named Desire*

B. *Desire Under the Elms*
C. *Who's Afraid of Virginia Woolf?*
D. *Death of a Salesman*

18. As a representative of the Confessional School, Robert Lowell's poems focus on the description of _____.
    A. human and nature   B. human internal world
    C. human external world   D. human spiritual world

19. Jack Kerouac is best known for his book, _____.
    A. *Wake Up*   B. *On the Road*
    C. *The Sea Is My Brother*   D. *Desolation Angels*

20. Who is often considered one of America's greatest modern playwrights, known for being on the vanguard of what would later be called "Theater of the Absurd"?
    A. Eugene O'Neill   B. Tennessee Williams
    C. Arthur Miller   D. Edward Albee

21. In terms of Toni Morrison's writing features, she widely used _____ and metaphor in her works.
    A. symbolism   B. synecdoche   C. hyperbole   D. irony

22. Thomas Pynchon's masterpiece _____ is regarded as the classic work of postmodern literature.
    A. *V*   B. *The Crying of Lot 49*
    C. *Gravity's Rainbow*   D. *Vineland*

23. Maxine Hong Kingston is a famous contemporary _____ writer.
    A. African-American   B. Indian-American
    C. Canadian-American   D. Chinese-American

24. Which of the following writers did not receive the Nobel Prize?
    A. Eugene O'Neill   B. Saul Bellow
    C. Toni Morrison   D. Ralph Ellison

25. One major characteristic of post-war poetry is its diversity. The following terms belong to this period except _____.
    A. the Black Mountain poets
    B. the Waste Land painters

C. poets of the Beat Generation
D. poets of the San Francisco Renaissance
E. poets of the New York School

26. Robert Lowell's famous poem *Skunk Hour* was written in response to *Armadillo*, which was written by _____.
    A. Thomas Stearns Eliot   B. Richard Wilbur
    C. Elizabeth Bishop   D. Marianne Moore

27. The American fiction after the 1960s is noted for _____.
    A. nonfiction
    B. science fiction
    C. black and absurd humor
    D. parody and pop
    E. experimental novelistic techniques
    F. all of the above

28. Which of the following novels is NOT written by Saul Bellow?
    A. *The Dangling Man*   B. *Herzog*
    C. *The Naked and the Dead* D. *Mr. Sammler's Planet*

29. The title of Jerome David Salinger's novel *The Catcher in the Rye* comes from _____'s poem *Comin' thro' the Rye*.
    A. William Wordsworth   B. William Black
    C. Alfred Tennyson   D. Robert Burns

30. There are Gothic elements and an obvious absurdist tendency in Flannery O'Connor's works. These include the following except _____.
    A. *Wise Blood*   B. *A Good Man Is Hard to Find*
    C. *Lie Down in Darkness*   D. *The Violent Bear It Away*

31. The novels of postmodernism after the 1960s include the following except _____.
    A. the absurd   B. metafiction
    C. avant-gardism   D. the sentimental

32. William Burroughs and Jack Kerouac belong to _____.
    A. the Confessional School   B. the Black Mountain Poets

C. novelists of absurdity   D. the Beat Writers
33. _____ has been placed next to Allen Ginsberg among the Beat Generation. He seems to think that the job of the poet is to catch sight of the poetic, which resides nowhere but in the natural world.
A. John Ashbery   B. Frank O'Hara
C. Gary Snyder   D. Jack Kerouac

III. Match-Making

Group One

Column A

1. Richard Wright
2. Toni Morrison
3. N. Scott Momaday
4. Amy Tan
5. Joseph Heller
6. Jack Kerouac
7. James Mercer Langston Hughes
8. Theodore Huebner Roethke
9. Ralph Ellison
10. Ken Kesey

Column B

a. *Praise to the End!*
b. *Native Son*
c. *Catch-22*
d. *The Moon Lady*
e. *House Made of Dawn*
f. *Dream Keeper*
g. *On the Road*
h. *Beloved*
i. *One Flew Over the Cuckoo's Nest*
j. *Juneteenth*

Group Two

Column A

1. Elizabeth Bishop
2. Saul Bellow
3. Tennessee Williams
4. Ralph Ellison
5. Robert Lowell

Column B

a. *Herzog*
b. *A Streetcar Named Desire*
c. *North and South*
d. *Death of a Salesman*
e. *Life Studies*

6. Arthur Miller
7. Mary Flannery O'Connor
8. Allen Ginsberg
9. Jack Kerouac
10. Edward Albee

f. *Invisible Man*
g. *The Fall of America*
h. *Who's Afraid of Virginia Woolf?*
i. *Wise Blood*
j. *The Sea Is My Brother*

Group Three
Column A
1. Thomas Pynchon
2. Toni Morrison
3. Maxine Hong Kingston
4. Tennessee Williams
5. Saul Bellow

Column B
a. *The Woman Warrior: Memoir of a Girlhood Among Ghosts*
b. *Gravity's Rainbow*
c. *The Glass Menagerie*
d. *The Bluest Eye*
e. *Seize the Day*

IV. Define the Literary Terms.

1. The Black Mountain poets
2. The Confessional School
3. Deep Image group
4. Expressionism
5. Impressionism
6. Existentialism
7. Modernism
8. American dream
9. Absurdism
10. The Theater of the Absurd
11. Black humor

V. Answer the Following Questions Briefly.

1. Give a brief account of the main images used in James Mercer Langston Hughes's poems.
2. Make a brief comment on *My Papa's Waltz*.
3. Discuss Saul Bellow's achievement in literature.
4. Comment briefly on Saul Bellow's themes.
5. How do you understand the novel of the absurd of the 1960s?
6. How is the effect of absurdity achieved in Joseph Heller's *Catch-22*?
7. How do you understand the meaning of the letter "V" in Thomas Pynchon's novel *V*?
8. Give an analysis of *Who's Afraid of Virginia Woolf?* by Edward Franklin Albee.
9. What are the writing features of Arthur Miller's plays?
10. Give an analysis of *Invisible Man* by Ralph Ellison.
11. Give an analysis of *Beloved* by Toni Morrison.
12. Talk about Toni Morrison's writing features.
13. How do you understand ethnic literature?
14. How do you understand the Beat Generation?

下 编
美国文学选段练习

Part Two
Exercises on Selected Readings of American Literature

Exercise 1

If ever two were one, then surely we.
If ever man were loved by wife, then thee;
If ever wife was happy in a man,
Compare with me, ye women, if you can.
I prize thy love more than whole mines of gold
Or all the riches that the East doth hold.
My love is such that rivers cannot quench,
Nor ought but love from thee, give recompense.
Thy love is such I can no way repay,
The heavens reward thee manifold, I pray.
Then while we live, in love let's so persevere
That when we live no more, we may live ever.

QUESTIONS:
1. This lyric is entitled _____, written by _____.
2. It is written in one single 12-line stanza of _____ couplets, that is, rhymed pairs of _____ pentameter, rhymed "aa, bb, cc, dd, ee, ff."
3. Paraphrase "If ever two were one" in the first line.
4. What's the theme of this poem?

Exercise 2

I heard the merry grasshopper then sing,
The black-clad cricket bear a second part;
They kept one tune and played on the same string
Seeming to glory in their little art.
Small creatures abject thus their voices raise,
And in their kind resound their Maker's praise,

Whilst I, as mute, can warble forth no higher lays?

QUESTIONS:
1. This is the ninth of the *Contemplations* written by the first noteworthy woman writer in the early period of the American literary history. What is her name?
2. Make a brief comment on this short poem.

Exercise 3

Huswifery

Make me, O Lord, thy spinning wheel complete.
Thy holy word my distaff make for me.
Make mine affections thy swift flyers neat,
And make my soul thy holy spool to be.
My conversation make to be thy reel,
And reel the yarn thereon spun of thy wheel.

QUESTIONS:
1. Identify the poet of this poem.
2. Make a brief comment on this poem.

Exercise 4

These are the times that try men's souls: The summer soldier and the sunshine patriot will in this crisis, shrink from the service of their country; but he that stands it now, deserves the love and thanks of woman. Tyranny, like hell, is not easily conquered; yet we have this consolation with us, that the harder the conflict, the more glorious the triumph. What we obtain too cheap, we esteem too lightly: —'Tis dearness only that gives everything its value. Heaven knows how to put a proper price upon its goods; and it would be strange indeed, if so celestial an article as FREEDOM should not be highly rated. Britain, with an army to enforce her tyranny, has declared that she has a right (not only to) TAX but "to BIND us in ALL CASES WHATSOEVER", and if being bound in that manner, is not slavery, then is there not such a thing as slavery upon earth. Even the expression is impious for so unlimited a power can belong only to God.

Whether the Independence of the Continent was declared too soon, or delayed too long, I will not now enter into as an argument; my own simple opinion is, that had it been eight months earlier, it would have been much better. We did not make a proper use of last winter, neither could we, while we were in a dependent state. However, the fault, if it were one, was all our own; we have none to blame but ourselves. But no great deal is lost yet. All that Howe has been doing for this month past is rather a ravage than a conquest, which the spirit of the Jersies, a year ago would have quickly repulsed, and which time and a little resolution will soon recover.

I have as little superstition in me as any man living, but my secret opinion has ever been, and still is, that God Almighty will not give up a people to military destruction, or leave them unsupportedly to perish, who have so earnestly and so repeatedly sought to avoid the calamities of war, by every decent method which wisdom could invent. Neither have I so much of the infidel in me as to suppose that He has relinquished the government of the world; and given us up to the care of devils; and as I do not, I cannot see on what grounds the king of Britain can look up to heaven for help against us: a common murderer, a highwayman, or a house-breaker, has as good a pretence as he. ...

QUESTIONS:

1. These paragraphs are taken from _____, written by _____.
2. It consists of several papers. 13 of the papers, starting December 23, 1776, and ending April 19, 1783, argue _____.
3. The argument starts to expound theoretical thoughts on _____, _____ and the colonial framework.

4. The role of the government considered by the author is to protect _____, _____ and _____.
5. What does the author discuss in the book?

Exercise 5

Fair flower, that dost so comely grow,
Hid in this silent, dull retreat,
Untouched they honied blossom blow,
Unseen thy little branches greet:
No roving foot shall crush thee here,
No busy hand provoke a tear.

By Nature's self in white arrayed,
She bade thee shun the vulgar eye,
And planted here the guardian shade,
And sent soft waters murmuring by;
Thus quietly thy summer goes,
Thy days declining to repose.

Smit with those charms, that must decay,
I grieve to see your future doom;
They died—nor were those flowers more gay,
The flowers that did in Eden bloom;
Unpitying frosts, and Autumn's power
Shall leave no vestige of this flower.

From morning suns and evening dews,
At first thy little being came:
If nothing once, you nothing lose,
For when you die you are the same:

The space between, is but an hour,
The frail duration of a flower.

QUESTIONS:
1. These lines are taken from _____ written by _____.
2. Before Freneau, some American poets wrote mostly on the religious theme. However, he was a pioneer who pay attention to the _____ of the New Continent and American subject matter.
3. In this poem, the poet shows his deep love of _____.
4. It is said to indicate the nineteenth-century Romantic use of simple _____.
5. Why does the poet choose the honey suckle as the object of depiction?

Exercise 6

To speak truly, few adult persons can see nature. Most persons do not see the sun. At least they have a very superficial seeing. The sun illuminates only the eye of the man, but shines into the eye and the heart of the child. The lover of nature is he whose inward and outward senses are still truly adjusted to each other; who has retained the spirit of infancy even into the era of manhood. His intercourse with heaven and earth becomes part of his daily food. In the presence of nature, a wild delight runs through the man, in spite of real sorrows. Nature says, —he is my creature, and maugre all his impertinent griefs, he shall be glad with me. Not the sun or the summer alone, but every hour and season yields its tribute of delight; for every hour and change corresponds to and authorizes a different state of the mind, from breathless noon to grimmest midnight. Nature is a setting that fits equally well a comic or a mourning piece. In good health, the air is a cordial of incredible virtue. Crossing a bare common, in snow puddles, at twilight, under a clouded sky, without having in my thoughts any occurrence of special good fortune, I have enjoyed a perfect exhilaration. Almost I fear to think how glad I am. In the woods too, a man casts off his years, as the snake his slough, and at what period soever of life, is always a child. In the woods is perpetual youth. Within these plantations of God, a decorum and sanctity reign, a perennial festival is dressed, and the guest sees not how he should tire of them in a thousand years. In the woods, we return to reason and faith. There I feel that nothing can befall me in life, —no disgrace, no calamity (leaving me my eyes,) which nature cannot repair. Standing on the bareground, —my head bathed by the blithe air, and uplifted into infinite space, —all mean egotism vanishes. I become a transparent eye-ball. I am nothing. I see all. The currents of the Universal Being circulate through me; I am part or particle of God. The name of the nearest friend sounds then foreign and accidental. To be brothers, to be acquaintances, —master or servant, is then a trifle and a disturbance. I am the lover of uncontained and immortal beauty. In the wilderness, I find something more dear and connate than in streets or villages. In the tranquil landscape, and especially in the distant line of the horizon, man beholds somewhat as beautiful as his own nature.

QUESTIONS:

1. These lines are taken from _____, written by _____.
2. This work paves the way for _____, which advocates a non-traditional admiration of nature.
3. Within the essay, Emerson divides nature into four usages: _____, _____, _____ and _____.
4. Emerson considers that the single way to be fully participated in the world of nature is _____.
5. What problem does the author try to deal with?

Exercise 7

But the Raven, sitting lonely on the placid bust, spoke only
That one word, as if his soul in that one word he did outpour.
Nothing farther then he uttered—not a feather then he fluttered—

Till I scarcely more than muttered, "Other friends have flown before—"
On the morrow he will leave me, as my hopes have flown before."
      Then the bird said, "Nevermore."

Wondering at the stillness broken by reply so aptly spoken,
"Doubtless," said I, "what it utters is its only stock and store,
Caught from some unhappy master whom unmerciful Disaster
Followed fast and followed faster—so, when Hope he would adjure,
Stern Despair returned, instead of the sweet Hope he dared adjure—
      That sad answer, "Nevermore!"

But the Raven still beguiling all my sad soul into smiling,
Straight I wheeled a cushioned seat in front of bird, and bust, and door;
Then upon the velvet sinking, I betook myself to linking
Fancy unto fancy, thinking what this ominous bird of yore—
What this grim, ungainly, ghastly, gaunt, and ominous bird of yore
      Meant in croaking "Nevermore."

This I sat engaged in guessing, but no syllable expressing
To the fowl whose fiery eyes now burned into my bosom's core;
This and more I sat divining, with my head at ease reclining
On the cushion's velvet lining that the lamplight gloated o'er,
But whose velvet violet lining with the lamplight gloating o'er,
      She shall press, ah, nevermore!

Then, methought, the air grew denser, perfumed from an unseen censer
Swung by angels whose faint foot-falls tinkled on the tufted floor.
"Wretch," I cried, "thy God hath lent thee—by these angels he hath sent thee
Respite—respite and Nepenthe from thy memories of Lenore!
Let me quaff this kind Nepenthe and forget this lost Lenore!"
      Quoth the Raven, "Nevermore."

QUESTIONS:

1. These lines are taken from _____, written by _____.
2. The poem was published in the _____ on January 29, 1845.
3. It was considered as the first poem with _____ in the West.
4. The whole poem was filled with a sense of _____.
5. In the poem, the poet strongly believes that human beings are _____ creatures in modern society.
6. In this poem, the Raven is a symbolic character. It may be varieties of symbolic meanings. How many symbolic meanings do you know?
7. In this poem, the poet takes advantage of a number of intricate musical expressions. Please find out three of them and quote the instances.

Exercise 8

A few days later a cry rang through the ship. Moby Dick had been spotted. The voice was Captain Ahab's, for none of the sailors, alert as they had been, had been able to sight him before their captain. Then boats were lowered and the chase began, with Captain Ahab's boat in the lead. As he was about to dash his harpoon into the side of the mountain of white, the whale suddenly turned on the boat, dived under it, and split it into pieces. The men were thrown into the sea, and for some time the churning of the whale prevented rescue. At length Ahab ordered the rescuers to ride into the whale and frighten him away, so he and his men might be picked up. The rest of that day was spent chasing the whale, but to no avail.

The second day the men started out again. They caught up with the whale and buried three harpoons in his white flanks. But he so turned and churned that the lines became twisted, and the boats were pulled every way, with no control over their direction. Two of them were splintered, and the men hauled into the sea, but Ahab's boat had not as yet been touched. Suddenly it was lifted from the water and thrown high into the air. The captain and the men were quickly picked up, but Fedallah was nowhere to be found.

When the third day of the chase began, Moby Dick seemed tired, and the Pequod's boats soon overtook him. They saw the body of Fedallah bound to the whale's back by the coils of rope from the harpoon poles. The first part of his prophecy had been fulfilled. Moby Dick, enraged by his pain, turned on the boats and splintered them. On the Pequod Starbuck watched and turned the ship toward the whale in the hope of saving the captain and some of the crew. The infuriated monster swam directly into the Pequod, shattering the ship's timbers. Ahab, seeing the ship founder, cried out that the Pequod—made of wood grown in America—was the second hearse of Fedallah's prophecy. The third prophecy, Ahab's death by hemp, was fulfilled when rope from Ahab's harpoon coiled around his neck and snatched him from his boat. All except Ishmael perished. He was rescued by a passing ship after clinging for hours to Queequeg's canoe-coffin, which had bobbed to the surface as the Pequod sank.

QUESTIONS:
1. It is an _____ novel written by _____.
2. The novel was regarded an outstanding work of _____ and the _____.
3. Ahab's ship, the Pequod, seemed to be _____, with characters ranging from the observer and narrator Ishmael to the savage harpooners and the motley crew.
4. Although *Moby Dick* can be considered as a whaling encyclopedia, it is essentially a _____.
5. How many times do Captain Ahab and other sailors meet the whale? What is the result?

Exercise 9

I celebrate myself, and sing myself,
And what I assume you shall assume,

For every atom belonging to me as good belongs to you.

I loafe and invite my soul,
I lean and loafe at my ease observing a spear of summer grass.

My tongue, every atom of my blood, form'd from this soil, this air,
Born here of parents born here from parents the same, and their parents the same,
I, now thirty-seven years old in perfect health begin,
Hoping to cease not till death.

Creeds and schools in abeyance,
Retiring back a while sufficed at what they are, but never forgotten,
I harbor for good or bad, I permit to speak at every hazard,
Nature without check with original energy.

QUESTIONS:
1. These lines are taken from "_____", the longest poem in _____.
2. The original name of this poem was _____.
3. The poet comes up with two principal beliefs: one is _____ and the other is in the _____ of all beings in values.
4. What does this part mainly describe?
5. What's the theme of this poem? What is the theme of most poems in *Leaves of Grass* according to your understanding?

Exercise 10

O Captain! my Captain! Our fearful trip is done,
The ship has weather'd every rack, the prize we sought is won,
The port is near, the bells I hear, the people all exulting,

While follow eyes the steady keel, the vessel grim and daring;
But O heart! heart! heart!
O the bleeding drops of red,
Where on the deck my Captain lies,
Fallen cold and dead.

O Captain! my Captain! Rise up and hear the bells;
Rise up—for you the flag is flung—for you the bugle trills,
For you bouquets and ribbon'd wreaths—for you the shores a-crowding,
For you they call, the swaying mass, their eager faces turning;
Here Captain! dear father!
This arm beneath your head!
It is some dream that on the deck,
You've fallen cold and dead.

My Captain does not answer, his lips are pale and still.
My father does not feel my arm, he has no pulse nor will,
The ship is anchor'd safe and sound, its voyage closed and done,
From fearful trip the victor ship comes in with object won:
Exult, O shores, and ring, O bells,
But I with mournful tread,
Walk the deck my Captain lies,
Fallen cold and dead.

QUESTIONS:

1. These lines are taken from _____, written by _____.
2. The poet takes advantage of writing skills of _____, imagery and _____ so that a good effect is attained in this poem.
3. This poem is crowded with metaphor. In it, the poet uses the "ship" to represent the _____; its "fearful trip" implied _____; the "prize we sought" stood for _____; the "captain" is used to symbolize _____.

4. What is the writing background of this poem?
5. What's the feature of this poem?

Exercise 11

On his bench in Madison Square Soapy moved uneasily. When wild geese honk high of nights, and when women without sealskin coats grow kind to their husbands, and when Soapy moves uneasily on his bench in the park, you may know that winter is near at hand.

A dead leaf fell in Soapy's lap. That was Jack Frost's card. Jack is kind to the regular denizens of Madison Square and gives fair warning of his annual call. At the corners of four streets, he hands his pasteboards to the North Wind, footman of the mansion of All Outdoors, so that the inhabitants thereof may make ready. Soapy's mind became cognizant of the fact that the time had come for him to resolve himself into a singular Committee of Ways and Means to provide against the coming rigor. And therefore he moved uneasily on his bench.

QUESTIONS:

1. These paragraphs are taken from _____, written by _____.
2. Please briefly describe the plots of *The Cop and the Anthem* and make a brief comment on it.
3. Try to illustrate the rhetorical devices employed in *The Cop and the Anthem* by giving examples.
4. What are the main characteristics of O. Henry's works?

Exercise 12

When Caroline Meeber boarded the afternoon train for Chicago, her total outfit consisted of a small trunk, a cheap imitation alligator-skin satchel, a small lunch in a paper box, and a yellow leather, snap purse, containing her ticket, a scrap of paper with her sister's address in Van Buren Street, and four dollars in money. It was in August, 1889. She was eighteen years of age, bright, timid, and full of the illusions of ignorance and youth. Whatever touch of regret at parting characterized her thoughts, it was certainly not for advantages now being given up. A gush of tears at her mother's farewell kiss, a touch in her throat when the cars clacked by the flour mill where her father worked by the day, a pathetic sigh as the familiar green environs of the village passed in review, and the threads which bound her so lightly to girlhood and home were irretrievably broken.

To be sure there was always the next station, where one might descend and return. There was the great city, bound more closely by these very trains which came up daily. Columbia City was not so very far away, even once she was in Chicago. What, pray, is a few hours—a few hundred miles? She looked at the little slip bearing her sister's address and wondered. She gazed at the green landscape, now passing in swift review, until her swifter thoughts replaced its impression with vague conjectures of what Chicago might be.

QUESTIONS:

1. These paragraphs are taken from _____, written by _____.
2. Make a brief comment on *Sister Carrie*.
3. Briefly analyze the personalities of the protagonist in *Sister Carrie*.
4. Try to illustrate the symbolic meaning used in *Sister Carrie* by giving examples.
5. From what angles can the emotional tragedy experienced by Carrie enlighten modern Chinese women?
6. What does *Sister Carrie* mainly talk about?
7. Does the disillusionment of the protagonist Carrie's personal ideal indicate the unreality of the American dream? If so, please give a concrete analysis.

Exercise 13

And he was rich—yes, richer than a king—
And admirably schooled in every grace:
In fine, we thought that he was everything
To make us wish that we were in his place.

So on we worked, and waited for the light,
And went without the meat, and cursed the bread;
And Richard Cory, one calm summer night,
Went home and put a bullet through his head.

QUESTIONS:
1. What is the title of the poem from which these two stanzas are taken?
2. Who wrote this poem?
3. How are the "we" of the poem different from Richard Cory?
4. Do you think the use of the adjective "calm" in the next-to-last line is an example of verbal irony? What is verbal irony?
5. Do you think there is an element of black humor in the mistaken ideas that the townspeople have of Richard Cory?

Exercise 14

Black riders came from the sea.
There was clang and clang of spear and shield,
And clash and clash of hoof and heel,
Wild shouts and the wave of hair
In the rush upon the wind:
Thus the ride of Sin.

QUESTIONS:
1. This is the first poem in _____ (1895) written by _____.
2. The title of the poem is _____.
3. This poem is written in _____.
   A. free verse
   B. sonnet
   C. blank verse
4. Appreciate the figures of speech used in this poem.
5. Make a comment on this poem.

Exercise 15

None of them knew the color of the sky. Their eyes glanced level, and were fastened upon the waves that swept toward them. These waves were of the hue of slate, save for the tops, which were of foaming white, and all of the men knew the colors of the sea. The horizon narrowed and widened, and dipped and rose, and at all times its edge was jagged with waves that seemed thrust up in points like rocks.

Many a man ought to have a bath-tub larger than the boat which here rode upon the sea. These waves were most wrongfully and barbarously abrupt and tall, and each froth-top was a problem in small boat navigation.

The cook squatted in the bottom and looked with both eyes at the six inches of gunwale which separated him from the ocean. His sleeves were rolled over his fat forearms, and the two flaps of his unbuttoned vest dangled as he bent to bail out the boat. Often he said: "Gawd! That was a narrow clip." As he remarked it he invariably gazed eastward over the broken sea.

The oiler, steering with one of the two oars in the boat, sometimes raised himself suddenly to keep clear of water that swirled in over the stern. It was a thin little oar and it seemed often ready to snap.

The correspondent, pulling at the other oar, watched the waves and wondered why he was there.

QUESTIONS:
1. This passage is the first part of a short story entitled _____ written by _____.
2. Interpret the first sentence of the passage "None of them knew the color of the sky".
3. Give a brief analysis of the story.
4. How does the author understand the relationship between man and nature in the short story?

Exercise 16

Whose woods these are I think I know.
His house is in the village though;
He will not see me stopping here
To watch his woods fill up with snow.

My little horse must think it queer
To stop without a farmhouse near
Between the woods and frozen lake
The darkest evening of the year.

He gives his harness bells a shake
To ask if there is some mistake.
The only other sound's the sweep
Of easy wind and downy flake.

The woods are lovely, dark and deep
But I have promises to keep,
And miles to go before I sleep,
And miles to go before I sleep.

QUESTIONS:
1. What is the title of this poem? Who wrote this poem?
2. What's the form of this poem?
3. The image of the "woods" is repeated several times in the poem. What does it imply?
4. Why does the poet repeat the line "And miles to go before I sleep" in the last stanza?
5. What does "sleep" mean?
6. How do you appreciate this poem?

Exercise 17

Two roads diverged in a yellow wood,
And sorry I could not travel both
And be one traveler, long I stood
And looked down one as far as I could
To where it bent in the undergrowth;

Then took the other, as just as fair,
And having perhaps the better claim,
Because it was grassy and wanted wear;
Though as for that the passing there
Had worn them really about the same,

And both that morning equally lay
In leaves no step had trodden black.
Oh, I kept the first for another day!
Yet knowing how way leads on to way,
I doubted if I should ever come back.

I shall be telling this with a sigh

Somewhere ages and ages hence:
Two roads diverged in a wood, and I—
I took the one less traveled by,
And that has made all the difference.

QUESTIONS:
1. What is the title of this poem? Who wrote this poem?
2. Identify the rhyme scheme of the poem.
3. This poem is a symbolic poem. Analyze the symbols in the poem.
4. Discuss the philosophical ideas in this poem.

Exercise 18

Some say the world will end in fire,
Some say in ice.
From what I've tasted of desire
I hold with those who favor fire.
But if it had to perish twice,
I think I know enough of hate
To say that for destruction ice
Is also great
And would suffice.

QUESTIONS:
1. What is the title of this poem? Who wrote this poem?
2. Identify the rhyme scheme of the poem.
3. There are two contrasted images "fire" and "ice" in this poem. How do you understand them?

Exercise 19

He went back to the text and lost himself. He did not notice that a young woman had entered the room. The first he knew was when he heard Arthur's voice saying: —

"Ruth, this is Mr. Eden."

The book was closed on his forefinger, and before he turned he was thrilling to the first new impression, which was not of the girl, but of her brother's words. Under that muscled body of his he was a mass of quivering sensibilities. At the slightest impact of the outside world upon his consciousness, his thoughts, sympathies, and emotions leapt and played like lambent flame. He was extraordinarily receptive and responsive, while his imagination, pitched high, was ever at work establishing relations of likeness and difference. "Mr. Eden," was what he had thrilled to—he who had been called "Eden," or "Martin Eden," or just "Martin," all his life. And "*Mister*!" It was certainly going some, was his internal comment. His mind seemed to turn, on the instant, into a vast camera obscura, and he saw arrayed around his consciousness endless pictures from his life, of stoke-holes and forecastles, camps and beaches, jails and boozing-kens, fever-hospitals and slum streets, wherein the thread of association was the fashion in which he had been addressed in those various situations.

QUESTIONS:
1. What is the title of the novel from which this passage is taken?
2. Whom does the first word "he" refer to?
3. Who is the author of this novel?
4. Make a brief comment on the character Mr. Eden.

Exercise 20

Hog Butcher for the World,
Tool Maker, Stacker of Wheat,

Player with Railroads and the Nation's Freight Handler;
Stormy, husky, brawling,
City of the Big Shoulders:

QUESTIONS:
1. These lines are talking about a big American city. What is it?
2. What is the title of the poem?
3. Who wrote this poem?
4. Why does the poet describe the city as "City of the Big Shoulders"?
5. Make a brief comment on the poem.

Exercise 21

The fog comes
on little cat feet.

It sits looking
over harbor and city
on silent haunches
and then moves on.

QUESTIONS:
1. What is the title of the poem? Who wrote this poem?
2. This poem is chosen from _____ (1916) written in _____.
3. Make a brief comment on the poem.

Exercise 22

I placed a jar in Tennessee,
And round it was, upon a hill.

It made the slovenly wilderness
Surround that hill.

The wilderness rose up to it,
And sprawled around, no longer wild.
The jar was round upon the ground
And tall and of a port in air.

It took dominion everywhere.
The jar was gray and bare.
It did not give of bird or bush,
Like nothing else in Tennessee.

QUESTIONS:
1. What is the title of the poem?
2. Who wrote the poem?
3. What is the relationship between the jar and the wilderness as shown in this poem?
4. Why does the poet choose Tennessee to place the jar?

Exercise 23

So much depends
upon

a red wheel
barrow

glazed with rain
water

beside the white

chickens.

QUESTIONS:
1. This poem is a typical _____ poem entitled _____.
2. Who wrote the poem?
3. This poem is a pattern poem. How does its pattern help express its meaning?
4. Pay attention to the images used in this poem. What is the effect of these images?

Exercise 24

The apparition of these faces in the crowd;

Petals on a wet, black bough.

QUESTIONS:
1. Who wrote this short poem?
2. What is title of this poem?
3. What two images are juxtaposed, or placed next to each other in this poem?
4. How do you appreciate this poem?

Exercise 25

Whirl up, sea—

whirl your pointed pines,

splash your great pines

on our rocks,

hurl your green over us,

cover us with your pools of fir.

QUESTIONS:
1. What's the title of the poem?
2. Who wrote the poem?
3. Explain the following words or phrases:
   Oread
   whirl up
   pointed pines
4. Make a brief comment on the poem.

Exercise 26

YANK—(*With a hard, bitter laugh.*) Welcome to your city, huh? Hail, hail, de gang's all here! (*At the sound of his voice the chattering dies away into an attentive silence.* YANK *walks up to the gorilla's cage and, leaning over the railing, stares in at its occupant, who stares back at him, silent and motionless. There is a pause of dead stillness. Then* YANK *begins to talk in a friendly confidential tone, half-mockingly, but with a deep undercurrent of sympathy.*) Say, yuh're some hard-lookin' guy, ain't yuh? I seen lots of tough nuts dat de gang called gorillas, but yuh're de foist real one I ever seen. Some chest yuh got, and shoulders, and dem arms and mits! I bet yuh got a punch in eider fist dat'd knock 'em all silly! (*This with genuine admiration. The gorilla, as if he understood, stands upright, swelling out his chest and pounding on it with his fist.* YANK *grins sympathetically.*) Sure, I get yuh. Yuh challenge de whole woild, huh? Yuh got what I was sayin' even if yuh muffed de woids. (*Then bitterness creeping in.*) And why wouldn't yuh get me? Ain't we both members of de same club—de Hairy Apes?

QUESTIONS:
1. Which play is this passage taken from?

2. The author was America's first dramatist of world renown. Who was he?
3. Who is the antagonist in the play? Make a brief analysis of the antagonist.

Exercise 27

Let us go then, you and I,
When the evening is spread out against the sky
Like a patient etherized upon a table;
Let us go, through certain half-deserted streets,
The muttering retreats
Of restless nights in one-night cheap hotels
And sawdust restaurants with oyster-shells:
Streets that follow like a tedious argument
Of insidious intent
To lead you to an overwhelming question...
Oh, do not ask, "What is it?"
Let us go and make our visit. In the room the women come and go
Talking of Michelangelo.

QUESTIONS:
1. This is the first 14 lines of a famous poem _____.
2. Who wrote this poem?
3. What image is created in these lines?
4. Is Prufrock a tragic figure? Why or why not?
5. Is this poem a dramatic monologue? Why?

Exercise 28

April is the cruellest month, breeding
Lilacs out of the dead land, mixing
Memory and desire stirring
Dull roots with spring rain.
Winter kept us warm, covering
Earth in forgetful snow, feeding
A little life with dried tubers.

QUESTIONS:
1. This is the first seven lines of a masterpiece poem. What is the title of this masterpiece?
2. Who is the author of this masterpiece?
3. What theme can you get from these lines?

Exercise 29

l(a

le

af

fa

ll

s)

one

l

iness

QUESTIONS:
1. This poem was published in _____ (1958) entitled "_____".
2. This poem was written by _____, a poet who defined independently his own universe by expressing conventional ideas through modern techniques.
3. How does the shape of the poem contribute to its theme?

Exercise 30

in Just—
spring   when the world is mud—
luscious the little
lame balloonman

whistles   far   and wee

and eddieandbill come
running from marbles and
piracies and it's
spring

when the world is puddle-wonderful

the queer
old balloonman whistles
far   and   wee
and bettyandisbel come dancing

from hop-scotch and jump-rope and

it's

spring
and
   the

      goat-footed

balloonMan   whistles
far
and
wee

QUESTIONS:
1. This poem was entitled _____, written by _____.
2. Explain the following words or phrases:
    eddieandbill
    marbles and / piracies
    bettyandisbel
    hop-scotch and jump-rope
3. Why is the balloonman "goat-footed"? How does this mythological allusion enrich the meaning of the poem?
4. How does the shape of the poem contribute to its theme?
5. Explain the repetition of "whistles far and wee" in the poem.

Exercise 31

For a moment the last sunshine fell with romantic affection upon her glowing face; her voice compelled me forward breathlessly as I listened—then the glow faded, each light deserting her with lingering regret, like children leaving a pleasant street at dusk.

The butler came back and murmured something close to Tom's ear, whereupon Tom frowned, pushed back his chair, and without a word went inside. As if his absence quickened something within her, Daisy leaned forward again, her voice glowing and singing.

"I love to see you at my table, Nick. You remind me of a—of a rose, an absolute rose. Doesn't he?" She turned to Miss Baker for confirmation: "An absolute rose?"

This was untrue. I am not even faintly like a rose. She was only extemporizing, but a stirring warmth flowed from her, as if her heart was trying to come out to you concealed in one of those breathless, thrilling words. Then suddenly she threw her napkin on the table and excused herself and went into the house.

Miss Baker and I exchanged a short glance consciously devoid of meaning. I was about to speak when she sat up alertly and said "Sh!" in a warning voice. A subdued impassioned murmur was audible in the room beyond, and Miss Baker leaned forward unashamed, trying to hear. The murmur trembled on the verge of coherence, sank down, mounted excitedly, and then ceased altogether.

"This Mr. Gatsby you spoke of is my neighbor—" I said.

QUESTIONS:

1. Which novel is this passage taken from?
2. Who wrote this novel?
3. What is the author's attitude toward such people as Tom and Daisy?
4. From this novel, talk about the author's achievements.

Exercise 32

When Miss Emily Grierson died, our whole town went to her funeral: the men through a sort of respectful affection for a fallen monument, the women mostly out of curiosity to see the inside of her house, which no one save an old manservant—a combined gardener and cook—had seen in at least ten years.

QUESTIONS:
1. This paragraph is taken from a short story. What's the title of the story?
2. Who is the author of the work?
3. Discuss the narration of the story.
4. This story seemed to be a detective story, but it goes beyond that. What does the author want to convey through the story?

Exercise 33

We went out doors. The sun was cold and bright.

"Where you heading for." Versh said. "You dont think you going to town, does you." We went through the rattling leaves. The gate was cold. "You better keep them hands in your pockets." Versh said. "You get them froze onto that gate, then what you do. Whyn't you wait for them in the house." He put my hands into my pockets. I could hear him rattling in the leaves. I could smell the cold. The gate was cold.

"Here some hickeynuts. Whooey. Git up that tree. Look here at this squirl, Benjy." I couldn't feel the gate at all, but I could smell the bright cold. "You better put them hands back in your pockets."

Caddy was walking. Then she was running, her book satchel swinging and jouncing behind her.

"Hello, Benjy." Caddy said. She opened the gate and came in and stooped down. Caddy smelled like leaves. "Did you come to meet me." she said. "Did you come to meet Caddy. What did you let him get his hands so cold for, Versh."
"I told him to keep them in his pockets." Versh said. "Holding on to that ahun gate."

QUESTIONS:
1. This passage is taken from the novel _____, the title of which is taken from the lines of William Shakespeare's tragedy _____.

2. Who wrote the novel?
3. This novel belongs to the "Yoknapatawpha saga," which took the author 33 years to complete. Make a brief analysis of the saga.
4. Analyze the character of Benjy.

Exercise 34

Poor, poor dear Cat. And this was the price you paid for sleeping together. This was the end of the trap. This was what people got for loving each other. Thank God for gas, anyway. What must it have been like before there were anaesthetics? Once it started, they were in the mill-race. Catherine had a good time in the time of pregnancy. It wasn't bad. She was hardly ever sick. She was not awfully uncomfortable until toward the last. So now they got her in the end. You never got away with anything. Get away hell! It would have been the same if we had been married fifty times. And what if she should die? She won't die. People don't die in childbirth nowadays. That was what all husbands thought. Yes, but what if she should die? She won't die. She's just having a bad time. Afterward we'd say what a bad time and Catherine would say it wasn't really so bad. But what if she should die? She can't die. Why would she die? What reason is there for her to die? There's just a child that has to be born, the by-product of good nights in Milan. It makes trouble and is born and then you look after it and get fond of it maybe. But what if she should die? She won't die. But what if she should die? She won't. She's all right. But what if she should die? She can't die. But what if she should die? Hey, what about that? What if she should die?

QUESTIONS:
1. This passage is taken from _____ by _____.
2. The title is taken from a poem by the 16th-century English dramatist _____.
3. Explain the double meanings of the title.
4. Discuss the language style as shown in the novel.

5. Give a brief introduction to the novel.

Exercise 35

"You are all a lost generation—."
—GERTRUDE STEIN IN CONVERSATION

"One generation passeth away, and another generation cometh; but the earth abideth forever... The sun also ariseth, and the sun goeth down, and hasteth to the place where he arose... The wind goeth toward the south, and turneth about unto the north; it whirleth about continually, and the wind returneth again according to his circuits. ... All the rivers run into the sea; yet the sea is not full; unto the place from whence the rivers come, thither they return again."
—ECCLESIASTES

BOOK ONE

1

Robert Cohn was once middleweight boxing champion of Princeton. Do not think that I am very much impressed by that as a boxing title, but it meant a lot to Cohn. He cared nothing for boxing, in fact he disliked it, but he learned it painfully and thoroughly to counteract the feeling of inferiority and shyness he had felt on being treated as a Jew at Princeton. There was a certain inner comfort in knowing he could knock down anybody who was snooty to him, although, being very shy and a thoroughly nice boy, he never fought except in the gym. He was Spider Kelly's star pupil. Spider Kelly taught all his young gentlemen to box like featherweights, no matter whether they weighed one hundred and five or two hundred and five pounds. But it seemed to fit Cohn. He was really very fast. He was so good that Spider promptly overmatched him and got his nose permanently flattened. This increased Cohn's distaste for boxing, but it gave him a certain satisfaction of some strange sort, and it certainly improved his nose. In his last year at Princeton he read too much and took to wearing spectacles. I never met any one of his class who remembered him. They did not even remember that he was middleweight boxing champion.

I mistrust all frank and simple people, especially when their stories hold together, and I always had a suspicion that perhaps Robert Cohn had never been middleweight boxing champion, and that perhaps a horse had stepped on his face, or that maybe his mother had been frightened or seen something, or that he had, maybe, bumped into something as a young child, but I finally had somebody verify the story from Spider Kelly. Spider Kelly not only remembered Cohn. He had often wondered what had become of him.

QUESTIONS:
1. This passage is taken from _____, which establishes its author _____ as a representative of writers who dealt with the Lost Generation.
2. Explain the two quotations in the front of the book.
3. Give a brief analysis of the novel.
4. Discuss the theme of the novel.

Exercise 36

The Mexicans were weak and fled. They could not resist, because they wanted nothing in the world as frantically as the Americans wanted land.

Then, with time, the squatters were no longer squatters, but owners; and their children grew up and had children on the land. And the hunger was gone from them, the feral hunger, the gnawing, tearing hunger for land, for water and earth and the good sky over it, for the green thrusting grass, for the swelling roots. They had these things so completely that they did not know about them anymore. They had no more the stomach-tearing lust for a rich acre and a shining blade to plow it, for seed and a windmill beating its wings in the air. They arose in the dark no more to hear the sleepy birds' first chitterling, and the morning wind around the house while they waited for the first light to go out to the dear acres. These things were lost, and crops were reckoned in dollars, and land was valued by principal plus interest, and crops were bought and sold before they were planted. Then crop failure, drought, and flood were no longer little deaths within life, but simple losses of money. And all their love was thinned with money, and all their fierceness dribbled away in interest until they were no longer farmers at all, but little shopkeepers of crops, little manufacturers who must sell before they can make. Then those farmers who were not good shopkeepers lost their land to good shopkeepers. No matter how clever, how loving a man might be with earth and growing things, he could not survive if he were not also a good shopkeeper. And as time went on, the business men had the farms, and the farms grew larger, but there were fewer of them.

Now farming became industry, and the owners followed Rome, although they did not know it. They imported slaves, although they did not call them slaves: Chinese, Japanese, Mexicans, and Filipinos. They live on rice and beans, the business men said. They don't need much.

They wouldn't know what to do with good wages. Why, look how they live. Why, look what they eat. And if they get funny—deport them.

QUESTIONS:
1. Which novel is this passage taken from?
2. Who is the author of this novel?
3. Where does the title of the novel come from?
4. What are the major themes of the novel?

Exercise 37

I've known rivers:
I've known rivers ancient as the world and older than
The flow of human blood in human veins.

My soul has grown deep like the rivers.
I bathed in the Euphrates when dawns were young.

I built my hut near the Congo and it lulled me to sleep.
I looked upon the Nile and raised the pyramids above it.
I heard the singing of the Mississippi when Abe Lincoln
Went down to New Orleans, and I've seen its
Muddy bosom turn all golden in the sunset

I've known rivers:
Ancient, dusky rivers.

My soul has grown deep like the rivers.

QUESTIONS:
1. The title of the poem is _____.
2. This poem was written by _____, the first prominent Black writer in American literary history. It is he who initiated a new movement in Black literature known as the "_____" of the 1920s.
3. In the poem the poet mentions several rivers. What are they? How do these rivers serve the meaning of the poem?

Exercise 38

stared and stared
and victory filled up
the little rented boat,
from the pool of bilge
where oil had spread a rainbow
around the rusted engine
to the bailer rusted orange,
the sun-cracked thwarts,
the oarlocks on their strings,
the gunnels—until everything

was rainbow, rainbow, rainbow!
And I let the fish go.

QUESTIONS:
1. These lines are chosen from the poem _____.
2. This poem was written by _____.
3. Identify the form of the poem.
4. Explain the image of rainbow at the end of the poem.
5. Make a brief comment of the poem.

Exercise 39

(Blanche enters)

Eunice: What's the matter, honey? Are you lost?

Blanche: They told me to take a street-car named Desire, and then transfer to one called Cemeteries and ride six blocks and get off at—Elysian Fields!

Euncie: That's where you are now.

Blanche: At Elysian Fields?

Eunice: This here is Elysian Fields.

Blanche: They mustn't have—understood—what number I wanted…

Eunice: What number you lookin' for?

Blanche: Six thirty-two.

Eunice: You don't have to look no further.

Blanche: I'm looking for my sister, Stella DuBois. I mean—Mrs. Stanley Kowalski.

Eunice: That's the party. —You just did miss her, though.

Blanche: This—can this be—her home?

Eunice: She's got the downstairs here and I got the up.

Blanche: Oh. She's—out?

Eunice: You noticed that bowling alley around the corner?

Blanche: I'm—not sure I did.

Eunice: Well, that's where she's at, watchin' her husband bowl. You want to leave your suitcase here an' go find her?

Blanche: No.

Woman: I'll go tell her you come.

Blanche: Thanks.

Woman: You welcome.

Eunice: She wasn't expecting you?

Blanche: No. No, not tonight.

Eunice: Well, why don't you just go in and make yourself at home till they get back.

Blanche: How could I—do that?

Eunice: We own this place so I can let you in. *(goes into their apartment)* It's sort of messed up right now but when it's clean it's real sweet.

Blanche: Is it?

Eunice: Uh-huh, I think so. So you're Stella's sister?

Blanche: Yes. Thanks for letting me in.

Eunice: Por nada, as the Mexicans say, por nada! Stella spoke of you.

Blanche: Yes?

Eunice: I think she said you taught school.

Blanche: Yes.

Eunice: And you're from Mississippi, huh?

Blanche: Yes.

Eunice: She showed me a picture of your home-place, the plantation.

Blanche: Bell Reve?

Eunice: A great big place with white columns.

Blanche: Yes…

QUESTIONS:

1. Which play is this passage taken from?
2. Who wrote this play?
3. To what does the street name "Elysian Fields" allude?
4. Symbols are frequently used in the play. Try to interpret these symbols.

Exercise 40

LINDA *(hearing Willy outside the bedroom, calls with some trepidation)*: Willy!

WILLY: It's all right. I came back.

LINDA: Why? What happened? *(Slight pause.)* Did something happen, Willy?

WILLY: No, nothing happened.

LINDA: You didn't smash the car, did you?

WILLY *(with casual irritation)*: I said nothing happened. Didn't you hear me?

LINDA: Don't you feel well?

WILLY: I'm tired to the death. *(The flute has faded away. He sits on the bed beside her, a little numb.)* I couldn't make it. I just couldn't make it, Linda.

LINDA *(very carefully, delicately)*: Where were you all day? You look terrible.

WILLY: I got as far as a little above Yonkers. I stopped for a cup of coffee. Maybe it was the coffee.

LINDA: What?

WILLY *(after a pause)*: I suddenly couldn't drive any more. The car kept going off onto the shoulder, y'know?

LINDA *(helpfully)*: Oh. Maybe it was the steering again. I don't think Angelo knows the Studebaker.

WILLY: No, it's me, it's me. Suddenly I realize I'm goin' sixty miles an hour and I don't remember the last five minutes. I'm—I can't seem to—keep my mind to it.

QUESTIONS:
1. Which play is this passage taken from?
2. Who wrote this play?
3. Make a brief analysis of the major character Willy.
4. Appreciate the play in your own words.

Exercise 41

If I am out of my mind, it's all right with me, thought Moses Herzog.

Some people thought he was cracked and for a time he himself had doubted that he was all there. But now, though he still behaved oddly, he felt confident, cheerful, clairvoyant, and strong. He had fallen under a spell and was writing letters to everyone under the sun. He was so stirred by these letters that from the end of June he moved from place to place with a valise full of papers. He had carried this valise from New York to Martha's Vineyard, but returned from the Vineyard immediately; two days later he flew to Chicago, and from Chicago he went to a village: in western Massachusetts. Hidden in the country, he wrote endlessly, fanatically, to the newspapers, to people in public life, to friends and relatives and at last to the dead, his own obscure dead, and finally the famous dead.

It was the peak of summer in the Berkshires. Herzog was alone in the big old house. Normally particular about food, he now ate Silvercup bread from the paper package, beans from the can, and American cheese. Now and then he picked raspberries in the overgrown garden, lifting up the thorny canes with absentminded caution. As for sleep, he slept on a mattress without sheets—it was his abandoned marriage bed—or in the hammock, covered by his coat. Tall bearded grass and locust and maple seedlings surrounded him in the yard. When he opened his eyes in the night, the stars were near like spiritual bodies. Fires, of course; gases-minerals, heat, atoms, but eloquent at five in the morning to a man lying in a hammock, wrapped in his overcoat.

QUESTIONS:
1. Which novel is this passage taken from?
2. This novel is written by _____, an important Jewish novelist.
3. Marginal man is often described in the author's novels so as in this one. Analyze his marginal characters together with the author's own experiences.
4. Appreciate the novel in your own words.

Exercise 42

Nautilus Island's hermit
heiress still lives through winter in her Spartan cottage;
her sheep still graze above the sea.
Her son's a bishop. Her farmer
is first selectman in our village,
she's in her dotage.

Thirsting for
the hierarchic privacy
of Queen Victoria's century,
she buys up all
the eyesores facing her shore,
and lets them fall.

The season's ill—
we've lost our summer millionaire,
who seemed to leap from an L. L. Bean
catalogue. His nine-knot yawl
was auctioned off to lobstermen.
A red fox stain covers Blue Hill.

And now our fairy
decorator brightens his shop for fall,
his fishnet's filled with orange cork,
orange, his cobbler's bench and awl,
there is no money in his work,
he'd rather marry.

One dark night,
my Tudor Ford climbed the hill's skull,

I watched for love-cars. Lights turned down,
they lay together, hull to hull,
where the graveyard shelves on the town…
My mind's not right.

A car radio bleats,
'Love, O careless Love…' I hear
my ill-spirit sob in each blood cell,
as if my hand were at its throat…
I myself am hell,
Nobody's here—

only skunks, that search
in the moonlight for a bite to eat.
They march on their soles up Main Street:
white stripes, moonstruck eyes' red fire
under the chalk-dry and spar spire
of the Trinitarian Church.

I stand on top
of our back steps and breathe the rich air—
a mother skunk with her column of kittens swills the garbage pail
She jabs her wedge-head in a cup
of sour cream, drops her ostrich tail,
and will not scare.

QUESTIONS:

1. This is a poem written by _____ in response to Elizabeth Bishop's _____.
2. The title of this poem is _____.
2. How do you understand the title of the poem?
4. What do you think of the poet's attitude toward life reflected in the

poem?

Exercise 43

"You know that song 'If a body catch a body comin' through the rye'? I'd like—"

"It's 'If a body meet a body coming through the rye'!" old Phoebe said. "It's a poem. By Robert Burns."

"I know it's a poem by Robert Burns."

She was right, though. It is "If a body meet a body coming through the rye." I didn't know it then, though.

"I thought it was 'If a body catch a body,'" I said. "Anyway, I keep picturing all these little kids playing some game in this big field of rye and all. Thousands of little kids, and nobody's around—nobody big, I mean—except me. And I'm standing on the edge of some crazy cliff. What I have to do, I have to catch everybody if they start to go over the cliff—I mean if they're running and they don't look where they're going I have to come out from somewhere and catch them. That's all I'd do all day. I'd just be the catcher in the rye and all. I know it's crazy, but that's the only thing I'd really like to be. I know it's crazy."

Old Phoebe didn't say anything for a long time. Then, when she said something, all she said was, "Daddy's going to kill you."

"I don't give a damn if he does," I said. I got up from the bed then, because what I wanted to do, I wanted to phone up this guy that was my English teacher at Elkton Hills, Mr. Antolini. He lived in New York now. He quit Elkton Hills. He took this job teaching English at N.Y.U. "I have to make a phone call," I told Phoebe. "I'll be right back. Don't go to sleep." I didn't want her to go to sleep while I was in the living room. I knew she wouldn't but I said it anyway, just to make sure.

QUESTIONS:
1. This passage is taken from _____, which propelled the author

onto the national stage.
2. Who is the author of the novel?
3. Who is the "I" in the passage? Talk about his or her story in the novel.
4. Please interpret the meaning of the name of the main character Holden.
5. Appreciate the novel in your own words.

Exercise 44

Junior used to long to play with the black boys. More than anything in the world he wanted to play King of the Mountain and have them pish him down the mound of dirt and roll over him. He wanted to feel their hardness pressing on him. Smell their wild blackness, and say "Fuck you" with that lovely casualness. He wanted to sit with them on curbstones and compare the sharpness of jackknives, the distance and crcs of spitting. In the toilet he wanted to share with them the laurels of being able to pee far and long.

He pulled her into another room, even more beautiful than the first. More doilies, a big lamp with green-and-gold base and white shade. There was even a rug on the floor, with enormous dark-red flowers. She was deep in admiration of the flowers when Junior said, "here!" Pecola turned. "Here is your kitten!" he screeched. And he threw a big black cat right in her face. She sucked in her breath in fear and surprise and felt fur in her mouth. The cat clawed her face and chest in an effort to right itself, then leaped nimbly to the floor.

QUESTIONS:
1. Which novel is this passage taken from?
2. This is the first novel written by _____, a woman novelist and a Nobel Prize winner.
3. Talk about the narration of the novel.
4. Please explain the connotation of the title *The Bluest Eye*.

上编参考答案

Key to Exercises of Part One

Part I

Literature of Colonial America

I. Fill in the Blanks.

1. English; European
2. Pilgrims; Puritans
3. Captain John Smith
4. hard work; thrift; piety; sobriety
5. chosen
6. family; Puritan
7. Anne Bradstreet
8. *Huswifery*
9. wheel
10. loom; God
11. John Smith
12. Reason; Revolution
13. Puritan values
14. simplicity; Bible
15. the Church of Rome
16. colonial Puritan
17. Anne Bradstreet
18. Anne Bradstreet
19. Virginia; Massachusetts
20. Captain John Smith
21. flee the Old World; a New Promised Land
22. would-be purifier
23. Separatists
24. English; mid-seventeenth
25. religion
26. 1937; 1960

II. Choose the Best Answer for Each Question.

1-5   B A A C B   6-10   C D C A C   11-15 A A C C A
16-20 A A B C C   21-25 B A A D D   26-30 A A B B B
31-35 A A C A B   36   A

III. Match-Making

1-3 b c a

IV. Define the Literary Terms.

1. American Enlightenment

   The Age of Enlightenment (or simply the Enlightenment or Age of Reason) was a cultural movement of intellectuals beginning in late 17th-century Europe emphasizing reason and individualism rather than tradition. Its purpose was to reform society using reason, to challenge ideas grounded in tradition and faith, and to advance knowledge through the scientific method. It promoted scientific thought, skepticism, and intellectual interchange. The Enlightenment was a revolution in human thoughts. The ideas of the Enlightenment continued to exert significant influence on the culture, politics, and governments of the Western world. It was also very successful in America, where its influence was manifested in the works of Benjamin Franklin and Thomas Jefferson, among others. It played a major role in the American Revolution. The political ideals of the Enlightenment influenced the *Declaration of Independence*, and the *Bill of Rights*.

2. American naturalism

   American naturalism refers to a new and harsher realism or pessimistic realism. Naturalism also came from Europe. Nature here means to put a man into a mechanized world, and the man is the victim of several forces hard to control in the world, including environment, heredity, serene and indifferent nature. Man is a weak, incompetent animal. He cannot control his fate. He is not free. This ideology of "framing up man" is the core of naturalistic literature. The milestones in the development of American naturalism were the publication of Emile Zola's novels in the 1870s and 1880s, the success of Stephen Crane's *The Red Badge of Courage* in the 1890s, and the continual appearance of Theodore Dreiser's *Sister Carrie* (1900), *The Financier* (1912), and *An American Tragedy* (1925). In poetry, it was represented by Edgar Lee Masters's *Spoon River Anthology* (1915), etc.

3. American Puritanism

American Puritanism is the beliefs and practices characteristic of Puritans (most of whom were Calvinists who wished to purify the Church of England of its Catholic aspects). The American Puritans accept the doctrine and practice of predestination, original sin, total depravity, and limited atonement through a special infusion of grace from God. Strictness and austerity in conduct and religion are characteristic of American Puritans. But due to the grim struggle for living in the new continent, they become more and more practical. American Puritanism is one of the most enduring shaping influences in American thought and American literature. It has become, to some extent, so much a state of mind, rather than a set of tenets, so much a part of the national cultural atmosphere that the Americans breathe. Without some understanding of Puritanism, there can be no real understanding of American culture and literature.

V. Answer the Following Questions Briefly.

1. What is the significance of American Puritanism in American literature?

The first settlers who became the founding fathers of the American nation were quite a few of them Puritans. They carried with them to America a code of values, a philosophy of life, and a point of view, which, in time, took root in the New World and became what is popularly known as American Puritanism. It is one of the most enduring shaping influences in American literature. It has become, to some extent, so much a state of mind, rather than a set of tenets, so much a part of national cultural atmosphere that the Americans breathe, that we may state with a degree of safety that, without some understanding of Puritanism, there can be no real understanding of American culture and literature.

The American Puritans were idealists, believing that the Church should be restored to the "Purity". They believed that they were God's chosen people enjoying His blessings on this earth as in heaven. It has been a critical commonplace that the American literature—or Anglo-American literature—is based on a myth, that is, the Biblical myth of the Garden of Eden. The Puritans dreamed of living under a perfect order and worked with indomitable courage and confident hope toward building a new Garden of Eden in America. Fired with such a sense of mission, the Puritans looked even the worst of life in the face with a tremendous amount of optimism. All this went, in due time, into the making of American literature. The optimistic Puritan has exerted a great influence on American literature.

The American Puritan's metaphorical mode of perception was chiefly instrumental in calling into being a literary symbolism which is distinctly American. Puritan doctrine and literary practice contributed to no small extend to the development of an indigenous symbolism.

With regard to technique, one naturally thinks of the simplicity, which characterizes the Puritan style of writing. The style is fresh, simple and direct; the rhetoric is plain and honest, not without a tough of nobility often traceable to the direct influence of the Bible.

All these have left an indelible imprint on American writing. Thus American Puritanism has been, by and large, a healthy legacy to the Americans.

2. Comment briefly on Charles Brockden Brown's contribution to

American novel.

Although Charles Brockden Brown was basically an imitator, he did a few things for which he has been remembered. One of these was his awareness that his inspiration was rooted in his own land, its new life and energy which, he felt, offer the writers with areas of exploration different from European subjects. Another thing of historic significance that Charles Brockden Brown did was his description of his characters' inner world. Some of his early writings indicate Charles Brockden Brown's consciousness of the complexity of the human emotional spectrum. Charles Brockden Brown explored the emotional world of his characters and found that man is not always controlled by reason and that sensual experiences, passion and illusion all impact human thinking and emotional responses. He was aware that the subconscious is mystic and unfathomable and that art is a necessary medium to externalize the deeper impulses of the human psyche. In a manner of speaking, Charles Brockden Brown's works can be read as psychological novels. Charles Brockden Brown is found wanting in depth and scope when compared with authors such as Edgar Allen Poe and Nathaniel Hawthorne, but it is important that he took that road first.

3. Give an introduction of the periods of American literature.

The following divisions of American literary history recognize the importance assigned by many literary historians to the Revolutionary War (1775-1783), the Civil War (1861-1865), World War I (1914-1918), and World War II (1939-1945). Under these broad divisions are listed some of the more widely used terms to distinguish periods and subperiods of American literature. These terms, it will be noted, are diverse in kind; they may signify a span of time, or else a form of political organization, or a prominent intellectual or imaginative mode, or a predominant literary form.

A. 1607-1775

This overall era, from the founding of the first settlement at

Jamestown to the outbreak of the American Revolution, is often called the Colonial Period. Writings were for the most part religious, practical, or historical. Notable among the 17th-century writers of journals and narratives concerning the founding and early history of some of the colonies were William Bradford, John Winthrop, and the theologian Cotton Mather. In the following century Jonathan Edwards was a major philosopher as well as the theologian, and Benjamin Franklin an early American master of lucid and cogent prose. Not until 1937, when Edward Taylor's writings were first published from manuscript, was Edward Taylor discovered to have been an able religious poet in the metaphysical style of the English devotional poets George Herbert and Richard Crashaw. Anne Bradstreet was the chief Colonial poet of secular and domestic as well as religious subjects.

The publication in 1773 of *Poems on Various Subjects* by Philis Wheatley, then a nineteen-year-old slave who had been born in Africa, inaugurated the long and distinguished, but until recently neglected, line of Black writers (or by what has come to be preferred name, African-America writers) in America. The complexity and diversity of African-American cultural heritage—both Western and African, oral and written, slave and free, Judeo-Christian and pagan, plantation and urban, integrationist and Black nationalist—have effected tensions and fusions that, over the course of time, have produced a highly innovative and distinctive literature, as well as musical forms that have come to be considered America's unique contribution to the Western musical tradition.

The period between the Stamp Act of 1765 and 1790 is sometimes distinguished as the Revolutionary Age. It was the time of Thomas Paine's influential revolutionary tracts; of Thomas Jefferson's *Statute of Virginia for Religious Freedom*, *Declaration of Independence*, and many other writings of *The Federalist Papers* in support of the Constitution, most notably those by Alexander Hamilton and James Madison; and of the patriotic and satiric poems by Philip Freneau and Joel Barlow.

B. 1775-1865

The years 1775-1828, the Early National Period ending with the triumph of Jacksonian democracy in 1828, signalized the first American comedy (Royall Tayler's *The Contrast*, 1787), the earliest American novel (William Hill Brown's *The Power of Sympathy*, 1789), and the establishment in 1815 of the first enduring American magazine, *The North American Review*. Washington Irving achieved international fame with his essays and stories; Charles Brockden Brown wrote distinctively American versions of the Gothic novel of mystery and terror; the career of James Fenimore Cooper, the first major American novelist, was well launched; and William Cullen Bryant and Edgar Allan Poe wrote poetry that was relatively independent of English precursors. In the year 1760 was published the first of a long series of slave narratives and autobiographies written by African-American slaves who had escaped or been freed. Most of these were published between 1839 and 1865, including Frederick Douglass's *Narrative of the Life of Frederick Douglass* (1845) and Harriet Jacob's *Incidents in the Life of a Slave Girl* (1861).

The span 1828-1865 from the Jacksonian era to the Civil War, often identified as the Romantic Period in America, marks the full coming of age of a distinctively American literature. This period is sometimes known as the American Renaissance, the title of Francis Otto Matthiessen's influential book about its outstanding writers, Ralph Waldo Emerson, Henry David Thoreau, Edgar Allan Poe, Herman Melville, and Nathaniel Hawthorne; it is also sometimes called the Age of Transcendentalism, after the philosophical and literary movement, centered on Ralph Waldo Emerson, that was dominant in New England. In all the major literary genres except drama, writers produced works of an originality and excellence not exceeded in later American history. Ralph Waldo Emerson, Henry

David Thoreau, and the early feminist Margaret Fuller shaped the ideas, ideals, and literary aims of many contemporary and later American writers. It was the age not only of continuing writings by William Cullen Bryant, Washington Irving, and James Fenimore Cooper, but also the novels and short stories of Edgar Allan Poe, Nathaniel Hawthorne, Herman Melville, Harriet Beecher Stowe, and the southern novelist William Glimore Simms; of the poetry of Edgar Allan Poe, John Greenleaf Whittier, Ralph Waldo Emerson, Henry Wadsworth Longfellow, and the most innovative and influential of all American poets, Walt Whitman; and of the beginning of distinguished American criticism in the essays of Edgar Allan Poe, William Glimore Simms, and James Russel Lowell. The Tradition of African-American poetry by women was continued by Francis Ellen Watkins Harper, and African-American novel was inaugurated by William Wells Browns's *Clotel* (1853) and Harriet E. Wilson's *Our Nig* (1859).

C. 1865-1914

The cataclysm of the bloody Civil War and the Reconstruction, followed by a burgeoning industrialization and urbanization in the North, profoundly altered the American sense of itself, and also American literary novels by Mark Twain, William Dean Howells, and Henry James, as well as by John William De Forest, Harold Frederic, and the African-American novelist Charles Waddell Chesnutt. These works, though diverse, are often labeled "realistic" in contrast to the "romances" of their predecessors in prose fiction, Edgar Allan Poe, Nathaniel Hawthorne, and Herman Melville. Some realistic authors grounded their fiction in a regional milieu, thus the term Local Colorism; these include (in addition to Mark Twain's novels on the Mississippi River region) Francis Bret Harte in California, Sarah Orne Jewett in Maine, Mary Wilkins Freeman in Massachusetts, and George Washington Cable and Kate Chopin in Louisiana. Kate Chopin has become prominent as an early and major feminist novelist. Walt Whitman continued writing poetry up to the last decade of the century, and (unknown to him and almost everyone else) was joined by Emily Dickinson; although only seven of Emily Dickinson's more than a thousand short poems were published in her lifetime, she is now recognized as one of the most distinctive and eminent of American poets. Sidney Lanier published his experiments in versification based on the meters of music; the African-American author Paul Lawrence Dunbar published both poems and novels between 1893 and 1905; and in 1890s Stephen Crane, although he was only twenty-nine when he died, published short poems in free verse that anticipate the experiments of Ezra Pound and the Imagists, and wrote also the brilliantly innovative short stories and short novels that look forward to two later narrative modes, naturalism and impressionism. The years 1900-1914—although Henry James, William Dean Howells, and Mark Twain were still writing, and Edith Wharthon was publishing her earlier novels—are discriminated as the Naturalistic Period, in recognition of the powerful though sometimes crudely wrought novels by Frank Norris, Jack London, and Theodore Dreiser, which typically represent characters who are joint victims of their instinctual drives and of external sociological forces.

D. 1914-1939

The era between the two world wars, marked also by the trauma of the great economic depression beginning in 1929, was that of the emergence of what is still known as "modern literature", which in America reached an eminence rivaling that of the American Renaissance of the mid-19th-century; unlike most of the authors of that earlier period, however, the American modernists also achieved widespread international recognition and influence. *Poetry* magazine, founded in Chicago by Harriet Monroe in 1912, published many innovative authors. Among the notable poets were Edgar Lee Maters, Edwin Arlington Robinson, Robert Frost, Robinson Jeffers,

Marianne Moore, Thomas Stearns Eliot, Edna St. Vincent Millay, and Edward Estlin Cummings—authors who wrote in an unexampled variety of poetic modes. These include the Imagism of Amy Lowell, H. D. (Hilda Doolittle), and others, the metric poems by Robert Frost and free verse poems by William Carlos Williams in American vernacular, the formal and typographic experiments of Edward Estlin Cummings, the poetic naturalism of John Robinson Jeffers, and the assimilation to their own distinctive uses by Ezra Pound and Thomas Stearns Eliot of the forms and procedures of French symbolism, merged with the intellectual and figurative methods of the English metaphysical poets. Among the major writers of prose fiction were Edith Wharton, Sinclair Lewis, Ellen Glasgow, Willa Cather, Gertrude Stein, Sherwood Anderson, John Roderigo Dos Passos, Francis Scott Key Fitzgerald, William Faulkner, Ernest Hemingway, Thomas Wolfe, and John Steinbeck. America produced in this period its first great dramatist Eugene O'Neill, as well as well as a group of distinguished literary critics that included Van Wyck Brooks, Malcolm Cowley, Thomas Stearns Eliot, Edmund Wilson, and the irreverent and caustic Henry Louis Mencken.

The literary productions of this era are often subclassified in a variety of ways. The flamboyant and pleasure-seeking 1920s are sometimes referred to as the Jazz Age, a title popularized by Francis Scott Key Fitzgerald's *Tales of the Jazz Age* (1922). The same decade was also the period of the Harlem Renaissance, which produced major writings in all the literary forms by Countee Cullen, Langston Hughes, Claude McKay, Jean Toomer, Zora Neale Hurston, and many other African-American writers.

Many prominent American writers of the decade following the end of World War I, disillusioned by their war experiences and alienated by what they perceived as the crassness of American culture and its "puritanical" repressions, are often tagged (in a term first applied by Gertrude Stein to young Frenchmen of the time) as the Lost Generation. A number of these writers became expatriates, moving either to London or to Paris in their quest for a richer literary and artistic milieu and a freer way of life. Ezra Pound, Gertrude Stein, and Thomas Stearns Eliot lived out their lives abroad, but most of the younger "exiles", as Malcolm Cowley called them, came back to America in the 1930s. Ernest Hemingway's *The Sun Also Rises* and Francis Scott Key Fitzgerald's *Tender Is the Night* are novels that represent the mood and way of life of two groups of American expatriates. In "the radical 30s", the period of the Great Depression and of the economic and social reforms in the New Deal inaugurated by President Franklin Delano Roosevelt, some authors joined radical political movements, and many others dealt in their literary works with pressing social issues of the time—including, in the novel, William Faulkner, John Roderigo Dos Passos, James Thomas Farrell, Thomas Wolfe, and John Steinbeck, and in the drama, Eugene O'Neill, Clifford Odets, and Maxwell Anderson.

1939 to present, the contemporary period. World War II, and especially the disillusionment with Soviet Communism consequent upon the Moscow trials for alleged treason and Joseph Vissarionovich Stalin's signing of the Russo-German pact with Hitler in 1939, largely ended the literary radicalism of the 1930s. A final blow to the very few writers who had maintained intellectual allegiance to Soviet Russia came in 1991 with the collapse of Russian Communism and the dissolution of the Soviet Union. For several decades the New Criticism—dominated by conservative southern writers, the Agrarians, who in the 1930s had championed a return from an industrial to an agricultural economy—typified the prevailing critical tendency to isolate literature from the life of the author and from society and to conceive a work of literature, in formal terms, as an organic and autonomous entity. The eminent and influential critics Edmund Wilson and Lionel Trilling, however—as well as other critics grouped with them as the New York Intellectuals, including Philip Rahv, Alfred Kazin, and Washington Irving—continued through the 1960s to deal with a work of literature humanistically and historically, in the context of its author's life, temperament, and social milieu, and in terms of the work's moral and imaginative qualities and its consequences for society.

The 1950s, while often regarded in retrospect as a period of cultural conformity and complacency, was marked by the emergence of vigorous anti-establishment and anti-traditional literary movements: the Beat writers such as Allen Ginsberg and Jack Karouac; the American exemplars of the literature of the absurd; the Black Mountain poets Charles Olson, Robert Creely, and Robert Duncan; and the New York Poets Frank O'Hara, Keneth Koch, and John Ashbery. It was also a time of confessional poetry and the literature of extreme sexual candor, marked by the emergence of Henry Miller as a notable author (his autobiographical and fictional works, begun in the 1930s, had earlier been available under the counter) and the writings of Norman Mailer, William Burroughs, and Vladimir Nabokov (*Lolita* was published in 1955). The counterculture of the 1960s and early 1970s continued some of these modes, but in a fashion made extreme and fevered by the rebellious youth movement and the vehement and sometimes violent opposition to the war in Vietnam.

Important American writers after World War II include, in prose fiction, Vladimir Nabokov (who emigrated to America in 1940), Eudora Welty, Robert Penn Watten, Bernard Malmud, James Gould Cozzens, Saul Bellow, Mary McCarthy, Norman Mailer, John Updike, Kurt Vonnegut, Jr., Thomas Pynchon, John Barth, Donald Barthelme, Edgar Lawrence Doctorow, and Cythia Ozick; in poetry, Marianne Moore, Robert Lowell, Allen Ginsberg, Adrienne Rich, Sylvia Plath, and John Ashbery; and in drama, Thorton Wilder, Lillian Hellman, Arthur Miller, Tennessee Williams, Edward Franklin Albee, and a number of more recent playwrights, including Sam Shepard,

David Mamet, Tony Kushner, and Wendy Wasserstein. Many of the most innovative and distinguished literary works of the latter decades of the 20th century were written by writers who are often identified as belonging to one or another "minority", or ethnic literary group. (An "ethnic group" consists of individuals who are distinguishable, within a majority cultural and social system, by shared characteristics such as race, religion, language, cultural modes, and national origin.) There is, however, much contention, both within and outside these groups, whether it is more just and enlightening to consider such writers simply as part of the American mainstream or to stress the identity of each writer as a participant in an ethnic culture with its distinctive subject matter, themes, and formal feature. This is the era of the notable African-American novelists and essayists Ralph Ellison, James Baldwin, Richard Wright, Albert Murray, Gloria Naylor, Alice Walker, and Toni Morrison; the poets Amiri Baraka, Gwendolyn Brooks, Maya Angelou, and Rita Dove; and the dramatists Lorraine Hansberry and August Wilson. It is also the era of the emergence of such prominent minority novelists as Leslie Marmon Silko (Native American); Oscar Jerome Hijuelos and Sandra Cineros (Hispanic); and Maxin Hong Kingston and Amy Tan (Chinese American).

The contemporary literary scene in America is crowded and varied, and these lists could readily be expanded. We must await the passage of time to determine which writers now active will emerge as enduringly major figures in the canon of American literature.

Part II

Literature of Reason and Revolution

I. Fill in the Blanks.

1. men of letters
2. mid-eighteenth
3. Boston
4. eight; 1783
5. Federative; democratic
6. Enlightenment
7. Puritan
8. Enlightenment
9. literary independence
10. English
11. proverbs
12. Benjamin Franklin
13. University of Pennsylvania
14. scientific achievements
15. electricity
16. Benjamin Franklin
17. *The General Magazine*
18. *The Autobiography*
19. Constitution
20. *Common Sense*
21. bridge
22. *Rights of Man*
23. *Agrarian Justice*
24. Thomas Paine
25. Thomas Jefferson
26. Reason; Revolution
27. James Madison
28. satirist
29. *National Gazette*
30. Father of American Poetry
31. post-Revolutionary

II. Choose the Best Answer for Each Question.

1-5   B A D B A   6-10 D D B A C   11-15 C B B A C
16-20 D B D C A   21-25 B D C A A   26-30 D B A B A

31-35 B D D C A   36-40 A C D B B   41-45 B C C A D
46-50 A A C C A

III. Match-Making

1-4   d c a b

IV. Define the Literary Terms.

1. *Declaration of Independence*

    It was drafted by Thomas Jefferson, together with John Adams, Benjamin Franklin, Roger Sherman and Robert R. Livingston. It shows the principles on which American government and the identity of Americans are based. It makes clear three main things: advance the nature of national sovereignty and the importance of human rights; display a list of the complaints and dissatisfaction which the American colonists had against the actions of the British government; declare the independence of the 13 British colonies on the east coast of North America on 4 July 1776. It continually inspires people around the world to fight for freedom and equality.

2. Autobiography

    An autobiography is a person's account of his or her life. Generally written in the first person, with the author speaking as I, autobiographies present life events as the writer views them. In addition to providing inside details about the writer's life, autobiographies offer insights into the beliefs and perceptions of the author. Autobiographies also offer a glimpse of what it was like to live in the author's time period. Autobiographies often provide a view of historical events that you won't find in history books. Benjamin Franklin's *The Autobiography* set the standard for what was then a new genre.

V. Answer the Following Questions Briefly.

1. Why does *The Autobiography* become a classic?

    The reasons are as follows.

    Firstly, it establishes in literary form the first example of the fulfillment of the American Dream. Franklin shows the possibilities in the New American World through his own rise from the lower middle class to one of the most admired men. Furthermore, he demonstrates that he achieved his success through a solid work ethic.

    The second reason is for historical reasons. The work was one of the premier autobiographies in the English language. The autobiography as a literary form had not emerged at the time Franklin lived, at least not in non-religious format. The book giving its list of virtues and ways in which one can achieve them, has influenced millions of readers over the last two centuries. Also, *The Autobiography* tells us today what life was like in 18th-century America. It is precious information to anyone who wants to learn more about that period of time.

2. Give a brief analysis of *The American Crisis*.

    "The American Crisis" is the formal name of the papers. The book was written by Thomas Paine. There are 13 papers arguing American independence, including theoretical thoughts on government, religion and the colonial framework. In this book, Paine differentiates government and society. He believes that society is good and constructive because people will join together in order to accomplish things. However, a government, as an institution, in Paine's opinion, needs to protect the people from their own immoral behavior. He moves on to attack the notion of the hereditary succession of the monarchy, claiming that monarchy is corrupt and corrupting.

Part III

Literature of Romanticism

I. Fill in the Blanks.

1. industrial and urban
2. Utopian
3. feminist movement
4. women
5. Transcendental
6. Emerson
7. Europe
8. Washington Irving
9. Romantic
10. materialism
11. absolute good; divinity
12. cultural nationalism
13. Hudson River School
14. artificial ruins
15. Gothic design
16. oratory
17. free expression
18. Noah Webster
19. Johnson
20. prose stylist
21. Washington Irving
22. *Washington*
23. Washington Irving
24. novelist
25. the Revolutionary War
26. U.S. Navy
27. frontier
28. 1817
29. *To a Waterfowl*
30. blank verse
31. *Nature*
32. Thomas Carlyle
33. Ralph Waldo Emerson
34. *The Scarlet Letter*
35. Franklin Pierce
36. symbolic
37. *Scarlet*
38. Herman Melville
39. European meters
40. Henry Wadsworth Longfellow
41. *Angelo*
42. Lowell
43. Edgar Allan Poe
44. modern short story

45. *Bells*
46. *Raven*
47. Ralph Waldo Emerson
48. transcendentalism
49. 19th century
50. James Fenimore Cooper
51. *Moby Dick*
52. prose epic
53. Scott
54. Pioneers
55. Natty
56. *Clarel*

II. Choose the Best Answer for Each Question.

1-5   B C D D B
6-10 A A D B A
11-15 B C D A D
16-20 A A A C C
21-25 A C A D C
26-30 B D B A A
31-35 B C B A C
36-40 A B A C A
41-45 D A C C C
46-50 C C D D C
51-55 D D D C C
56-60 A A C B A
61-65 B B B C A

III. Match-Making

Group One
1-9   i j b h a e f d c
Group Two
1-9   i f j e c d b a h

IV. Define the Literary Terms.

1. Transcendentalism

   As a moral philosophy, transcendentalism was neither logical nor systematized. It exalted feeling over reason, individual expression over the restraints of law and custom. It appealed to those who disdained the harsh God of their Puritan ancestors, and it appealed to those who scorned the pale deity of New England Unitarianism. Transcendentalists took their ideas from the Romantic literature of Europe, from neo-Platonism, from German idealistic philosophy, and from the revelations of Oriental mysticism. They spoke for cultural rejuvenation and against the materialism of American society. They believed in the transcendence of the "Oversoul," an all-pervading power for goodness from which all things come and of which all things are a part.

2. Romanticism

The literature term was first applied to the writers of the 18th century in Europe who broke away from the formal rules of classical writing. When it was used in American literature it referred to the writers of the middle of the 19th century who stimulated the sentimental emotions of their readers. They wrote of the mysteries of life, love, birth and death. The Romantic writers expressed themselves freely and without restraint. They wrote all kinds of materials: poetry, essays, plays, fiction, history works of travel and biography.

3 Symbolism

Symbolism is a movement in literature and the visual arts that originated in France in the poetry of Charles Baudelaire in the late 19th century. In literature, symbolism was an aesthetic movement that encouraged writers to express their ideas, feelings and values by means of symbols or suggestions rather than by direct statements. Hawthorne and Melville are masters of symbolism in America in the 19th century.

V. Answer the Following Questions Briefly.

1. What are the manifestations of romanticism in America?

Its manifestations were as varied, as individualistic, and as conflicting as the cultures and the intellects from which it sprang. Yet Romantics frequently share certain general characteristics: moral enthusiasm, faith in the value of individualism and intuitive perception, and a presumption that the natural world is a source of goodness and human societies a source of corruption.

2. What's Washington Irving's main contribution to American literature?

Irving's contribution to American literature is unparalleled in more than one way. He was a forerunner in many things. He was the first American writers, especially as the first American writer of imaginative literature, to earn an international fame, and the first belletrist in American literature, writing for pleasure when people of his times wrote for useful purposes. His *The Sketch Book* probably made story a genre in American literature and he also was regarded as one of the "inventors" of the modern short story. He invented the expression "the almighty dollar". American people considered his success in literature as a sign that American literature was emerging as an independent entity. It is not much exaggerated that he was called a father of American literature.

3. Give an analysis of Edgar Allan Poe's poem *Annabel Lee*.

Annabel Lee was the last poem of Poe and has always been regarded as the best of Poe's poems, dedicated to his late wife, Virginia Clemm. However, the poet did not use her real name, nor did he use the real background. Instead, he gave a false name and an imagined "kingdom by the sea." Poe did so to add some mythical or fabulous color to their love; on the other hand, Poe wanted to imply that such kind of true love could exist nowhere else but in a mythical kingdom of ancient time. In the whole poem, "Annabel Lee" is mentioned more than once, this could be for the sake of rhyme and to emphasize the importance of her name, which represents the speaker's tremendous feelings of solitude.

Part IV
Literature of Realism

I. Fill in the Blanks.

1. 1865
2. the Civil War; World War I
3. women
4. Catherine Beecher
5. *National Era*
6. *Uncle Tom's Cabin*
7. *Leaves of Grass*
8. free verse
9. Milton
10. brotherhood
11. modern poetry
12. hymns
13. Mark Twain
14. Mark Twain
15. *Autobiography*
16. H. L. Mencken
17. 20th-century
18. Mark Twain
19. *Stranger*
20. *Innocents*
21. *Mississippi*
22. colloquial speech
23. Mark Twain
24. World War I
25. *Daisy Miller*
26. stream of consciousness
27. regionalist and local color
28. feminist
29. children; poor people
30. New York
31. O. Henry
32. *The Four Million*
33. *The Gift of the Magi*
34. *Sister Carrie*
35. *Jennie Gerhardt*
36. *The Financier*; *The Titan*; *The Stoic*
37. *The "Genius"*
38. *An American Tragedy*
39. Theodore Herman Albert Dreiser
40. lowest

41. *The People of the Abyss*; *The Iron Heel*
42. *The Call of the Wild*; *The Sea Wolf*
43. *Martin Eden*
44. *Windy McPherson's Son*
45. *Winesburg, Ohio*
46. short stories

II. Choose the Best Answer for Each Question.

1-5   C B A C D
6-10 D B C A D
11-15 C C A B C
16-20 D B B B C
21-25 A C A C B
26-30 C A B C D
31-35 D C B C B
36-40 C A D A C
41-45 D C A A A
46-50 B D B A D
51-55 C B B A A
56-60 D D A B A
61-65 A A A B A
66-70 D C A A B
71   B

III. Match-Making

1-10   e i j g f h a c b d

IV. Define the Literary Terms.

1. Free verse

   Free verse is the rhymed or unrhymed poetry composed without attention to conventional rules of meter. Free verse was first written and labeled by a group of French poets of the late 19th century. Their purpose was to deliver poetry from the restrictions of formal metrical patterns and to recreate instead the free rhythms of natural speech. Pointing to the American poet Walt Whitman as their precursor, they wrote lines of varying length and cadence, usually not rhymed. Free verse has been characteristic of the work of many modern American poets, including Ezra Pound and Carl Sandburg.

2. O. Henry-style ending

O. Henry is a popular American short story writer who loves to arrange unexpected endings at the end of the novel. For example, he suddenly makes the protagonist's mood change surprisingly or makes the protagonist's fate suddenly reversed. This kind of ending is highly dramatic and is called an O. Henry-style ending. *The Police and the Hymn* possesses a typical O. Henry-style ending. Just like the person who sees the dawn falls into the darkness again, the delicate plots make the reader's heart shake with fear and the ending is memorable, thought-provoking, and unforgettable for a long time. O. Henry makes good use of this method to deeply reflect the reality that there is no distinction between good and evil in a disordered society.

V. Answer the Following Questions Briefly.

1. What are the literary characteristics of the Realistic Age?

A. In the latter half of the nineteenth century, women became the nation's dominant culture force. Therefore, ladies' journalism began to flourish. A new generation of women authors appeared whose poetry and fiction enlivened the pages of popular ten-cent monthly and weekly magazines.

B. From 1865 to 1905 the total number of periodicals published in the United States increased from about seven hundred to more than six thousand to satisfy the demands of a vast new reading audience that was hungry for articles, essays, fictions, and poems.

C. A host of new writers appeared, among them Bret Harte, William Dean Howells, Hamlin Garland, and Mark Twain, whose background and training, unlike those of the older generation they displaced, were middle-class and journalistic rather than gentled or academic.

D. American most noteworthy new authors established a literature of realism. They sought to portray American life as it really was, insisting that the ordinary and the local were as suitable for artistic portrayal as the magnificent and the remote.

2. How much do you know about realism?

A. Realism originated in France as réalisme, a literary doctrine that called for "reality and truth" in the depiction of ordinary life.

B. "Realism" first appeared in the United States in the literature of local color.

C. The arbiter of nineteenth-century literary realism in America was William Dean Howells. He defined realism as "nothing more and nothing less than the truthful treatment of material".

D. The greatest of American realists, Henry James and Mark Twain, moved well beyond a superficial portrayal of nineteenth-century America. James probed deeply into the individual psychology of his characters, writing in a rich and intricate style that supported his intense scrutiny of complex human experience. Mark Twain, breaking out of the narrow limits of local color fiction, described the breadth of American experience and he created, in *Huckleberry Finn* (1884), a masterpiece of American realism that is one of the great books of world literature.

E. Although it was the product of the nineteenth century, their final triumph came in the twentieth century.

3. What is the relationship between realism and local color in America?

A. "Realism" first appeared in the United States in the literature of local color, and an amalgam of Romantic plots and realistic descriptions of things was immediately observable: the dialects, customs, sights, and sounds of regional America. Bret Harte in the 1860s was the first American writer of local color to achieve wide popularity, presenting stories of western mining towns with colorful gamblers, outlaws, and scandalous women.

B. Local color is a variation of American literary realism.

4. Please briefly define realistic literature and try to conclude its characteristics.

Realism originated in France as réalisme, a literary doctrine that called for "reality and truth" in the depiction of ordinary life. "Realism" first appeared in the United States in the literature of local color, and an amalgam of Romantic plots and realistic descriptions of things was immediately observable: the dialects, customs, sights, and sounds of regional America. The trend of realistic literature is the outcome of the establishment of the Western European capitalist system. It focuses on truthfully reflecting real life and possesses strong objectivity. It advocates inspecting real-life objectively and calmly, describing it accurately and delicately according to the original style of life, and striving to truly reproduce the typical characters in the typical environment. The literature and art of all countries in the world have realistic factors and characteristics to varying degrees from the beginning and they developed gradually with the social and historical conditions.

5. Briefly summarize the storyline of *The Call of the Wild*.

Buck, a strong and impressive dog, lives the good life in California then he is stolen and put into slavery of dogs. He is forced to pull the heavy sled along the frozen ice and suffers from hunger and beatings.

Day by day, Buck begins to adapt to his surroundings and learn from the other domestic dogs. He has some strong dreams about the primitive days of dogs and men. In his dreams, there are no rules or morality, only the law of club and fang, a kill-or-be-killed, rather ruthless and hard way of thinking.

Buck struggles for power against Spitz, another dog. They fight and Buck wins, becoming leader of the sled dog team. The new human management (new drivers) is incompetent to manage the team. They kill everyone and even themselves. Fortunately, Buck is saved by a kind man called John Thornton just before the death of the whole team in an icy river.

Buck becomes the intimate friend of Thornton and saves his life several times. Buck begins a journey with his new master and several other people. Although he loves his new life, he cannot repress the primal urge to run off and kill things in the woods once in a while.

Buck is in a dilemma: should he stay with his new master... or kill things? Be civilized... or be wild? At the end of the novel, Thornton is killed by the Yeehat tribe, and Buck makes a revenge on the people who murder his master. Buck's now free to run with the wild dog packs.

6. Is *The Call of the Wild* a simple dog's story? Make a brief comment on the novel.

The Call of the Wild is not just a story of a simple dog. In writing the story, Jack Griffith London deliberately used "he" to refer to Buck, a dog, instead of "it". Thus, the story must be read as a human's story.

The Call of the Wild brings readers a unique experience by means of feeling the tough life of sled dogs and people who live in the world of ice and snow in the north of the United States. The plots are interesting and thought-provoking, the exciting ups and downs affect the reader's heart. With a dog as the protagonist, it expresses the main idea incisively and vividly. The novel not only embodies Darwin's natural law of "survival of the fittest", the concept of maintaining the ecological balance between species and nature, but also the passionate love between animals and humans. The theme of "love and sympathy" offsets the cruelty described in the novel to a great extent. After fleeing from human civilization, Buck returns to nature and his wild instinct. The multiple themes of the novel make the content more profound and connotative. Great changes that happened to Buck express the author's yearning for freedom and his beautiful vision of returning to nature. By the vivid description of the fierce struggle of the wild animal and the animals' loss of humanity, Jack Griffith London is presenting the reality of American society.

7. How is the idea of "survival of the fittest" displayed in *The Call of the Wild*?

The Call of the Wild fully embodies Jack London's naturalistic artistic techniques. In naturalistic literary works, the protagonist often falls into all kinds of desperate plight, such as death, panic, hunger, and extremely cold weather, and faces all kinds of survival pressure. In this work, the naturalistic creed of "natural selection, survival of the fittest" occurs repeatedly, which shows that human character is gradually formed in the process of making peace with the natural environment. Buck's transformation from dog to wolf fully reflects the view of "survival of the fittest". In his struggle with the natural environment, Buck is molded as the image of "the fittest". In judge Miller's home, Buck lives a comfortable and carefree life. Since he is smuggled to the north by a dealer, his fate changes dramatically. Buck masters various survival skills so that he can quickly adapt to the harsh environment. When he first arrives in the snowfield, Buck doesn't know what posture he should adopt to keep warm when he sleeps. He is inspired when he sees Billy lying under the snow, curling up like a hairball. To avoid starvation, Buck immediately gets rid of its picky eating habits. No matter how hard the food is to digest or swallow, he will gobble them down to store enough energy for his body. Living in the world of ice and snow, Buck changes from a gourmet to a predator, showing his extraordinary adaptability to the natural environment.

8. Why did the author use "he" to refer to a dog in *The Call of the Wild*?

In the novel, Buck is just a dog, but Jack Griffith London replaced "it" with "he" in order to personify Buck and his surroundings, depicting the world in Buck's eyes and human essence incisively and vividly. This novel uncovers the coldness and cruelty of capitalist society as well as the objective reality of "survival of the fittest". Buck longs for freedom and finally makes it come true, which is exactly the embodiment of London's pursuit and ideal. Buck overcomes many difficulties and finally regains his kingdom, his process of struggling insinuates that of mankind. The harsh environment faced by Buck is just the epitome of human society. The author intends to let readers reflect on their current situation while striking a chord with them and shortening the distance.

The novel does not describe too much about Buck's life together with judge Miller's family. But we know that the author endows Buck with spirituality by using "he" instead of "it". He feels the warmth of his family and the respect of other family members.

Buck has his inherent curiosity, selfless love, sense of shame and justice, which is fully reflected in his relationship with Thornton. He is just a dog, but he is more conscientious than many people around him. The author uses "he" instead of "it" to satirize the indifference of human nature and the cruelty of capitalist society.

9. Make a brief comment on *Winesburg, Ohio*.

Winesburg, Ohio contains 22 stories. In structure, it lies midway between a novel and a mere collection of stories. It is a cycle of stories with several unifying elements, including a single background, a prevailing tone, a central character, and an underlying plot that is advanced or enriched by each of the stories.

Winesburg, Ohio is described as a place with a stressful atmosphere, especially for "the grotesques." This is a book of the grotesque, of people each having seized upon a single truth that distorts their personalities. The underlying plot in *Winesburg, Ohio* is the growing up of young George Willard who is too young to understand the hope held for him by people in the small Midwestern town. Since they cannot truly communicate with others, they have all become emotional cripples. Most of the grotesques are attracted one by one to George Willard with the belief that he might be able to speak what is in their hearts and thus re-establish their connection with mankind. In the last story "Departure", George leaves Winesburg, promising that he will become the voice of inarticulate men and women in small towns. In this sense, this book is a work of love, an attempt to break down the walls that divide one person from another. At the same time, this book is a celebration of small town life in the lost days of goodwill and innocence.

10. Comment briefly on the contribution Sherwood Anderson made to American literature.

Sherwood Anderson did a few things for which he is remembered today. Thematically, he had the courage to explore new material for fiction: the psychological and emotional aspect of American small-town life, with emphasis chiefly on lower-class figures, the unsuccessful, the depraved, and the inarticulate. In more ways than one, Anderson was a writer of an important period in American history, one in which America passed from a rural to a predominantly industrial society. The transition, which was drawing to a close in the first years of this century, had been a painful experience in small towns. Alienation, loneliness, and want of love and understanding made life intolerable, and turned people into "grotesques". Thwarted emotions, repressed drives, frustrated lives, and distorted natures became the distinct features of America's small-town life. The historic importance of Anderson lies in the fact that he offered in his best works a rather timeless record of these for posterity. *Winesburg, Ohio*, which has become an American classic, is a good illustration.

Anderson was a highly original writer. He depended on inspiration in his creative endeavor. Like the old writer in "The Book of the Grotesque", Anderson seemed to have a "young thing" active within him, directing his pen. He must have often had the same experience, again like the old writer, of falling into a half-dream in which he meets a procession of figures, some amusing, some almost beautiful, but all grotesques of one kind or another: He felt there was something, "the young indescribable thing within him" as he called it, that was driving this long procession before him. Listening to the call from inside, Anderson wrote his stories that appeal not through careful fabrications of incidents or episodes, but by the sheer emotional force of the moments of revelation, or the Joycean epiphany, that these stories describe. Here lies Anderson's contribution to the art of fiction. He observed human grotesqueness and eccentricity from a Freudian psychological point of view and tried to reveal the abnormal states of mind in a more or less accurate way. As Malcolm Cowley puts it, Anderson was endowed with "a gift for pouring a lifetime into a moment".

Then there is his style to consider. Anderson was probably the first writer since Mark Twain to write in the colloquial style. He regarded the vernacular as an honest medium and developed a style the major features of which included clarity, directness, and a deceptive simplicity. This style, though its power was very much vitiated by its weakness like monotony, crudity, and sentimental expansiveness, was to influence such writers as Ernest Hemingway and William Faulkner. For Hemingway, Anderson served as his stylistic guide for some time, and for Faulkner, the young writer expressed his respect for the older more than adequately when he stated that Anderson was "the father of my generation of American writers and the tradition of American writing which our successors will carry on." Anderson has been called "a writer's writer". In addition to Hemingway and Faulkner, there were also Hart Crane, Thomas Wolfe, and John Steinbeck, to name just a few, who owed a debt to him. Modern American literature would not have been the same had there not been such a seminal figure as Sherwood Anderson.

Part V

Twentieth-Century Literature I: Before WWII

I. Fill in the Blanks.

1. realism; naturalism
2. historical romances
3. *Poetry: A Magazine of Verse*
4. First World War
5. the 1920s
6. *The Waste Land*
7. *Main Street*
8. Harlem Renaissance
9. Great Depression
10. *The Grapes of Wrath*
11. Francis Scott Key Fitzgerald; William Faulkner; Sigmund Freud
12. ideas of order
13. *Harmonium*
14. Imagist
15. transcendentalist
16. *The Necessary Angel*
17. Wallace Stevens
18. *Opus Posthumous*
19. Tilbury Town
20. Edwin Arlington Robinson
21. Edwin Arlington Robinson
22. The futility of human life
23. The Children of the Night
24. Stephen Crane
25. naturalism; realism; impressionism
26. Sin
27. *A Man Said to the Universe*
28. *The Open Boat*
29. *Maggie: A Girl of the Streets*
30. *The Red Badge of Courage*
31. *A Boy's Will*; an authentic poet
32. New England; the daily life of ordinary people
33. sophisticated society
34. road; traveler
35. conversational
36. suicide
37. *Design*
38. innocence; evil; victim

· 177 ·

39. Robert Frost
40. *New Hampshire*
41. Populist radical
42. *Cool Tombs; Flash Crimson*
43. Carl Sandburg
44. simple; simple; *The People, Yes*
45. Abraham Lincoln; *The War Years*
46. Walt Whitman; Emily Dickinson
47. Carl Sandburg; Ezra Pound
48. new life
49. William Carlos Williams
50. *Kora in Hell: Improvisations*
51. *Spring and All*
52. *Paterson*
53. No ideas but in things; *Spring and All*
54. Thomas Stearns Eliot; *The Waste Land*
55. Thomas Stearns Eliot; Ezra Pound
56. reconstructions; Chinese; *Homage to Sextus Propertius*
57. Ezra Pound
58. *Hugh Selwyn Mauberley*
59. *The Cantos*
60. Ezra Pound
61. Chinese
62. Sinclair Lewis; *Babbitt*
63. *Hike and the Aeroplane; Our Mr. Wrenn*
64. *Dodsworth*
65. *Babbitt*
66. Angry American
67. *Main Street*
68. *Beyond the Horizon; Anna Christie; Strange Interlude; Long Day's Journey into Night*
69. Eugene Gladstone O'Neill
70. *The Iceman Cometh*
71. *Bound East for Cardiff*
72. Ezra Pound
73. Thomas Stearns Eliot
74. *The Waste Land*
75. *Murder in the Cathedral*
76. *Four Quartets*
77. Tradition and the Individual Talent
78. *Homage to John Dryden*
79. *This Side of Paradise*
80. *Tender Is the Night*
81. *The Last Tycoon*
82. Edward Estlin Cummings; *The Enormous Room*
83. love for nature; children; normal
84. picture-poems

family life; artistic work
85. *Marble Faun*
86. *Sherwood Anderson*
87. *Yoknapatawpha saga*
88. *Soldier's Pay*
89. *Sartoris*
90. *The Sound and the Fury*
91. *As I Lay Dying*; subjective monologues
92. *A Fable*; *The Reivers*
93. *Lafayette, Oxford*
94. *Exhaustion*
95. *The Sound and the Fury*
96. *Light in August*
97. *Carson McCullers*
98. *The Sun Also Rises*
99. *A Farewell to Arms*
100. *A Farewell to Arms*
101. *For Whom the Bell Tolls*; John Donne
102. *Of Mice and Men*
103. *The Long Valley*
104. *The Grapes of Wrath*
105. *Tortilla Flat*
106. *The Pearl*

II. Choose the Best Answer for Each Question.

1-5	C D D D A	6-10	A B B D C	11-15 A D D A D
16-20	A D B B A	21-25	A D D C D	26-30 D A A B D
31-35	D B C D C	36-40	A B A B C	41-45 A D D A B
46-50	A D D C D	51-55	D D A D D	56-60 D D C B C
61-65	A B A A C	66-70	B B A D D	71-75 D A B D D
76-80	A A A D B	81-85	A B C D C	86-90 B B D D C
91-95	A D B D B	96-100	A A A A B	101-105 A C C D D
106-108	D D D			

III. Match-Making

Group One

1-8 g c b f e d a h

Group Two
1-8 b a e d c h f g

IV. Define the Literary Terms.

1. Harlem Renaissance

    Harlem Renaissance, also known as the "New Negro Movement", is a burst of literary achievement in the 1920s by Negro playwrights, poets, and novelists who presented new insights into the American experience and prepared the way for the emergence of numerous Black writers after mid-20th century (Black Arts Movement—the mid 1960's to the mid 1970's). Harlem Renaissance was more than just a literary movement. It included racial consciousness, "the back to Africa" movement led by Marcus Garvey, racial integration, the explosion of music, particularly jazz, spirituals and blues, painting, dramatic revues, and others.

2. Hemingway heroes

    Hemingway heroes refer to some protagonists in Ernest Hemingway's works. Such a hero usually is an average man of decidedly masculine tastes, sensitive and intelligent. And usually he is a man of action and of few words. He is such an individualist, alone even when with other people, somewhat an outsider, keeping emotions under control, stoic and self-disciplined in a dreadful place where one cannot get happiness. Frederic Henry in *A Farewell to Arms* is completely disillusioned. He has been to the war, but has seen nothing sacred and glorious. Like Jake Barnes in *The Sun Also Rises* who hates to talk about the war, Henry is shocked into the realization that "abstract words such as glory, honor, courage, or hallow were obscene", and feels "always embarrassed by words such as glory, sacred and sacrifice." Hemingway heroes stand for a whole generation. In a world which is essentially chaotic and meaningless, a Hemingway hero fights a solitary struggle against a force he does not even understand. The awareness that it must end in defeat, no matter how hard he strives, engenders a sense of despair. But a Hemingway hero possesses a kind of "despairing courage" as Bertrand Russell terms. It is this courage that enables a man to behave like a man, to assert his dignity in face of adversity. This is the essence of a code of honor in which all of Ernest Hemingway's heroes believe, whether he is Nick Adams, Jake Barnes, Frederic Henry, Robert Jordan, Santiago or the undefeated bullfighter. But surely, they differ, some from others, in their views of the world. The difference which comes gradually in view is an index to the subtle change which Ernest Hemingway's outlook had undergone.

3. Imagism

Imagism was a movement in early 20th-century Anglo-American poetry that favored precision of imagery and clear, sharp language. It came into being as a reaction to the traditional English poetry to express the sense of fragmentation and dislocation. Imagism called for a return to what were seen as more classical values, such as directness of presentation and economy of language, as well as a willingness to experiment with non-traditional verse forms. Imagists used free verse. Imagist publications appearing between 1914 and 1917 featured works by many of the most prominent modernist figures, both in poetry and in other fields. The Imagist group was centered in London, with members from Great Britain, Ireland and the United States. A characteristic feature of Imagism is its attempt to isolate a single image to reveal its essence. The poem of Ezra Pound entitled *In a Station of the Metro* is the most outstanding representative poem of this movement.

4. Southern Renaissance

Southern Renaissance refers to the reinvigoration of American Southern literature that began in the 1920s and 1930s with the appearance of writers such as William Faulkner and others. For writers in the South, the questions often involved a desire to protect tradition and myth from being destroyed by the influx of new ways of thinking and living. "Southern Renaissance" explores some of the ways that the writers, who either lived in, wrote about, or were otherwise associated with the South between 1920 and 1950, responded to the many changes during the period. Among the writers of the Southern Renaissance, William Faulkner is arguably the most influential and famous, having won the Nobel Prize in Literature in 1949 (for his anti-racist *Intruder in the Dust*).

5. Stream of consciousness

Stream of consciousness or "interior monologue" (内心独白) is one of the modern literary techniques. It was first used in 1922 by the Irish novelist James Joyce. This modernistic trend in 1920s, deeply influenced by the psychoanalytic theories of Sigmund Freud, adopted the psychoanalytic approach in literary creation to explore the existence of sub-conscious and unconscious elements in the mind. In English fiction, the novelists of stream of consciousness were represented by James Joyce and Virginia Woolf. Their novels break through the bounds of time and space, and vividly and skillfully depict the unconscious activities of the mind, particularly the hesitant, misted, distracted and illusory psychology people have when they face reality. Britain was the center of stream of consciousness. The modern American writer William Faulkner successfully advanced this technique. In his stories, action and plots are less important than the reactions and inner musings of the narrators. Time sequences are often dislocated. The reader feels as if he has been a participant rather than an observer in the stories. A high degree of emotion can be achieved by this technique. But it also makes the stories hard to understand.

6. The Beat Generation

The Beat Generation is a term used to describe a group of American writers who came to prominence in the late 1950s and early 1960s, and the cultural phenomena that they wrote about and inspired: a rejection of mainstream American values, experimentation with drugs and alternate forms of sexuality, and an interest in Eastern spirituality. The major works of Beat writing are Allen Ginsberg's *Howl* (1956), William Seward Burroughs II's *Naked Lunch* (1959) and Jack Kerouac's *On the Road* (1957). During the 1960s, the rapidly expanding Beat culture underwent a transformation: the Beat Generation gave way to the 1960s counterculture, which was accompanied by a shift in public terminology from "beatnik" to "hippie".

7. The Jazz Age

The Jazz Age refers to the 1920s in America characterized by frivolity and carelessness. It was brought vividly to life in Francis Scott Key Fitzgerald's *The Great Gatsby*. To many, World War I was a tragic failure of old values, old politics and old ideas. The social mood was one of confusion and despair. Yet, on the surface the mood in America did not seem desperate. It entered a decade of prosperity and exhibitionism. Fashions were extravagant; more and more automobiles crowded the roads; advertising flourished. This was the Jazz Age, when New Orleans musicians moved "up the river" to Chicago and the theater of New York's Harlem pulsed with the music that had become a symbol of the time. These were the roaring twenties. It served to mask a quiet pain, the sense of loss.

8. The Lost Generation

The Lost Generation is also termed as the Sad Young Men, which was created by Francis Scott Key Fitzgerald in his book *All the Sad Young Men*. The term in general refers to the post-World War I generation, but specifically a group of US writers who came of age during the war and established their reputation in the 1920s. It stems from a remark made by Gertrude Stein to Ernest Hemingway, "You are all a lost generation." Ernest Hemingway used it as an epigraph to *The Sun Also Rises*, a novel that captures the attitudes of a hard-drinking, fast living set of disillusioned young expatriates in postwar Paris. The generation was "lost" in the sense that its inherited values were no longer relevant in the postwar world and because of its spiritual alienation from US, they seemed hopelessly provincial, materialistic, and emotionally barren. The term embraces Ernest Hemingway, Francis Scott Key Fitzgerald, John Dos Passos, Edward Estlin Cummings and so on.

9. The Waste Land Painters

It refers to Francis Scott Key Fitzgerald, Ernest Hemingway, Thomas Stearns Eliot and William Faulkner. They all painted the post-war western world as a waste land, lifeless, and hopeless. Thomas Stearns Eliot's *The Waste Land* depicts a picture of modern social crisis, in which modern civilized society turns into a waste land due to ethnical degradation and disillusionment with dreams. *The Hollow Men* is no less depressing. Francis Scott Key Fitzgerald's *The Great Gatsby* is about the frustration and despair from the failure of the American dream. Ernest Hemingway's *The Sun Also Rises* and *A Farewell to Arms* portray the dilemma of modern man utterly thrown upon himself for survival in an indifferent world, revealing man's impotence and his despairing courage to assert himself against overwhelming odds.

V. Answer the Following Questions Briefly.

1. Give an analysis of Ezra Pound's *In the Station of the Metro*.

The excellent image in this short poem is not a decoration. It is central to the poem's meaning. In fact, it is the poem's meaning.

The "Metro" is the underground railway of Paris. In this brief poem, Ezra Pound uses the fewest possible words to convey an accurate image, according to the principles of the "Imagists". He tries to render exactly his observation of human faces seen in an underground railway station. He sees the faces, turned variously toward light and darkness, like flower petals which are half absorbed by, half resisting, the wet, dark texture of a bough.

The word "apparition", with its double meaning, binds the two aspects of the observation together:

A. Apparition meaning "appearance", in the sense of something which appears, or shows up; something which can be clearly observed.

B. Apparition meaning something which seems real but perhaps is not real; something ghostly which cannot be clearly observed.

2. Give an analysis of Edwin Arlington Robinson's *Richard Cory*.

Richard Cory is a narrative poem written by Edwin Arlington Robinson. It was first published in 1897, as part of *The Children of the Night*, having been completed in July of that year; and it remains one of Edwin Arlington Robinson's most popular and anthologized poems. The poem describes a person who is wealthy, well educated, mannerly, and admired by the people in his town. Despite all this, he fatally shoots himself in the head.

Edwin Arlington Robinson's world is naturalistic in nature. Here God is no longer caring, men suffer from frustrations and want of mutual understanding and life is in general futile and meaningless. These reveal Edwin Arlington Robinson as a modern poet, capable of a tragic vision in step with the modern spirit, trying to suggest a despairing courage to seek out the meaning of life. Take *Richard Cory* for example. Richard Cory is a gentleman, rich and human and clean and graceful, the way he is dressed, walks downtown, speaks to people, "In fine, we thought that he was everything / To make us wish that we were in his place." But, all of a sudden, we hear of his suicide: "And Richard Cory, one calm summer night, / Went home and put a bullet through his head." The poem is thus also an illustration of Edwin Arlington Robinson's fascination with "psychological enigmas", enigmas that were the product of modern life.

3. Give an analysis of Robert Frost's *The Road Not Taken*.

"The Road Not Taken" is a poem by Robert Frost, published in 1916 as the first poem in the collection *Mountain Interval*. This poem is written in classic five-line stanzas, with the rhyme scheme a-b-a-a-b and conversational tone or style. The poem seems to be about the poet, walking in the woods in autumn, choosing which road he should follow on his walk. In reality, it concerns the important decisions which one must make in life, when one must give up one desirable thing in order to possess another. Then, whatever the outcome, one must accept the consequences of one's choice for it is not possible to go back and have another chance to choose differently.

In the poem, the poet hesitates for a long time, wondering which road to take, because they are both pretty. In the end, he follows the one which seems to have fewer travelers on it. Symbolically, he chooses to follow an unusual, solitary life; perhaps he is speaking of his choice to become a poet rather than some commoner profession. But he always remembers the road which he might have taken, and which would have given him a different kind of life.

4. Give an analysis of Robert Frost's *Fire and Ice*.

Fire and Ice

Some say the world will end in fire,

Some say in ice.

From what I've tasted of desire

I hold with those who favor fire.

But if it had to perish twice,

I think I know enough of hate

To say that for destruction ice

Is also great

And would suffice.

"Fire and Ice" is one of Robert Frost's most popular poems, published in December 1920 in *Harper's Magazine* and in 1923 in his

Pulitzer Prize-winning book *New Hampshire*. It discusses the end of the world, likening the elemental force of fire with the emotion of desire, and ice with hate. It is one of Robert Frost's best-known and most anthologized poems. Certain scientists say that the earth will someday be burned up by the sun. Other scientists say that a new Ice Age will kill all life on the earth. The poet compares the strong emotion of desire to fire. Knowing its destructive force on mankind, he thinks it likely that the world will end by fire. On the other hand, he compares hatred to ice. This, too, is a powerfully destructive emotion. Ice would also be capable of ruining the earth in the same way that hatred can ruin men.

5. Give an appreciation of Robert Frost's *Departmental*.

    Departmental is one of the most frankly comic of Robert Frost's poems. As originally printed, there was a subtitle that contained a pun: "The End of My Ant Jerry." The high humor was (and still is) emphasized by the comic rhymes, especially the rhymes for "Jerry" and "Formic", the latter proving that the poor victim was a house ant, Formica.

    But, though the lines provoke laughter, the poem is much more than a set of burlesque verses. Before the reader is halfway through, he is aware that *Departmental* is a satire, a criticism of standardization. The irony of regimentation is wryly pronounced by the rueful end.

6. Give an appreciation of Robert Frost's *Design*.

    The poet has a special sympathy for the persistent firefly and the patient spider. He does not laugh at the "emulating flies" who try to imitate stars, even though "they can't sustain the part."

    The "heal-all" is a common country plant supposed to have healing properties; it is almost always blue in color. The poet has found a strange white variety and, stranger still, attached to it a white spinner, "a snow-drop spider", holding a white moth, completing a pattern of whiteness. Here, in a world of chaos and darkness, there is purpose and design—"if" (the poet speculates whimsically) "design govern in a thing so small".

7. Give an analysis of Wallace Stevens's *Anecdote of the Jar*.

"Anecdote of the Jar" is a poem from Wallace Stevens's first book of poetry, *Harmonium* (1919). We can only decipher the meaning of *Anecdote of the Jar* by placing it in the larger context of his aesthetic credo and thematic concerns. Here lies the wild—and chaotic and formless—rural Tennessee, which we assume to be a symbol of the world of nature. Then the "I" of the poem places in it a tall, round jar, a man-made object, which is suggestive of the world of art, and by extension, the world of imagination. What happens when the jar is standing there is almost a miracle: it controls the whole disorderly landscape, so that "The wilderness rose up to it, / And sprawled around, no longer wild." The poem seems to be talking about the relationship between art and nature. The world of nature, shapeless and slovenly, takes shape and order from the presence of the jar. The world of art and imagination gives form and meaning to that of nature and reality, thus suggesting, as Wallace Stevens may be doing, that any society without art is one without order and that man makes the order he perceives, and the world he inhabits is one he half creates. Wallace Stevens firmly believes that the poet is the archetype of creative power on which all human understanding depends. His poet is "the necessary angel of the earth", in whose sight man sees the earth again. The poet is, in other words, an instrument by means of which man is made to see life whole again.

8. Give a brief summary of *The Waste Land*, the masterpiece of Thomas Stearns Eliot.

The Waste Land is a long poem by Thomas Stearns Eliot. It is widely regarded as one of the most important poems of the 20th century and a central text in modernist poetry. Published in 1922, *The Waste Land* is 433 lines long. The Waste Land itself is a desolate and sterile country ruled by an impotent king. The whole poem is divided into five parts: I. "The Burial of the Dead", representing the stirring life in the land after the barren winter; II. "The Game of Chess", contrasting the splendors of the past represented by Cleopatra with uneasiness and despair of modern life; III. "The Fire Sermon", making an imaginative silhouette sketch of the ugliness of cities and the mechanization of modern life and emotion; IV. "Death by Water", presumptively proving by the vision of a drowned Phoenician sailor that water is not only the constructive source of life, but also the destructive source of death; and V. "What the Thunder Said", presenting a picture, through symbols of the Grail legend, of the drought, the decay and emptiness of modern life.

The theme of the poem is modern spiritual barrenness, the despair and depression that followed the First World War, the sterility and turbulence of the modern world, and the decline and break-down of Western culture. The noticeable characteristics of the poem are varied length and rhythm to harmonize with the changing subject matter, the unrhymed lines, lots of borrowings from some thirty-five different writers, the employment of materials such as the legends of the Holy Grail, Sir James Frazer's anthropological work *The Golden Bough*, several popular songs, and passages in six foreign languages, including Sanskrit. The poem, therefore, is obscure and hard to understand, needless to say its absence of logical continuity. The poem, nevertheless, is broadly acknowledged as one of the most recognizable landmarks of modernism.

9. Give an analysis of Thomas Stearns Eliot's *The Love Song of J. Alfred Prufrock*.

The Love Song of J. Alfred Prufrock, commonly known as *Prufrock*, is a poem by American-British poet Thomas Stearns Eliot. It depicts a timid middle-aged man going (or thinking of going) to propose marriage to a lady but hesitating all the way there. It takes the form of soliloquy, an interior monologue like that of Robert Browning's. Whether the man actually leaves his spot at all remains a question. Most probably he stays where he is all the while, allowing his imagination to run wild. Prufrock is the image of an ineffectual, sorrowful, tragic 20th-century Western man, possibly the modern intellectual who is divided between passion and timidity, between desire and impotence. His tragic flaw is timidity; his "curse" is his idealism. Knowing everything, but able to do nothing, he lives in an area of life and death; and caught between the two worlds, he belongs to neither. He craves love but has no courage to declare himself. He despairs of life. He discovers its emptiness and yet has found nothing to replace it. Thus the poem develops a theme of frustration and emotional conflict.

The title of the poem is ironic in that the "love song" is in fact about the absence of love. The name of Prufrock is that of a furniture dealer in St Louis. His initial "J" sounds tony and classy, giving one a sense of the upper class to which he belongs. The epigraph, taken from Dante's *Inferno*, is in fact a confessional, a kind of "I'll tell you all." The speaker in it is the flame of Guido suffering in the eighth circle of Hell for fraud. Through the tongue of the flame Guido says to the effect that, since nobody ever goes out of Hell, I can answer you without fear, which is another way of saying that we can talk candidly about our sins. The implication of all this is that Prufrock is, like Guido, also in Hell or a hellish situation. Since Prufrock is not guilty of anything and Guido is, the resemblance is highly ironic. The epigraph also implies that modern man inhabits a nightmarish inferno. The first line, "Let us go then, you and I", suggests that what follows is a dramatic monologue with an audience. It reminds us of Robert Browning's *My Last Duchess* where there is the impregnated line, "Nay, we'll go / Together down, sir." The identity of "you" has invited a variety of comment. Thomas Stearns Eliot himself says that it is "an unidentified male companion". Some critics see it as "the generalized reader". But most seem to agree that it is Prufrock's alter ego, symbolizing the split nature of this divided person; "I" represents his inner self.

Prufrock is a middle-aged dandy, well dressed and self-conscious to a fault. He lives in an urban world, seedy, raw, more or less Zolaesque as the first few lines suggest and the third section of the poem (Lines 15-22) confirms. It is a world where there is no social unity, and where there is elegance and beauty of a kind such as divorced from force and vitality. It is a trivial world of total emptiness ("I have measured out my life with coffee spoons"). Here walks (or he imagines himself walking) this man with an obsession he cannot handle in the natural way, afraid of rejection, of being misinterpreted, of forcing the moment to its crisis. Here is an extreme example of the Hamlet problem: a man harassed with self-doubt, never reaching that "Readiness is all" state with his inability to act and be alive at the moment. Neurotically desperate, Prufrock can conceive a heroic action which he is incapable of fulfilling; he can see his actions on the grandest level but do not a thing. He sees himself as Lazarus coming back from the dead, but cannot break through his deadness. He sees himself as John the Baptist, that vigorous, dynamic, committed human being that he is by all standards not, with his aimless, silly, repetitive way of wasting his life in a purposeless social environment. At the end of the poem he fancies himself "in the chambers of the sea / By sea girls wreathed with seaweed red and brown," but the "human voices" wake him up from his revelry. Unable to bring himself and his world together, to build a base for meaningful action, Prufrock represents the spiritual impotence of archetypal modern man. What is redeeming is probably his self-perception: he sees his own absurdity.

The poem is interesting also for its method of presentation. We do not move in a sequential fashion. Apart from the surreal vividness which characterizes certain parts of the poem, there are elliptical structures, strange juxtapositions, an absence of bridges, so that the whole seems broken; nothing is explained in a logical manner. We have to make leaps in our reading and appreciation, as the poet seems to jump from one scene to another and from one idea to another. It is important to note here, however, that the association of images establishes the general feeling. Nothing is discordant, irrelevant, or abrupt any more when the overall mood of the poem is perceived.

10. Give a story summary and an analysis of chapter 3 of *The Great Gatsby*.

The Great Gatsby is a 1925 novel written by American author Fitzgerald Scott Key Fitzgerald that follows a cast of characters living in the fictional town of West Egg on prosperous Long Island in the summer of 1922. Considered to be Fitzgerald Scott Key Fitzgerald's magnum opus, *The Great Gatsby* explores themes of decadence, idealism, resistance to change, social upheaval, and excess, creating a portrait of the Jazz Age or the Roaring Twenties that has been described as a cautionary tale regarding the American Dream.

The novel describes the life and death of Jay Gatsby, as seen through the eyes of a narrator who does not share the same point of view as the fashionable people around him. The narrator learns that Gatsby became rich by breaking the law. Gatsby pretends to be a well-educated war hero, which he is not, yet the narrator portrays him as being far more noble than the rich, cruel, stupid people among whom he and Gatsby live. Gatsby's character is purified by a deep, unselfish love for Daisy, a beautiful, silly woman who, earlier, married a rich husband instead of Gatsby and moved into high society. Gatsby has never lost his love for her and, in an era when divorce has become easy, he tries to win her back by becoming extravagantly rich himself. He does not succeed, and in the end he is killed almost by accident because of his determination to shield Daisy from disgrace. None of Gatsby's upper class friends come to his funeral. The narrator is so disgusted that he leaves New York and returns to his original home in the provinces.

Chapter 3 describes one of Gatsby's fabulous parties at his expensive, rented estate near New York; it is the first such party that the narrator has attended. There is a passage which begins with a description of the elaborate preparations, which he watches from the house next door, and continues with his observations as one of the guests. He evokes a vivid atmosphere of contradiction: the party is crowded yet empty of warmth or friendship, the charm and sweetness of youth is spoiled by triviality and tawdriness, the splendid house and garden have been purchased not for enjoyment but for the purpose of making an impression.

11. Give an analysis of John Steinbeck's *The Grapes of Wrath.*

The Grapes of Wrath is an American realist novel written by John Steinbeck and published in 1939. It is one of the major American books. *The Grapes of Wrath* is a crisis novel. It is John Steinbeck's clear expression of sympathy with the dispossessed and the wretched. The Great Depression throws the country into abject chaos and makes life intolerable for the luckless millions. One of the worst stricken areas is the central prairie lands. There farmers become bankrupt and begin to move in a body toward California, where they hope to have a better life. The westering is a most tragic and brutalizing human experience for families like the Joads. There are unspeakable pain and suffering on the road, and death occurs frequently. Everywhere they travel, they see a universal landscape of decay and desolation. When they reach California and try to settle down, they meet with bitter resistance from the local landowners. Iniquity is widespread and wrath is about to overwhelm patience. The prophecy of an imminent explosion is sent forth from the anger-saturated pages: "When a majority of the people are hungry and cold they will take by force what they need", John Steinbeck is saying. "Burn coffee for fuel in the ships. Burn corn to keep warm, it makes a hot fire... Slaughter the pigs and bury them, and let the putrescence drip down into the earth." But John Steinbeck then says, "There is a crime here that goes beyond denunciation." The day of wrath is coming. In the souls of the people the grapes of wrath are filling and growing heavy. Something in the nature of a social revolution would be imminent, the book is in effect saying, if nothing is done to stop the detonation. This is perhaps one of the reasons why the book was for many years banned.

Structurally, *The Grapes of Wrath* consists of two blocks of material: the westward trek of the Joads and the dispossessed Oklahomans, and the general picture of the Great Depression. The fact that the intercalary chapters are dispersed in between others tends to give one the impression of a formal looseness not to be tolerated in a good work of art. However, critical research has revealed a close relationship between the two parts of the book. The interchapters function as informational and informative, offering, for instance, the social and historical background against which the characters move. We read the appalling description of drought at the beginning of the book to get ready for the unnerving population movement that constitutes its action. The dismal look of Highway 66 enables us to visualize the tragic nature of the trek of the Oklahomans. The chapters dealing with migrant life appear in between the narrative chapters of the actual westering journey, while the last interchapter describes the rain in which the action of the novel ends. These are but some of the illustrations of the inherent unity of the novel.

The novel is structurally interesting for another, perhaps more important, reason, that its structure is dictated by the Bible. There are suggestions that the author was thinking about the Bible when writing the novel. The 30 chapters fall neatly into three sections, with the description of the drought in the first ten, the journeying in chapters 13 through 18, and the remaining 12 devoted to a narrative of the life of the migrants in California. These three sections correspond to the Exodus story in the Old Testament. The Exodus tells about the bondage of the ancient Jews in Egypt, their escape out of it and journeying toward Canaan, the Promised Land. In distant times, so the story goes, the Jews went to Egypt in search of food and, having stayed there for some 400 years, became the slaves of the Egyptian Pharoah. Their suffering was such that God sent Moses as His prophet to lead them out. This Moses did, and the great host traveled through the desert toward Canaan, only to meet with bitter resistance there. *The Grapes of Wrath*, in emphasizing the fact of the Oklahomans coming from the Oklahoma desert, crossing the big Death Valley desert and into California, the land of hope for them, works out the parallel to the Exodus admirably well. John Steinbeck is not stating this very explicitly, but the suggestion is very strong, and is supported by symbols such as that of the grapes.

12. Give an analysis of William Faulkner's *The Sound and the Fury*.

The Sound and the Fury (1929) is a novel written by the American author William Faulkner. It employs a number of narrative styles, including the technique known as stream of consciousness, pioneered by 20th-century European novelists such as James Joyce and Virginia Woolf.

Let us take a look at *The Sound and the Fury*. Here is "a tale / Told by an idiot, full of sound and fury. / Signifying nothing." There is enough despair and nihilism but not much love and emotion in this sad story of the Compsons. Mr. Compson is disenchanted with life and the society he lives in. Unable to find meaning in the moral verities he was brought up with, he escapes into alcoholism and cynicism. Mrs. Compson is spiritually effete and has little love to spare for her children. Of the four children, Caddy is the only one capable of loving, but she loses her virginity. The youngest brother, Benjy, is an idiot, a curse on the family. Another, Quentin, lives in the ideal world of his youth with his dreams of love, honor, and integrity, and, when he fails to keep off the intrusion of the "loud, harsh world", he destroys himself. The life of the eldest brother, Jason, is empty and meaningless. Love is alien to him, and so are other traditional humanistic values.

The Sound and the Fury tells a story of deterioration from the past to the present. The past is idealized to form a striking contrast with the loveless present. There is in the book an acute feeling of nostalgia toward the happy past. Quentin's section offers a good illustration. A miserable creature in the modern world, Quentin frequently casts a backward glance at the time of his childhood when life was innocent, romantic, and secure. He just cannot bring himself to come to terms with the present which is, to him, purposeless, futile, and devoid of the values which make life worth living. His suicide offers an example of a complete negation of the present. In a sense, Quentin's value system may represent William Faulkner's own idea of an ideal way of life, that of an ante-bellum society. The fact that Benjy's section begins the book is not a haphazard arrangement on the part of the author, for it is Benjy who feels most keenly the loss of love. Benjy lives on the emotional support of love. Although an idiot with no sense of time, he knows who loves him best. When Caddy is gone, his world of love vanishes with her; and nobody can take her place, not even Dilsey. Thus, this section helps to dramatize the theme of loss from the very beginning of the story. With the story of Jason whose life embodies all the vices of the modern world, the contrast between the ante-bellum society and the present one is brought out in the most poignant manner possible. The triumph of rationalism over feeling and compassion is best illustrated in this sterile and loveless individual.

13. Summarize American poetic revolution of the 20th century.

The years 1912-1914 witnessed the appearance of all kinds of innovations. Here were indications that a new poetic revolution was taking place, comparable in scope and significance to (if not greater than) the one Walt Whitman represented in 1855. The new poets wrote poetry that defied most of the accepted rules, and dealt with subjects which had not been dealt with except, perhaps, by Walt Whitman, thus pushing the boundaries of poetry further back. And they wrote in new ways and techniques. These people were in effect creating a poetic revolution in America and also a very large American poetry reading audience. This audience was in large part a very fragmented one, because modern life was fragmented and dislocated; the West was, philosophically and religiously, a fragmented civilization with no longer a unified set of beliefs which characterized the world of Dante Alighieri's *Divine Comedy*, Geoffrey Chaucer's *The Canterbury Tales*, Edmund Spenser's *Faerie Queene* or the world of William Shakespeare, John Milton, and Alexander Pope. The new verse was responsive to the fragmentized nature of modern life. Within a little over two decades, it scored a complete triumph over old poetry. Ezra Pound, Thomas Stearns Eliot, William Carlos Williams, Wallace Stevens, Carl Sandburg, Edward Estlin Cummings and Hart Crane, to name just a few, all made their presence felt, and Thomas Stearns Eliot became, by 1925, the acknowledged leader of the new verse and criticism.

14. What is Thomas Stearns Eliot's style of poetry? What is his main contribution to literature?

At first, Thomas Stearns Eliot, like Ezra Pound, attempted to produce "pure imagery" with no added meaning or symbolism. Then he began adding one image to another in such a way that his attitude and mood became clear. In his best works, the image, his own philosophy and the music of words are all harmoniously blended. Thomas Stearns Eliot mingled grand images with commonplace ones, he combined trivial and tawdry images with traditional poetic subjects. Thomas Stearns Eliot rarely made his meaning explicit. The internal logic of his poems is carried out by swiftly accumulating images, suggestions and echoes, depending for their interpretation upon the imagination of the reader.

Thomas Stearns Eliot is the author of the epochal poem, *The Waste Land*, a graphic illustration of the spiritual poverty of the West of the time. The poem has been recognized as representing a solid body of literary works, fiction, poetry, and other genres which came out of the decade of the 1920s and the years immediately after it.

15. What is Ezra Pound's main contribution to American literature?

Ezra Pound (1885-1972) is regarded rightly as the father of modern American poetry. Impatient with the fetters of English traditional poetics, he led the experiment in revolutionizing poetry. It was he who first discovered Thomas Stearns Eliot and blue-penciled the latter's famous poem, *The Waste Land*. It was he who helped William Butler Yeats, James Joyce, David Herbert Lawrence, and William Carlos Williams in their literary careers. And he survived them all, writing continually right up to his death. Ezra Pound's contribution to the development of modern poetry is very great.

16. How do you understand the Jazz Age in America under Francis Scott Key Fitzgerald's pen?

As one of the most celebrated of American writers, famed for his evocative stories of the 1920s, Francis Scott Key Fitzgerald is usually credited with coining the term the "Jazz Age" to describe that era, which he defined as "a new generation grown up to find all Gods dead, all wars fought, all faiths in man shaken". Francis Scott Key Fitzgerald was both a flamboyant participant and a detached observer of the high life he wrote about, giving his work its unique perspective.

Francis Scott Key Fitzgerald's greatest contribution to American literature, even the whole world literature, is that he found intuitively, in his own experience, the manifestation of the intense agony of the nation and created a myth of American life. Francis Scott Key

Fitzgerald wrote the life of young people, especially those of the middle class of that time—their dream of success, their discontent, and their suffering in mind. Fitzgerald's greatness lies in the fact that he found in his personal experience the embodiment of the nation and created a myth out of American life—at first, a dream, then, a disenchantment and realization of the truth, finally a sense of failure and despair. The implications of this simmer beneath the alluring surfaces of his fiction, where hedonistic youth and the idle rich party relentlessly to escape the moral and spiritual emptiness of their lives. And these could be best illustrated in *The Great Gatsby*.

Francis Scott Key Fitzgerald's fiction unfolds the sterility of Americans who have a drastically mad admiration for wealth and American dream of a new world. He put his eyes on the double theme of love and money and had an unprecedented power in depicting the corrupting relationship between the two. He was convinced that crazy pursuit of wealth destroyed American morality and values and drove one astray to emptiness.

17. Discuss William Faulkner's style, theme and point of view.

William Faulkner used a remarkable range of techniques, themes and tones in his fiction. His stylistic innovations were often adapted from the experiments of other modern writers, which he then used in his own way. His books are sometimes difficult to read, and need close study by the reader. His works are distinguished by complex plots, sometimes extending over several novels in which the same characters appear. The hero of one story may appear as a minor character in another. He successfully advanced two modern literary techniques: stream of consciousness and multiple points of view.

Stream of consciousness, first used by James Joyce, the Irish novelist, in 1922, tells a story by recording the thoughts of one character. Action and plot are less important than the reactions and inner musings of the narrator. Time sequences are often dislocated. The reader feels himself to be a participant in the story, rather than an observer, and a high degree of emotion can be achieved by this technique. William Faulkner has the ability to recreate the thought patterns of the human mind. It was an essential development in the stream of consciousness narrative technique.

William Faulkner became a master at presenting multiple points of view, showing within the same story how the characters reacted differently to the same person or the same situation. The use of this technique gives the story a circular form—wherein one event is the center, with various points of view radiating from it—rather than a linear structure, with one event following another by cause and effect, in a logical progression of time. The multiple point of view technique makes the reader recognize the difficulty of arriving at a true judgment.

William Faulkner's frequent themes are history and race. He sought to explain the present time by examining the past, particularly by telling the story of several generations of one family as history altered their lives. He was deeply interested in the relationship between Blacks and Whites in the South, where both races exist side by side in almost equal numbers. He was especially concerned about the social problems of people who were of mixed race, unacceptable to either Blacks or Whites.

William Faulkner generally shows a grim picture of human society, where violence and cruelty are frequently included. His later books show more optimism, and his last book is a comedy. His intention was to show the evil, harsh events in contrast to such eternal virtues as love, honor, pity, compassion and self-sacrifice, and thereby expose the faults of society. He felt that it was a writer's duty to remind his readers constantly of true values and virtues.

18. What's Ernest Hemingway's contribution to American literature?

Ernest Hemingway's contribution to American literature is unequalled in more than one way. He was endowed with the spiritual monument of American nation and the founder of narrative/literary journalism. He was a great American writer, especially a successful war correspondent of the 20th century, who centered his novels on personal experiences and affections and earned an international fame.

And he is among the renowned writers called the Lost Generation. He could not deal with post-war America, and thus he introduced a new type of character in writing named "code hero" who struggled with the mixture of their tragic faults and the surrounding environment.

And in many novels he presents the stripped-down "Hemingway style", that is, iceberg theory, sometimes referred to as "theory of omission", as Ernest Hemingway said, "If a writer knows enough about what he is writing, he may omit things that he knows. The dignity of movement of an iceberg is due to only one ninth of it being above water. So I always try to write on the principle of the iceberg." This was in fact what Ernest Hemingway tried to achieve in writing. His economical style of writing is striking: sentence short, uncomplicated, but active; words simple but filled with emotion; few modifiers and great control of pause with action of the story continuing during the silence. There are times when the most powerful effect comes from restrain and understatement for he believed the strongest effect comes with an economy of means. In short, his essay is simple, apparently natural. It has the effect of directness, clarity and freshness, and is highly suggestive and connotative. In the later part of his life, Ernest Hemingway came to be called as "Papa Hemingway". This compliment mainly referred to his contribution to the development of a new writing style in American, that is, the colloquial style.

American people considered his success in literature as a landmark that promoted the development of American literature. It is no exaggeration to say that he was a real author of American literature.

Part VI

Twentieth-Century Literature II: After WWII

I. Fill in the Blanks.

1. Harlem
2. *Native Son*; *Beloved*
3. *House Made of Dawn*
4. Saul Bellow; J. D. Salinger
5. *On the Road*
6. Poet Laureate of Harlem
7. human beings
8. *North and South*
9. Impressionist
10. poet's poet
11. *The Fish*
12. *The Glass Menagerie*
13. *The Waste Land*; *Invisible Man*
14. Ralph Ellison
15. *Invisible Man*
16. Nobel
17. happy
18. *Death of a Salesman*
19. Robert Lowell; confessional poets
20. *The Catcher in the Rye*
21. Jack Kerouac
22. southern
23. Allen Ginsberg; free; breathing
24. spontaneous prose
25. *The American Dream*
26. Toni Morrison
27. Beat Generation
28. Thomas Pynchon
29. *Catch*
30. *Slaughterhouse*
31. Kesey
32. Pynchon
33. spontaneous
34. Confessional
35. gardism
36. *The American Dream*

II. Choose the Best Answer for Each Question.

1-5　D D B A C　　6-10　D A C D B　　11-15　A C B C A
16-20　C D B B D　　21-25　A C D D B　　26-30　C F D D C
31-33　D D A

III. Match-Making

Group One
1-10　b h e d c g f a j i
Group Two
1-10　c a b f e d i g j h
Group Three
1-5　b d a c e

IV. Define the Literary Terms.

1. The Black Mountain poets

The Black Mountain poets, sometimes called projectivist poets, were a group of mid-20th century American avant-garde or postmodern poets centered on Black Mountain College. In 1950, Charles Olson published his seminal essay, Projective Verse. In this, he called for the poetry of "open field" composition to replace traditional closed poetic forms with an improvised form that should reflect exactly the content of the poem. This form was to be based on the line, and each line was to be a unit of breath and of utterance. The content was to consist of "one perception immediately and directly (leading) to a further perception". This essay was to become a kind of de facto manifesto for the Black Mountain poets. One of the effects of narrowing the unit of structure in the poem down to what could fit within an utterance was that the Black Mountain poets developed a distinctive style of poetic diction (e.g. "yr" for "your"). In addition to Charles Olson, the poets most closely associated with Black Mountain include Larry Eigner, Robert Duncan, Ed Dorn, Paul Blackburn, Hilda Morley, John Wieners, Joel Oppenheimer, Denise Levertov, Jonathan Williams and Robert Creeley.

2. The Confessional School

Confessional poetry or "confessionalism" is a style of poetry that emerged in the United States during the 1950s. It has been described as poetry "of the personal", focusing on extreme moments of individual experience, the psyche, and personal trauma, including previously taboo matter such as mental illness, sexuality, and suicide, often set in relation to broader social themes. It is sometimes also classified as postmodernism. The school of confessional poetry was associated with several poets who redefined American poetry in 1950s and 1960s, including Robert Lowell, Sylvia Plath, John Berryman, Anne Sexton, Allen Ginsberg, and William De Witt Snodgrass.

3. Deep Image group

Deep Image group is a school of poetry founded by Robert Bly, James Wright, and William Edgar Stafford in the late 1950s and early 1960s. It calls for breaking the bondage of European (mainly British) traditional culture on the spirit of American poetry, emphasizing "new imagination", making poetry more open, pointing to the depths of the soul, and exploring the pure life world behind nature. They translated a large number of contemporary surrealist poets' works in Spanish, German, French, and Nordic, and introduced Chinese Lao-Zhuang philosophy and the artistic conception of classical pastoral poetry. Their fresh, natural, profound works have influenced the whole American poetry world. Today, "Deep Image" has become a very common creative consciousness of American poets.

4. Expressionism

   Expressionism refers to an avant-garde movement in Germany at the beginning of the 20th century. It is a reaction against Impressionism and its goals are not to reproduce the impression suggested by the surrounding world, but to project a highly personal or subjective vision of the world. In a further sense, the term is sometimes applied to the belief that literary works are especially expressions of their authors and moods. Literary works like Eugene O'Neill's *The Emperor Jones* and T.S. Eliot's *The Waste Land* are typical examples of Expressionism.

5. Impressionism

   The term "impressionism" is coined by French art critic Louis Leroy as a way to describe a late-nineteenth century art movement with a distinctive style. In literature, impressionism refers to writing, whether that be prose, verse, or drama, that depends on a character's impressions of a scene, event, or experience. In other words, this type of literature is centered on the character's mental life and the way they feel and sense things.

6. Existentialism

   The word "existentialism" comes from the Latin meaning "to stand out." It is a philosophy that emphasizes the uniqueness and isolation of the individual experience in an irrational or indifferent universe. And its famous motto is "existence precedes essence", which means that the individual should be concerned with their own individuality rather than with labels or roles they're supposed to play. Kurt Vonnegut's masterpiece *Slaughterhouse-Five* is an example of existentialism in literature.

7. Modernism

   Modernism is a general term applied to the wide range of experimental and avant-garde trends in the literature of the early 20th century, including symbolism, futurism, Expressionism, Imagism, Dadaism and surrealism. It is characterized by a rejection of 19th-century literary traditions: the conventions of realism and a self-conscious break with traditional ways of writing, in both poetry and prose fiction. The modernist writers pay more attention to the private and subjective than the public and objective. Writers like Elizabeth Bishop, Ernest Miller Hemingway and F. Scott Fitzgerald are all of the modernist type.

8. American dream

American dream refers to material success which one can gain by making efforts and good fortune regardless of the social status. The roots of the idea behind the American dream can be traced back to Colonial Period when settlers and pilgrims from England saw the States as a promised land of opportunities. And it was at its peak in the 1920s or the Jazz Age. Since America is a country formed through immigration, people need something that could unify them and American dream plays a significant role in constructing the nation.

9. Absurdism

"Absurdism" refers to a dramatic movement, strongly influenced by existentialism that emerged from Europe during the mid-twentieth century. It means the internal conflict between human tendency to find the inherent value and the meaning of life and his inability to find any. The term "Literature of the Absurd" is applied to a number of works and drama and prose fiction which have in common the sense that the human condition is essentially absurd, and that this condition can be adequately represented only in works of literature that are themselves absurd. Absurdist plays do not have conventional notions of character, plot, action, and setting but employ deliberately unrealistic methods. Plays of this type explore the absurdity of the human condition and expose the experiences of alienation, insanity, and despair inherent in modern society.

10. The Theater of the Absurd

The Theater of the Absurd refers to some plays the theme of which centers on the meaninglessness of life with its pain and suffering that seems funny, even ridiculous. Works like Samuel Becket's *Waiting for Godot* and *Endgame* belong to absurdist plays. Edward Franklin Albee wrote in this spirit. His plays seem to have dwelled on one problem only, that is, the absurdity of human life built very much on a frail illusion and spiritual emptiness. *Who's Afraid of Virginia Woolf?* is a good illustration.

11. Black Humor

Black humor, also called black comedy, is a literary device used in novels and plays to add grotesque elements with humorous ones in order to shock the readers. It is a humor out of despair and laughter out of tears referring as much to the tone of anger and bitterness as it does to morbid situation. It is often used to present any serious, gruesome or painful incidents lightly. As an important element in the anti-hero novels, it prevails in modern American literature. Kurt Vonnegut's *Slaughterhouse-Five* and Joseph Heller's *Catch-22* are classic examples of Black Humor.

V. Answer the Following Questions Briefly.

1. Give a brief account of the main images used in James Mercer Langston Hughes's poems.

    He was the leader of the "Harlem Renaissance" and was known as "Poet Laureate of Harlem". Hughes was the spokesman for black Americans. He used his sharp opinions to touch those extremely sensitive social topics and inspire black Americans to awaken. Hughes wrote countless well-known poems in the tone of an outsider. He focused his attention on his black compatriots, traced the history of blacks, wrote the good qualities of blacks, told their pain and anger, and expressed their enthusiasm and hope for life.

    Image 1: Black

    Whether in the east or the west, black is considered to have the meaning of sadness, melancholy, and desolation. However, the image of "black" can be seen everywhere in Hughes's poetry. In Hughes's mind, "black refers to beauty", and "black" expresses the poet's infinite enthusiasm for his own nation and culture. As a black American poet, Hughes has always been proud of his skin color. The poet called on black compatriots not to abandon themselves because of their black skin, but to treat their nation objectively and proudly, rediscover themselves and realize their own values.

Image 2: Dreams

In the world of ordinary people, dreams are mainly beautiful and majestic. It embodies people's joyous vision and hope for the future. However, in Hughes's poetry, "dream" has a completely different meaning. There are two main aspects of dreams in Hughes's poetry: one is the dream of African Americans; the other is the American dream. He used his dreams to arouse the awakening consciousness of blacks and inspire his compatriots to work hard for their dreams. "Dream" is the most common theme in Hughes's poetry. He wrote many poems about dream, such as *Dream*, *Dream Variations*, and other famous poems.

Image 3: Blues

As we all know, blues originated in the late 19th century. It is the music created by black Americans while working. It is their voice against their painful life. Blues has multiple characteristics, such as plaintive, narrative, and so on.

Hughes's introduction and utilization of black music in his poetry are mainly reflected in two aspects: one is the reference to the form of black music, and the other is the development of the internal characteristics of black music.

2. Make a brief comment on *My Papa's Waltz*.

Theodore Huebner Roethke was an outstanding representative of "the Middle Generation" in the United States. He was influenced by Romantic poets William Wordsworth and Walt Whitman, but he was mainly a naturalistic poet. He was good at mixing traditional skills and modern style, adopted the rigorous and realistic poetic style and comfortable rhythm. *My Papa's Waltz* is an excellent masterpiece of Roethke. It is a short lyric poem created by the author in his middle age showing the author's deep remembrance of his dead father.

This poem was selected from *The Lost Son* (1948), a collection of the autobiographical poems about his childhood days together with his father. After a whole day's labor and drinking of some whiskey, the father was dancing with his little son. Although the father's steps were clumsy and the son was too short, they all enjoyed the crazy waltz round the house in spite of the mother's frowning. The rough hand touched the boy with all the affection a father can afford; while the boy was so attached to that until he was too tired to go on. The poem presented a living scene of a happy family of the laboring class and deep affection between father and son.

3. Discuss Saul Bellow's achievement in literature.

Saul Bellow's early works earned him the reputation as a major novelist of the 20th century, and by his death he was widely regarded as one of the greatest living novelists. He was the first writer to win three National Book Awards in all award categories. His friend and protégé Philip Roth said of him, "The backbone of 20th-century American literature has been provided by two novelists—William Faulkner and Saul Bellow. Together they are Herman Melville, Nathaniel Hawthorne, and Mark Twain of the 20th century."

His novels explore some problems of the modern urban man in search of his identity, such as displacement, alienation and masochism. His major achievement lies in a double heritage of modernist concerns and Jewish humanist responsibility. Saul Bellow is famous for his flexibility and variety of style and idiom. Obeying the realistic tradition in literature, he is also influenced by the modern literature.

Therefore, he merges realism, romanticism and existentialism into his literary creation.

Saul Bellow is a controversial person. Martin Amis once described Saul Bellow as "the greatest American author ever". Some people like Martin Amis consider that Bellow breaks all the rules and he just likes the power of nature. People in Bellow's fiction are all real. However, Saul Bellow's detractors think that his writing style is old-fashioned and rigid. No one is perfect, we cannot deny that Saul Bellow is a brilliant writer, he has made his own contribution to the literature, and his works influenced people who love him.

4. Comment briefly on Saul Bellow's themes.

Saul Bellow's basic themes are essentially three-folded:

First, he views contemporary society as a threat to human life and human integrity. Modern civilization tends to dehumanize, making people lose their distinction and turning them into what he calls "fat goods". Material affluence distracts and produces a sense of alienation.

Second, living in such an environment, people tend to become paranoid, high-strung, and impotent, and so lose their sanity. Bellovian characters suffer most from a kind of psychosis. They go through a phase before they regain their mental balance and serenity.

Third, there is the motif of quest, a quest for truth and values, difficult, excruciating, but successful in a way. To Saul Bellow, the human search for affirmation should end happily, and people should see light at the end of the tunnel. His fictional world is full of people both tragic and comic, but happy in the end. He is a very human writer indeed.

5. How do you understand the novel of the absurd of the 1960s?

The notion that the universe is absurd, that neither God nor man, nor theology nor philosophy can make sense of the human situation, was not really new to American authors. The modern American novels as written by Ernest Hemingway and William Faulkner in the 1920s and 1930s and by Saul Bellow and Norman Maier near the end of the forties and throughout the fifties always treated the theme of "an absurd universe". The major difference between these authors and the "absurd" novelists of the sixties lies in the fact that, while the former represents the absurdity theme essentially in traditional novelistic devices, the latter tends to regard the conventional novel as "literature of exhaustion". To them, the old ways of presentation are no longer good enough, and even obsolete. To reflect the new, stupefying and sickening reality, these conventions must be updated, while at the same time new devices should be found. If, in the earlier decades, only the thinking minds felt the chaos and meaninglessness of modern existence, the 1960s and 1970s proved to be a period in which the common run of humanity had also come to sense absurdity existing on all conceivable levels of life, and it fell to the "absurd" novelists to discover a new rhetoric effective enough to voice that feeling in literature. Incidentally, these novelists appeared, responded to the call of the time, and took it upon themselves to present a vision of absurdity in what have been termed "absurdist" techniques.

The novelists of the absurd tend to burlesque traditional novelistic devices. They parody other novels, other styles and forms and take them with highly equivocal attitudes: they want to prove the artificiality of any literary art which, by pretending to bring order to reality, falsifies it and keeps people from comprehending its absurdity. They embrace the theory of Einsteinian relativity and quantum physics which hold that truth and reality are multiple, elusive, and uncertain; they regard any pretension of any traditional form to represent reality authentically as illegitimate and misleading. In doing these the novelists intend to upset all traditions and deliberately create in the readers, so as to jostle them into the recognition that the absurdity of their universe does not disappear simply because they have come to terms with it. The universe is out of joint. It is a tragic place to live in. But as the contemporary novelists tend to be more nihilistic, they cannot produce tragedy. Instead, they offer a kind of comedy which verges on being grotesque. The tragic absurdity of the human condition is often seen in their works as a cosmic joke. The response they intend to provoke in the readers to the blackness of modern life is laughter, that is, laughing in face of a tragic situation. Hence black humor, or black comedy, which is one of the commonly employed devices of the novelists of the absurd. These authors generally do not laugh at their characters; in fact, they take them seriously. But if they do laugh at some of them at times, it is because they feel amused at their attempt to try to create order in their disordered and absurd world. what occurs is a sense of grief and pain coming through the laughter, a feeling of frustration and being bottled up.

The attitude of the novelists of the absurd is not always an unmitigated "No." The modernist feeling of the world as a random, contingent and chaotic place is intensified in contemporary times. If the modernist novelists tried to control the meaninglessness and disorder through the agency of art, hoping to transcend it by shaping it and giving it an art form, the contemporary novelists of the absurd tend to accept the world as it is, and as they are skeptical of their self-integrity and their own ability to "give shape and significance to the immense panorama of futility and anarchy," they open themselves to that disorder and contingency which they believe no art can mediate. They regard these features of modern existence as normal and locate themselves within the messiness of their world. Rejecting the modernist nostalgia for an organic wholeness and feeling that life's quandaries are not resolvable, the contemporary authors attempt to generate meaning in the face of, but without denying, chaos and absurdity. For them uncertainty is the rule.

6. How is the effect of absurdity achieved in Joseph Heller's *Catch-22*?

Catch-22 was the first book in America to treat the absurdist theme with absurdist techniques. It protests against the absurdity of modern America as embodied by the military power structure it describes. The world of Yossarian, one of the protagonists, is an absurd one, and the way Joseph Heller exposes it is through the ruthless burlesque of the military unreason, as Charles Harris puts it, as best represented by its three major features: the structured chaos of the military build-up, the military logic, one symbol of which is a "rule" known as "Catch-22", and the widespread absurdity on all levels of existence.

First, the chaos in the military structure is well illustrated in the novel. Here is a place where the absurd is the norm: people still very much alive like Doc Daneeka are declared dead and people long dead such as Mudd are kept "alive" on the official roster; one officer, Major Major, welcomes visitors in his office only when he is out; and only those are allowed to attend "educational sessions" who never ask question. These are only a few from many of life's bizarre manifestations. What the author castigates is the absurdity of not only the military bureaucracy but the whole of the capitalist world in which a traitor like Milo, who profiteers in the war and plots the German bombing of the American squadron, is set free simply because he has made money.

Another object of ridicule is the military logic inherent in the monstrous establishment. The bureaucracy has more faith in paper work than in the stark reality of the war. Then there is this overriding "Catch-22", which does its work effectively in absurd situations. For instance, all bomber pilots are afraid of flying bombing mission. They have to fly unless they are crazy. Orr is crazy and can be grounded. All he has to do is to ask to be grounded, but as soon as he starts asking, he is no longer considered crazy and must fly more bombing mission. This is the simple logic of *Catch-22*.

Furthermore, Joseph Heller uses an absurd linguistic surface to reflect the depth of the absurdity of the modern world. Devices such as "circular conversations", to Harris's terms, constructions with their comic, unexpected responses, the "wrenched cliché" which results from the change of "a key word in an otherwise hackneyed expression", juxtaposed incongruities, sudden tonal changes from seriousness to triviality—all these are skillfully employed to convey the illogicality and the unpredictability of a mad world. The effect of the burlesque and its absurd verbal expression is irrepressible laughter on the part of the readers; everyone would have a good laugh if they care to read the book through. The laughter is, however, inevitably followed by the acute awareness that it is based on the suffering and misfortunes of their fellow creatures. This is what is meant by "black humor".

7. How do you understand the meaning of the letter "V" in Thomas Pynchon's novel *V*?

The uncertainty and multiple nature of reality are best illustrated by the letter "V". Its meaning is obscure and protean. It can be names such as Victoria, Vena, and Veronica. It can be places like Valletta of Malta or Venezuela. And it can be a good many other things, the "V" shape of spread thighs, say, or the Virgin Mother. There is an amount of truth in all these suggestions which fall, nonetheless, short of the whole truth. Its obscurity further increases with the ambiguous narrative of the novel. The readers are placed in a quandary where they are hard put to it to tell fact from fiction. Thomas Pynchon wants to show that it is impossible to gain access to the truth.

8. Give an analysis of *Who's Afraid of Virginia Woolf?* by Edward Franklin Albee.

In the history of drama, Edward Albee is often considered one of America's greatest modern playwrights, known for being on the vanguard of what would later be called the "Theater of the Absurd." *Who's afraid of Virginia Woolf?* is a dark comedy, which portrays husband and wife George and Martha in a searing night of dangerous fun and games.

Virginia Woolf was a brilliant writer and women's rights advocate. In addition, she sought to live her life without false illusions. So then, the question of the play's title becomes: "Who is afraid of facing reality?" And the answer is: most of us. Certainly, the tumultuous characters George and Martha are lost in their drunken, everyday illusions. By the play's end, each audience member is left to wonder, "Do I create false illusions of my own?"

The "Virginia Woolf" in the title is significant in a couple of ways. First, Martha is well read and has a kind of respect for language. Has she been younger, she would have identified herself with Virginia Woolf who had an incredible amount of verbal wit. Martha is afraid of Virginia Woolf who committed suicide in the end. She could have done the same, given the enormous amount of despair she feels all her life, if she had not lived on her frail illusion that she had a son. Second, "Virginia Woolf" is used as a homophone for "wolf", and the title is in fact a humorous way of repeating a line from a ballad, "Who's afraid of the big, bad wolf?" The wolf here is a metaphor for something terrible like poverty etc., and the wolf that has scared the four people in the play is the hopelessness that stretched before them. At the end of the play, however, they seem to have to come to terms with the absurd life that they are made to live, and face with courage that darkness which it offers them.

9. What are the writing features of Arthur Miller's plays?

Arthur Miller is one of the most renowned and important American playwrights. Throughout his life and work, Arthur Miller remained socially engaged and wrote with conscience, clarity, and compassion. His plays were not only for entertainment, but for exposing the flaws in the American government. In his plays, he showed what was happening to the American citizens. The theme of his plays mainly concerns the dilemma of modern man in relation to his family and work.

Miller thought of playwriting as a way to change America. In his plays, he also gave a reality check to the American dream that not everything is golden. His writings give a realistic quality to characters acknowledging they are people and not perfect. His plays spoke to the common person by making average characters in exaggerated settings and events. After World War II Arthur Miller wrote plays that gave an honest view of life and the direction the country was going. He wrote about human morality in a desperate working class. He was so great because he did not only write amazing plays, but also change the views of America.

10. Give an analysis of *Invisible Man* by Ralph Ellison.

Ralph Ellison was one of the most important black literature writers of the United States since the 1950s, who made a landmark contribution to American black literature and American literature and broke new ground for the future of African American literary and the development of its literary theory. *Invisible Man* is one of his masterpieces. This novel addresses the social issues as well as the intellectual issues that most African-Americans faced in the early twentieth century, including Black nationalism, politics, and the relationship between black identity and Marxism.

The novel *Invisible Man* begins with a stranger arriving at the town of Iping. He doesn't get along well with all villagers in the town. He is busy with his scientific research in his room privately. But when he is accused of robbery by villagers, he takes off his clothes and becomes invisible. After fighting with the villagers, the invisible man flees without carrying his research notes. In order to find them, he forces Marvel, a homeless guy, to help him. When they want to get those scientific things back, the villagers attack them. The invisible man beats them and wins the fight. And then they go to another town Port Stowe. The invisible man steals money and puts it into Marvel's pockets to frame him up. Failing to do so, the invisible man wants to kill Marvel, but a group of people come to help Marvel to fight the invisible man off. The invisible man runs to a house as a shelter and it turns out that the house's owner is an old college friend of the invisible man named Kemp. Here we know that the real name of the invisible man is Griffin. Then Griffin tells Kemp his previous stories: he wanted to learn invisibility to get rid of poverty, so he stole money from his father. After learning the key points of invisibility, he burned the house of his landlord, stole money from a department store, and went to work in Iping. However, Kemp tells the police where Griffin hides, but when the police come, Griffin runs away again. Then a group of people in Burdock catch him and kill him. Finally, Marvel gets Griffin's scientific notes, and gets the skill of invisibility.

In conclusion, Ellison uses the narrator's struggles throughout the novel to show how American society perpetuates racist political and social ideologies, which emphasize his theme of racism and the loss of self-identity.

11. Give an analysis of *Beloved* by Toni Morrison.

Toni Morrison is best known for her fifth novel, *Beloved*. The book is remarkable in its skillful fusion of its formal with its thematic concerns. The novel depicts a mother being haunted and destroyed by the ghost of her daughter who was killed by the mother 18 years earlier in order to stop a vicious slave master to take her daughter. The novel involves so many important themes and techniques, from love and guilt to history's role in clarifying the past influence on the present, all told in a style of magical realism that transforms (without denying) more mundane facts. In May 2006, *The New York Times Book Review* praised *Beloved* the best American novel published in the previous 25 years.

The major formal feature of *Beloved* is the use of magic realism.

Toni Morrison's ghost does not make the book a ghost story. There is an obvious magic and supernatural element in the narrative: first the baby ghost causing strange voices, lights, and violent shaking, and then the ghost assuming actual human form, but behaving in uncanny ways, becoming invisible, appearing mysteriously, moving Paul D. out of Sethe's house, and exhibiting her growing psychic powers. This element shocks and jostles readers as well as the characters out of their normal way of living and thinking. It fits well into the larger realistic scheme to serve the author's purpose. Talking about her book, Toni Morrison states the importance of "dwelling on" and "coming to terms with" the truth about the past in a land where the past is either erased, absent or romanticized. The "rememory" of the past is to Toni Morrison a very important subject to write about. Toni Morrison feels that her people have to come to some kind of terms with their past in order to find peace and happiness. Their past is a hurdle they have to jump over in order to cope well now and in the future. Sethe is guilt-ridden. Her physical scar is an emblem of her inner bleeding scar. The appearance of the ghost is in fact an externalization of the emotional wound in her life. The disruption of "normal" life Beloved causes forces her mother and also Paul D., to face the fact that they need healing and renewal. She makes it imperative for them to dive deep into the past when they suffered injustice and inhuman treatment and felt such despair that the only way to emancipation was death. The ghost offers Sethe a good opportunity to explain her act and subconsciously exonerate herself from the sense of "sin" and self-condemnation that cripple her life all along. Sethe is supposed to be free, but she is not. She has to address the "unspeakable", hidden deep down in her, which would weaken and humiliate her if she dare remember and speak about it. She has to face it in order to heal and live on a new basis. Beloved thus reopens Sethe's rebuilding self-identity. Sethe is not an isolated case. What Beloved does to her is in fact also what the African Americans need as a once enslaved race. The grandmother Baby Suggs talks about "the Misery", which indicates the harsh condition of the African slaves. It was worse than death. It was the reason why some salves like Sethe chose death rather than slavery: as there was nothing they could do about it, they inflicted death and pain on themselves. The sense of self-mortification afflicts and debilitates all survivors as a ghost of the past after their physical emancipation. In this sense, *Beloved* offers a medication and a cure for all African Americans.

12. Talk about Toni Morrison's writing features.

Toni Morrison was a novelist of great importance in her own right and was the central figure in putting fiction by and about African American women at the forefront of the late twentieth-century literary canon. The main content of her works is about the life of the black people in the United States. Her writing style is delicate, and characters, languages and plots in her works are live and vivid, which shows her rich imagination. Western critics generally agreed that Toni Morrison inherited the black literary tradition of Ralph Ellison and James Baldwin. She was not only familiar with black folklore, Greek mythology and Christian Bible, but also benefited from the influence of Western classical literature. In the writing skill, her economical style is compared with Ernest Hemingway's, and a mysterious and dark sense of plot is approximate to Southern writer William Faulkner, obviously influenced by Latin American magical realism. But Toni Morrison dared to explore and innovate, and abandoned the language that the white people used to describe the black.

In her work, Toni Morrison explores the experience and roles of black women in a society where racists and the male dominate. In the center of her complex and multilayered narratives is the unique cultural inheritance of African-Americans.

In terms of her writing features, symbolism and metaphor are widely used in her works. Her works are also filled with Gothic, post-modernism, narrative techniques, esthetic language, and artistic characteristics and so on.

13. How do you understand ethnic literature?

    Literature is the mirror of any country. Since the United States has different cultures, customs, languages, and traditions, the literature of America can present the diversity of its culture. It is believed that American history and culture should be defined by Americans of all national and ethnic backgrounds, which is the theoretical basic of ethnic or, more precisely, multiethnic literature.

    Generally speaking, American ethnic literature includes Native American literature, Mexican American or Chicano literature, African American literature and Asian American literature. The multiethnic writers mainly focus on questioning and challenging the ideology of "Manifest Destiny", decoding and recoding the norms of American culture, and exploring identity construction. The Nobel Prize in Literature winner, Toni Morrison was a major figure of American ethnic literature. The main content of her works is about the life of the black people in the United States. She played a crucial role in putting fiction by and about African American women at the forefront of the late twentieth-century literary canon.

14. How do you understand the Beat Generation?

    The Beat Generation is a group of American writers in the late 1950s and 1960s. Jack Kerouac and poet Allen Ginsberg, along with the writer William Burroughs, formed the nucleus of the group. Writers of the Beat Generation rejected literary formalism and the capitalistic and materialistic features of American life. They championed personal freedom and the expression of free-flowing thoughts and ideas, incorporating the use of drugs, new ideas about sex and sexuality, and the experimental nature of jazz music into their works. The representative works of the Beat Generation are Allen Ginsberg's *Howl* and Jack Kerouac's *On the Road*.

下编参考答案

Key to Exercises of Part Two

Exercise 1

1. *To My Dear and Loving Husband*; Anne Bradstreet
2. heroic; iambic
3. If there had ever been two persons, a husband and a wife, living in perfect harmony in this world, they must be you and me.
4. In the poem, Anne Bradstreet wrote on the everlasting theme of love and eulogized the true love between her husband and her. She strongly praised the sincerity of their love and felt grateful for all the love she had enjoyed from her husband. When they were alive, that love was so abundant and burning hot that "rivers cannot quench"; when they die, their death would just prove the love constant. The true love has overgrown the power of time and space.

Exercise 2

1. Anne Bradstreet
2. This short poem offers the reader an insight into the mentality of the early Puritan pioneering in a new world. When she, the poet, heard the grasshopper and the cricket sing, she thought of this as their praising their creator and searched her own soul accordingly. It is evident that she saw something metaphysical inhering in the physical, a mode of perception which was singularly Puritan.

Exercise 3

1. Edward Taylor
2. The poem indicates that the poet saw religious significance in a simple daily incident like a housewife spinning. The spinning wheel, the distaff, the flyers, the spool, the reel and the yarn have all ac-

quired a metaphorical significance in the symbolic, Puritan eyes of Edward Taylor.

Exercise 4

1. *The American Crisis*; Thomas Paine
2. American independence
3. government; religion
4. life; liberty; property
5. Paine first begins by differentiating government and society. He believes that society is good and constructive. As an institution, the government needs to protect the people from their own immoral behavior.

    Paine moves on to attack the notion of the hereditary succession of the monarchy, claiming that monarchy is corrupt and corrupting. He believes that this kind of government is inherently evil and uses Bible verses to prove it.

Exercise 5

1. *The Wild Honey Suckle*; Philip Freneau
2. natural surroundings
3. nature
4. nature imagery
5. It is "wild" in order to convey the fresh perception of the natural scenes on the new continent.

    The flowers, similar to the early Puritan settlers, used to believe they were the selects of God to be arranged on the abundant land, but now have to wake up from that fantasy and be more respectful to natural law.

Exercise 6

1. *Nature*; Ralph Waldo Emerson
2. transcendentalism
3. commodity; beauty; language; discipline
4. solitude
5. Emerson attempts to solve an abstract problem: humans do not fully accept nature's beauty. He writes in this essay that people are distracted by worldly concern, but fail to grasp the things that nature gives them. The essay consists of eight sections, and each section takes a different perspective on the relationship between humans and nature.

Exercise 7

1. *The Raven*; Edgar Allan Poe
2. *New York Evening Mirror*
3. hazy conceptions
4. melancholy
5. apathetic
6. The symbolic meanings are as follows:
   A. The Raven symbolizes disaster and misfortune.
   B. The bird may symbolize the soul of the radiant maiden, the "lost Lenore."
   C. The bird may be taken as a symbol of the sub-consciousness of the poet.
   D. The Raven is the symbol of modern reality.
7. Three intricate musical expressions and the instances are as follows.
   A. Alliteration. Example:
   Followed fast and followed faster

B. End rhyme. Example:

But the Raven still beguiling all my sad soul into smiling,

Straight I wheeled a cushioned seat in front of bird, and bust, and door;

Then upon the velvet sinking, I betook myself to linking

Fancy unto fancy, thinking what this ominous bird of yore—

C. Refrain. In the last sentence of every chapter, there must be "nevermore".

Exercise 8

1. adventure; Herman Melville
2. romanticism; American Renaissance
3. a world in miniature
4. revenge tragedy
5. They meet the whale three times, and after three bloody battles, the captain Ahab and his crew harpoon the whale, but it carries the Pequod along with it to its doom. All on board get drowned except Ishmael, who is rescued by another whaler and survives to tell the story.

Exercise 9

1. Song of Myself; *Leaves of Grass*
2. *Poem of Walt Whitman, an American*
3. the theory of universality; singularity and equality
4. First of all, the author cordially celebrates himself to unfold the theme of "a leaf of grass is no less than the journey-work of the stars". Later, he "extols the ideals of equality and democracy and celebrates the dignity, the self-reliant spirit and the joy of the com-

mon man."
5. According to the title "Song of Myself" of this poem, we can conclude that the theme of this poem is man/human being. Most of the poems in *Leaves of Grass* are about man and nature.

Exercise 10

1. *O Captain! My Captain!*; Walt Whitman
2. symbol; repetition
3. United States; the American Civil War; the Union's victory; Lincoln
4. It was finished at the end of the Civil War in 1865 when Abraham Lincoln who symbolized democracy and progress was assassinated. Lincoln's death plunged the war-weary nation into shock. He eulogized the beloved president who made monumental contributions to Americans and confided his own deep mourning for the murder of the president against the background of the victory of the Civil War.
5. A. Metaphor runs throughout the whole poem. In the poem, the poet uses the "ship" to represent the United States while its "fearful trip" implies the American Civil War which was ended with the Union's victory, that is, the "prize we sought". The "captain" is used to symbolize Lincoln.
B. Phonetic recurrence is the main feature of the poem such as "O Captain! my Captain!" in the first and second stanza and "heart" in the first stanza.
C. The stanzaic form looks like a ship, with the word "captain" at the head of each stanza. The stanzaic form was deliberately chosen and designed.

Exercise 11

1. *The Cop and the Anthem*; O. Henry
2. *The Cop and the Anthem* is one of the representative works of O. Henry, a famous American writer. The novel tells such a story: Soapy, a poor tramp wandering on the streets of New York, tried every means to be put in prison in the cold winter by doing all kinds of criminal acts, but failed. Finally, inspired by the hymn of the church, he wanted to turn over a new leaf but was thrown to prison by the police on an unwarranted charge. The story has a typical O. Henry-style ending. It tells a serious story through humorous and vivid diction. In the story, Soapy is representative of the lower class at that time. In such an absurd story, Soapy's experience also reflects the social condition at that time. Human nature is complex. O. Henry intends to arouse people's attention to the lower class and explore the plight of such a group at that time through such a story. It is also an expression of humanism in such a ruthless era.
3. There are four main rhetorical devices used by O. Henry in this novel:

   A. Simile

   The simile used in the novel expression is mainly marked by words such as "like" and "as", which makes the irrelevant concepts have the necessary relevance. For example, in the novel, O. Henry wrote: "As Caesar had his Brutus, and every bed of charity must have its toll of a bath, and every loaf of bread its compensation of a private and personal acquisition." This sentence shows Soapy's clear understanding of the municipal government and the relief efforts organized by it. Soapy believes that these charities will make him lose his freedom. Through the description of the social situation at that time, the author used the method of simile to show the ruthless society where Soapy lives and analyzes the pain and despair of people under this social background.

B. Metaphor

Metaphor means that both the tenor and the vehicle appear in a sentence. It shows the relationship between them both implicitly. It is not as straightforward as simile and requires readers to think independently. For instance, the first fallen leaf in winter for Jack Frost's cards for the Rangers in the park, and the asphalt highway for the vast ocean, which reflect the author's longing for beauty and freedom. "Strong and ready hands turned him about and conveyed him in silence and to the sidewalk and averted the ignoble fate of the menaced mallard." This sentence compares Soapy to a poor duck on the chopping block. He can't have his own ideas but can only be slaughtered by others. O. Henry enhances the connotation of the novel by using metaphorical rhetoric.

C. Metonymy

Metonymy is to replace the tenor with the vehicle. Neither the tenor nor the indicator of resemblance appears in the sentence, such a rhetorical device directly says A into B. Because the only element reader could find is the vehicle, it can produce more profound and implicit effects, and make the language more concise. "The island" used in the novel is the name of the island where the prison is located, which is still a prison in essence. In Soapy's mind, prison is not a place to obliterate freedom, but a place to help Soapy escape from reality. Such a symbol shows Soapy's yearning for a better life.

D. Personification

Personification is a figure of speech to compare abstract things to people and to endow them with abilities and emotions that only human beings possess. "And then to the waiter, he betrayed the fact that the minutest coin and himself were strangers." This sentence personifies the coin and makes the coin a stranger to Soapy. The author wants to express that Soapy has always been destitute and penniless, and even the most worthless coin is the thing that

Soapy doesn't deserve to own.

4. O. Henry's own experience provides a lot of materials for his creation. Complicated experience has become a great wealth of his life, enabling him to be familiar with the life of all levels of society. His novel is ingenious in conception, witty and humorous in language, and the ending is like a thunderbolt, which makes readers gasp with admiration at his superb skill of plot designing. With humorous stories, vivid images, and funny language, it truly reflects some essential aspects of American capitalist society and has immortal artistic value. He and his short stories are known as "the humorous encyclopedia of American life" and "the poet laureate of Manhattan". His novels mainly boast the following characteristics:

A. Unexpected layout and delicate foreshadowing

O. Henry's novels are different from American classical short stories that pay attention to character and psychological description. They mainly win by plot, and its "O. Henry-style ending" is famous all over the world. He often leads readers to predict the ending through the trend of development. When the reader believes that the outcome must be the same as he predicted, O. Henry will give an unexpected ending. Because the author is adept at drawing a foreshadow in advance, the ending will not be viewed as unreasonable, but in line with the logic of the development of things.

B. Making good use of rhetoric

At the beginning of the novel, metaphor, personification, and other techniques are used, and the language is humorous and witty. In addition, there are many other rhetorical devices in the book.

C. Accurate and vivid depiction

In *The Cop and the Anthem*, the author does not use the blunt word "police" but refers to it through the extension of the meaning, such as "blue uniform" and "brass button" thus making the language style interesting. O. Henry uses his unique, accurate, and vivid words and sentences to interpret the content of the story, depict the characters and reveal the meaning of the theme. The author's sympathy for the bitter experience of nobodies and the pungent satire of the police as a symbol of the law are also vividly reflected.

Exercise 12

1. *Sister Carrie*; Theodore Herman Albert Dreiser
2. *Sister Carrie* is a remarkable debut novel of Theodore Herman Albert Dreiser, a great American naturalist writer, and it is one of the most famous works in the history of American literature. It tells the process of how Carrie, a rural girl, escapes from the bottom of society and becomes a popular actress. The novel delicately shows Carrie's outlook on life and her mental journey. With the distinctive feature of authentic realism, this work truly reveals the tragic fact that people enthusiastically pursued the American dream in the early 20th century, and shows that there can be no real happiness in the money-centered American capitalist society.

   From the beginning, Dreiser lays out for the readers a dimensional panorama of American ripening capitalism. He evades the current "genteel tradition" in literature to record the cruel reality based on large quantities of material and detailed descriptions of people's clothes, speech, and physical environment.

   Uniquely, Dreiser strikes the American myth that success and fame are to be achieved by work and virtue, and he dramatizes chance as a means of compelling characters to pay or gain for actions of their own. He presents Carrie, a new woman figure, drifts with the tide without judgment of her own. She follows whatever comes along. She has no self-control, no freedom of will. But Dreiser neither condemns her nor praises her. This was the way she has to be.

Dreiser sometimes stands out as an omniscient God teaching that "the world is full of desirable situations but, unfortunately, we can occupy but one at a time. It doesn't do us any good to wring our hands over the far-off things." A vague, uncritical pursuit always lends itself to ridicule and too much of it might be a danger.

3. *Sister Carrie* is the first novel of famous American novelist Theodore Herman Albert Dreiser in the 20th century. It is also a remarkable naturalist one of his works. Carrie is the major character of this book.

   In my opinion, Carrie is an innocent, simple, hard-working, and romantic girl. Also, she is realistic, enterprising but vainglorious.

   First, because of her simplicity and naivety, she is easy to be moved by man's complaisance.

   Second, she is diligent and enterprising. Carrie's diligence is shown principally in her work.

   Third, she is romantic and practical. Her romance is reflected in her fantasy of life and emotion.

   Fourth, Carrie is a woman with strong vanity and desire for material, which helps to make her succeed in the future. Her heart is filled with the desire for wear and beauty.

   The objective evaluation of Carrie needs to involve both positive and negative aspects. It is commendable that she is simple and beautiful, full of passion for life, harboring beautiful fantasies about her youth, and striving to achieve her own goals. What is not worth advocating is her love for vanity and greed for material enjoyment. She lacks correct moral concepts, keen observation and analysis abilities, and the ability to distinguish right from wrong.

4. Theodore Herman Albert Dreiser, the author of *Sister Carrie*, was a pioneer of modern novels and an outstanding representative of American naturalism in the 20th century. The use of symbolic meaning is an important feature of this novel. Dreiser intends to use symbols to reveal more profound connotations.

   A. Money

In this novel, money plays an important role. For each character, money has its special significance. There is no doubt that the author symbolizes people's social status and identity with money. This could be shown up completely through Carrie's comprehension of money, meanwhile, the changing process of her attitude towards money can be vividly reflected. At the same time, money also determines a person's position in the family. Although there is extreme disharmony between Hurstwood's family members, he is still the head of the family. Finally, money also symbolizes the indifferent exchange relationship between the characters in the novel.

B. Clothing

In the novel, clothing is equally important for men and women. It symbolizes a person's social class, economic status, and upbringing. Because her husband has not bought new clothes for a long time, Carrie realizes his loneliness and failure, and then resolutely leaves him. After that, Carrie becomes a popular film star by chance. She has enough money to buy fashionable clothes, and she has become a member of the upper-class. At the end of the novel, Hurstwood is penniless and reduced to living in a dirty inn, and his fur coat becomes shabby due to the erosion by wind and rain, which symbolizes that he has been descended to the bottom of society. The novel seems to say that a person's status can be judged by people's clothes.

C. Newspapers

Newspapers symbolize outdated news, things that happened in the past, and newspaper readers also belong to the product of the past. They are people who no longer look forward to the future and long for a rise to the top of society. The newspaper appears as a symbolic meaning several times in the whole book. In Chapter 43, the newspaper performs its symbolic meaning for the last time. Carrie becomes a social celebrity and appears in the newspaper together with other eminent people, while Hurstwood can only gain some information about Carrie in the newspaper. This once again symbolizes the conflict between the courageous young people represented by Carrie and the old people represented by Hurstwood, who would rather be intertwined with the past than look forward to the future.

5. American writer Theodore Herman Albert Dreiser's novel *Sister Carrie* is about a country girl named Carrie who goes to Chicago to seek refuge with her sister. It depicts the tortuous life experience and legend of the heroine and reveals the fragility of love and family affection, as well as the complexity and ugliness of human nature in the money-mad society. It reminds people to be cautious and self-disciplined, to restrain their impulsive behavior, and avoid mistakes in major choices during their whole life.

    As intellectual women in the new era, we should:

    Firstly, insist on correct values. As the old saying goes, gentlemen love money in a right way. The accumulation of wealth must rely on personal efforts. Don't believe in some so-called shortcuts.

    Secondly, establish a correct view of love. In addition, we should resist temptation, resolutely reject improper relations between men and women, and make a clear distinction between right and wrong.

    Thirdly, strive to enrich our spiritual world, improve our cultural level, and remember that knowledge changes destiny. We should cultivate inner beauty, and not be affected by bad social atmospheres such as vanity-chasing and money worship.

6. The novel is about an innocent and beautiful rural girl Carrie's experiences of making a living in a big city, Chicago. What she suffers here is heavy labor, poverty, unemployment, and loneliness. The harsh reality breaks her dream. Forced by life, she lives with the salesman Drouet and then becomes the mistress of the hotel manager Hurstwood. After eloping with Hurstwood, she becomes a popular actress in New York by chance, ascends to the upper class, and realizes her dream. However, what does the so-called "upper-class

social life" bring to her? She still feels empty and cannot find the meaning of real life. In loneliness and desolation, she sits in the rocking chair and dreams of unreachable happiness.

7. In *Sister Carrie*, Theodore Herman Albert Dreiser vividly reproduces the American society at that time and describes the heroine Carrie's pursuit of the American dream with his fine and smooth emotions. The American dream is an American spirit, which represents Americans' inexhaustible pursuit of democracy and freedom, as well as their perseverance and courage to realize their ideals. Carrie's American dream seems to be achieved, but in fact, Dreiser sets off the disillusionment of her dream with her success. Carrie's every material gain means her spiritual decline. Carrie's American dream is illusory and superficial. It is synonymous with her ambition and desire. Dreiser reflects the impetuous and money-worship trend of American society at that time by describing the gain of such a dream. In Dreiser's view, it is almost impossible for the people at the bottom of the capitalist society to obtain wealth and social status through their own efforts. The ideal American dream can only be a fantasy cut apart from reality. The success of the superficial female image of *Sister Carrie* is actually a strong counterattack and ridicule to the American society and the American dream at that time. The collapse of Carrie's American dream cruelly indicates that the dream of the whole United States will eventually break.

Exercise 13

1. *Richard Cory*
2. Edwin Arlington Robinson
3. The "we" in the poem refers to the poor townspeople who live a hard life and admire the rich. But Richard Cory is the rich person who is admired by the poor, and appears to be calm and smart, but

with a heart of suicidal despairing.
4. Yes, it is an example of verbal irony. Verbal irony occurs when words that appear to be saying one thing are really saying something quite different.
5. Yes.

Exercise 14

1. *The Black Riders and Other Lines*; Stephen Crane
2. *Black Riders Came from the Sea*
3. A
4. This poem, despite the short size, is written with figurative speeches: the alliteration in "hoof and heel"; the repetition of "clang and clang", "clash and clash", which makes the work read rhythmical though it is done without rhyme schemes. Besides, since the "Black riders" came from a distance, the poet first leads us to hear them by the words as "clangs", "clash", "shouts"; then we can use our eyesight to enjoy the waves of hair; finally, appears the whole figure of the impending catastrophe—the Sin.
5. Black riders are the heroes of this poem. They first appear exactly as real heroes: "came from the sea" implies the distance and adventurous spirit; "clang and clang of spear and shield" and "clash and clash of hoof and heel" indicate they are armed warriors and thus rather violent; "wild shouts" means they come recklessly; "the wave of hair" suggest their handsome appearance; "In the rush upon the wind" tells us the speed of their approaching; they are every piece a hero but who are they? The poet offers the real hero in the last word of the last line—Sin. The reader may be quite shocked to find a "Sin" is so honored. However, with a sincere consideration, one has to boldly face the cruel reality of modern society that all the evils are malicious, destructive and impossible,

which are, unfortunately, the most vigorous, most pervasive but disastrous elements in nature; as a striking contrast to this, the individuals, who had always been self-reliant and self-important since Ralph Waldo Emerson's transcendentalist declaration, are now discovered to be rather frail and vulnerable. What's worse, evils are, as well as every other substance, parts of nature created by God! People were born to confront them and have to devote part of their precious life to resistance against them. This sounds cruel but it is the reality of the modern world. As a naturalist poet, Stephen Crane just reveals the true face of nature so as to warn the unrealistic optimists about the dangerous circumstances in this godless world.

Exercise 15

1. *The Open Boat*; Stephen Crane
2. This implies the idea that "all sense of certainty" in the lives of these men is gone.
3. *The Open Boat* is a realistic account of the thoughts and emotions of four men who escape in a small dinghy from the wrecked steamer *Commodore* off the Florida coast. The captain, the cook, an oiler, and a newspaper correspondent, unable to land because of the dangerous surf, see the beach tantalizingly near, but are forced to spend the night on the sea. They must rely on each other in the dangerous situation and try to survive. Next morning, they employ their last strength to swim ashore, and all but the oiler survives.
4. The nature and the people of the story form a vivid comparison. In the story nature is cruel and indifferent. It has no sense of morality, is indifferent or cold to see those survivors to escape. In the final of reaching beach, the oiler is swallowed by strong wave, which fully shows the cruelty and coldness of nature. In front of indifferent nature, the four characters experience the subtle brotherhood of men

because they know they cannot give up, they have the same goal to work. Their friendship contrasts the indifferent nature and shows the greatness of human nature.

Through this experience, everyone has reached a new understanding of nature, life, friendship and love. As the author says at the end of the story, "When night falls, the white waves paced to and fro in the moonlight, and the wind brought the sound of the great sea's voice to the men on shore, and they felt they could then be interpreters", they can be interpreters of everything.

Exercise 16

1. *Stopping by Woods on a Snowy Evening*; Robert Frost
2. Iambic, aaba bbcb ccdc dddd.
3. This image frequently appears in Robert Frost's poems, symbolizing the mystery of nature, death or catastrophe.
4. The repetition of the last two lines reinforces the speaker's determination to carry on his life journey and fulfil his "promises", that is, his social duty and responsibilities.
5. "Sleep" refers to the final rest—death.
6. It is one of the most quietly moving of Robert Frost's lyrics. On the surface, it seems to be simple, descriptive verses, records of close observation, graphic and homely pictures. It uses the simplest terms and commonest words. But it is deeply meditative, adding far-reaching meanings to the homely music. It uses its superb craftsmanship to come to a climax of responsibility: the promises to be kept, the obligation to be fulfilled. Few poems have said so much in so little.

Exercise 17

1. *The Road Not Taken*; Robert Frost
2. abaab
3. This is a symbolic poem. The "yellow wood" may symbolize sophisticated society, in which most people are likely to follow a profitable but easier way; each "road" symbolizes a possibility in life; the "traveler" is the embodiment of every individual in the human world; the road which is "grassy and wanted wear" refers to a solitary life style; while "way leads to way" implies the complicated circumstances of the human world. Through the description of "a road not taken", the poet presents to the reader his experience of taking a road. With simple words and profound connotation, Robert Frost teaches. However, in the form of a natural poem, he teaches delightfully.
4. This poem, as many of Frost's poems, begins with the observation of nature, as if the poet is a traveler sightseeing in nature. By the end, all the simple words condense into a serious, philosophical proposition: When anyone in life is confronted with making a choice, in order to possess something worthwhile, he has to give up something which seems as lovely and valuable as the chosen one. Then, whatever follows, he must accept the consequence of his choice for it is not possible for him to return to the beginning and have another chance to choose differently. Frost is asserting that nature is fair and honest to everyone. Thus all the varieties of human destiny result from each person's spontaneous capability of making choices.

Exercise 18

1. *Fire and Ice*; Robert Frost

2. abaabcbcb
3. This is a symbolic poem. The two images "fire" and "ice" are two central symbols of the poem. In this poem, Robert Frost, of course not scientifically but humanistically, first reveals his identical view with those "in fire", for he is inclined to believe, that fire, as the symbol of desire, is destructive. However, at the same time, Robert Frost is worried about the power of "ice", the symbol of hatred, which is believed to be as dangerous as "desire" in ruining the world.

Exercise 19

1. *Martin Eden*
2. Martin Eden
3. Jack London
4. Martin Eden represents the writers' frustration with publishers by speculating that when he mails off a manuscript, a "cunning arrangement of cogs" immediately puts it in a new envelope and returns it automatically with a rejection slip. The central theme of Martin Eden's developing artistic sensibilities places the novel in the tradition of the *Künstlerroman*, in which is narrated the formation and development of an artist.

    Martin Eden differs from Jack London in that Martin Eden rejects socialism, attacking it as "slave morality", and relies on a Nietzschean individualism. In a note to Upton Sinclair, Jack London wrote, "One of my motifs, in this book, was an attack on individualism (in the person of the hero). I must have bungled, for not a single reviewer has discovered it."

Exercise 20

1. Chicago
2. *Chicago*
3. Carl Sandburg
4. It is used to describe the aggressive feature of this industrial city.
5. This is the best-known of Carl Sandburg's early poems. It vividly describes the common labor and people in Chicago. Its language is common and simple, but its craftsmanship is impressive. The poet uses personification, parallel constructions and other devices to glorify the optimistic and aggressive spirit of Chicago. The images of the working people, the present participles, and the frequent use of verbs best exemplify the mobility and vitality of Chicago.

Exercise 21

1. *Fog*; Carl Sandburg
2. *Chicago Poems*; free verse
3. This poem depicts a vivid fog scene in Chicago, an important city and harbor in America in the early 20th century. Short and simple, it is a typical poem of Imagism, with "cat" as the central image. The poet compares the immaterial, lifeless fog to a material, living cat. Through the description of the cat's movement, from the static to the dynamic, from the near to the distant, it may also reflect the alienated relationship between the country and the city, nature and man or the modern industrial civilization.

Exercise 22

1. *Anecdote of the Jar*

2. Wallace Stevens
3. This poem is a symbolic poem with the jar as the central image, which symbolizes art. It discusses the relationship between art and nature. The jar stands in contrast to the wilderness, which represents nature.
4. Tennessee is a state in the middle south of America. The eastern part of the state is covered by wilderness, and the area of forests in this state is nearly equal to half of the whole area. Here it symbolizes nature.

Exercise 23

1. Imagist; *The Red Wheelbarrow*
2. William Carlos Williams
3. On the first glance this poem is like an ordinary prose sentence broken up in a peculiar way. Actually, it is a pattern poem. The line arrangement of long and short pattern in each stanza imitates the zigzag course in which a red wheelbarrow went in the yard.
4. This is a famous representative of Imagist poetry. The poet conveys to the reader a common sight of the farmyard: Each stanza is shaped like a wheelbarrow. A heavy loaded red wheelbarrow is glazing in rain beside some white chickens. However, in the glazing transparent rain, the colors stand out because of their contrast with each other: the white chickens contrast with the red wheelbarrow; the static contrast with the dynamic; living thing contrasts with object without life; natural object contrasts with man-made object.

By contrasting the colors, the poet actually merges some images into the descriptions of the concrete objects. The wheelbarrow, as a farm tool, stands for human labor; rain and chickens are obviously symbols of natural existence. In the first 4 lines, the wheelbarrow, in the thick color of red and with "so much depends on" it, looks dignified and solemn; while in the next two lines, when the heavy loaded barrow is glazing with rain water, the solemnity is weakened into a bright scene. Finally, when the wheelbarrow appears beside white chickens, the serious mood of the poem is completely lightened into a fresh and vivid picture of words.

One can see the close relation between the poetry of Imagism and painting in this poem. The juxtaposition of different objects of different colors is quite fresh, full of visual beauty. Yet, when a picture is composed of words, it is presented as if seeing a film, one frame after another, with few differences to each but changes distinguish themselves gradually from solemnity to liveliness. William Carlos Williams, as one of the representative Imagist poets, through very fresh image, conveys to the reader Imagist ideas in "things". This poem is the representative expression of William Carlos Williams's poetic theory about "No ideas but in things!"

Exercise 24

1. Ezra Pound
2. *In a Station of the Metro*
3. The writer uses the image of "petals" on another image, that is, "wet, black bough".
4. In *In a Station of the Metro*, Ezra Pound attempts to produce the emotion he felt when he walked down into a Paris subway station and suddenly saw a number of faces in the dim light. To capture the emotion, Ezra Pound uses the image of petals on a wet, black bough. The image is not decoration: It is central to the meaning of the poem. In fact, it is the meaning of the poem.

Exercise 25

1. *Oread*
2. Hilda Doolittle
3. Oread: the goddess of forests in Greek mythology
   whirl up: move upward quickly by turning round and round
   pointed pines: In the poet's eyes, the high waves of the sea are like mountains and the sharp tops of the waves.
4. This poem is a representative work of Imagist poetry just like Ezra Pound's *In a Station of the Metro*. When looking at the whirling sea, the poet brings in the image of a roaring forest. Yet, the forest is acting as water—it whirls up, splashes, hurls, and covers with pools of fir. Actually, the poet is presenting neither the sea nor the forest in a conventional way; instead, the sea and the forest combine into an image of the momentary eruption of human emotion. "We", the embodiment of land, appeals to experience every aspect of the sea: the shape, the color, and the motions, until all is immersed in water.

    Some critics believe this poem is metaphorically written with the Freudian theories about subconscious sexual ideas, with all the waves and motions of sea symbolizing the masculine vigor, and as well, the land and "covering of us" symbolizing the sexual impression of a woman.

Exercise 26

1. *The Hairy Ape*
2. Eugene O'Neill
3. YANK is the play's antagonist. YANK works as a fireman on a transatlantic ocean liner. The play follows his quest to find a sense of belonging in modern, industrial society. YANK, whose real name

is Bob Smith, was born in New York City and was brought up in a lower class family. YANK is a burly, sometimes menacing figure who has difficulty with thought. He is known to take the physical position of Rodin's *The Thinker* when processing information or dealing with a problem.

YANK does not reveal many details of his family history, but, from what he does say, it is clear that it was painful. His mother died of the "tremens" and his father, a shore-worker, was abusive. YANK tells Long that on Saturday nights his parent's fighting was so intense that his parents would break the furniture. Ironically, his parents made him attend church every Sunday morning. After his mother died, YANK ran away from home, tired of lickings and punishment.

In the beginning of *The Hairy Ape*, YANK seems fairly content, if not proud, to be a fireman. He defends the ship as his home and insists that the work he does is vital—it is the force that makes the ship go twenty-five knots an hour. Mildred Douglas's reaction to YANK is the catalyst which makes YANK come to class awareness. His attempt to get revenge on Mildred Douglas widens to revenge on the steel industry and finally the entire Bourgeois. Throughout this struggle YANK defines "belonging" as power. When he thinks he "belongs" to something he gains strength, when YANK is rejected by a group, he is terribly weak. However, YANK is rejected by all facets of society: his fellow firemen, Mildred, the street goers of 5th Ave., The I.W.W., and finally the ape in the zoo. YANK symbolizes the struggle of modern man within the industrial society—he cannot break class or ideological barriers, nor create new ones. YANK is the outsider and eventually just the freak at the zoo for people to cage and point at.

Exercise 27

1. *The Love Song of J. Alfred Prufrock*
2. Thomas Stearns Eliot
3. A patient etherized upon a table.
4. Prufrock is a tragic figure. The plight of this hesitant, indecisive man, an aging dreamer trapped in decayed, shabby-genteel surroundings, aware of beauty and faced with sordidness, mirrors the plight of the sensitive in the presence of the dull.
5. Yes, it is a dramatic monologue. Prufrock is a character created by Thomas Stearns Eliot, and he speaks directly to us. He tells us his thoughts in leaps and bounds, jumping from one image to another, just as a human mind does.

Exercise 28

1. *The Waste Land*
2. Thomas Stearns Eliot
3. The theme of the poem is modern spiritual barrenness, the despair and depression that followed the First World War, the sterility and turbulence of the modern world, and the decline and breakdown of Western culture.

Exercise 29

1. *95 Poems*; l(a)
2. Edward Estlin Cummings
3. It is a pattern poem in which the form of the poem expresses its content. The poem consists of the word "loneliness" outside and "a leaf falls" inside the parentheses. It is typographically arranged as

the movement of a leaf falling down, which arouses the feeling of loneliness. That is the right emotion that the poet wants to convey.

Exercise 30

1. *in Just*—; Edward Estlin Cummings
2. eddieandbill: two boys' names, Eddie and Bill
   marbles and / piracies: two children's games often played by boys
   bettyandisbel: two girls' names, Betty and Isbel
   hop-scotch and jump-rope: two children's games often played by girls
3. The character of the "goat-footed" balloonman with his whistle strongly suggests the god of shepherds, Pan, who is half-man, half-animal in Greek myth and carries the sense of spring to the world with a pipe. The image of this little lame balloonman alludes to Pan, which reinforces the pastoral bliss.
4. This poem displays the innocent happiness of the children in spring. Edward Estlin Cummings makes good use of the line arrangement and typographical to express its meaning. The space left on the page and the invented compounds in the poem create a vivid scene of children playing and laughing in spring.
5. In the poem, "whistles far and wee" is repeated three times. When it appears for the first time in the fifth line, there are pauses between words which remind us of a peddler's whistles sound now and then and from a long distance. When "whistles far and wee" appears for the second time, the pauses come out regularly between "far" and "wee" just to imply that the balloonman is now surrounded by children and can be heard clearly. By the end, each word takes the space of a whole line just to show the gradual disappearance of the peddler and his whistle. As an eye-poem, the shape of the poem, as well as its words, contributes greatly to the

presenting of a particular childhood world of playfulness and innocence.

Exercise 31

1. *The Great Gatsby*
2. Francis Scott Key Fitzgerald
3. The author criticized them as selfish, hypocritical persons.
4. Francis Scott Key Fitzgerald's greatness lies in the fact that he found intuitively in his personal experience the embodiment of that of the nation and created a myth out of American life. The story of *The Great Gatsby* is a good illustration. Gatsby is a poor youth from the Midwest. He falls in love with Daisy, a wealthy girl, but is too poor to marry her. The girl is then married to a rich young man, Tom Buchanan. Determined to win his lost love back, Gatsby engages himself in bootlegging and other "shady" activities, thus earning enough money to buy a magnificent imitation French villa. There he spreads dazzling parties every weekend in the hope of alluring the Buchanans to come. They finally come and Gatsby meets Daisy again, only to find that the woman before him is not quite the ideal love of his dreams. A sense of loss and disillusionment comes over him. Then Daisy kills a woman in an accident, and plots with Tom to shift the blame on Gatsby. So Gatsby is shot and the Buchanans escape.

   Now Gatsby's life follows a clear pattern: There is, at first, a dream, then disenchantment, and finally a sense of failure and despair. In this, Gatsby's personal experience approximates the whole of the American experience up to the first few decades of this century. America had been "a fresh, green breast of the new world," had "pandered to the last and greatest of all human dreams" and promised something like "the orgiastic future" for humanity. Now the virgin forests have vanished and made way for a modern civilization, the only fitting symbol of which is the "valley of ashes," the living hell. Here modern men live in sterility and meaninglessness and futility as best illustrated by Gatsby's essentially pointless parties. The crowds hardly know their host; many come and go without invitation. The music, the laughter, and the faces, all blurred as one confused mass, signify the purposelessness and loneliness of the party-goers beneath their masks of relaxation and joviality. The shallowness of Daisy whose voice is "full of money", the restless wickedness of Tom, the representative of the egocentric, careless rich, and Gatsby who is, on the one hand, charmingly innocent enough to believe that the past can be recovered and resurrected, but is on the other hand, both corrupt and corrupting, tragically convinced of the power of money, however it was made—the behavior of these and other people like the Wilsons all clearly denote the vanishing of the great expectations which the first settlement of the American continent had inspired. The hope is gone; despair and doom have set in. Thus Gatsby's personal life has assumed a magnitude as a "cultural-historical allegory" for the nation. Here, then, lies the greatest intellectual achievement that Francis Scott Key Fitzgerald ever achieved.

Exercise 32

1. *A Rose for Emily*
2. William Faulkner
3. The narration follows a sequence of events not chronologically arranged and includes story details that contribute to our impression that Emily Grierson is an anachronistic woman who physically exists in the narrative present but psychologically lives in the past, in the Old South. The style compels us to piece together various frag-

ments of her life so that we can find out why she is the way she is. Also, the narrator who speaks on behalf of "we" (the townspeople) makes us (readers) sense a tension between Emily and the community, and this, too, is one of several clues for our effort to solve the mysteries.

4. *A Rose for Emily* (1931) seems to be a detective story, at least initially. But soon readers realize that the purpose of reading the story is not to find out who has committed a crime but to do a different kind of detective work. Half way through reading the story, readers become aware that Emily has killed Homer, and has been sleeping with the dead body for 40 years (a crime called necrophilia). Through the reading of the story, there are a few possible explanations a well-informed reader can come up with. But it is clear that *A Rose for Emily* is not just about a woman who has committed the monstrous crime of murder and necrophilia; the story is, more importantly, one that allows us to explore the problematic legacies of the Old South.

Exercise 33

1. *The Sound and the Fury*; *Macbeth*
2. William Faulkner
3. The "Yoknapatawpha saga" is a long, loosely constructed series of 14 novels and novellas. The Yoknapatawpha County is a fictional name for Lafayette County in northern Mississippi. Its capital, Jefferson, is also a fictional name for Oxford where the author lived. William Faulkner's Yoknapatawpha novels mainly have something to do with the three Sagas in Yoknapatawpha County: the Sartoris family, the Compson family and the Snopes family, about the contradiction and conflict between the decayed aristocratic traditions and the new upstart, including *The Sound and the Fury*, *As I lay Dy-*

ing, *Light in August*, and *Absalom, Absalom!* as well as other short stories. It's the representatives of the Old South, in the imaginary kingdom—Yoknapatawpha country.

4. *The Sound and the Fury* is set in the fictional Yoknapatawpha County. The novel centers on the Compson family, former Southern aristocrats who are struggling to deal with the dissolution of their family and its reputation.

Benjamin "Benjy" Compson is a 33-year-old man with severe mental handicaps. Benjy, the youngest of the Compson children and narrator of the novel's first chapter, has no concept of time. He portrays all events in the present—April Seventh, 1928—regardless of when they actually occurred in his life. The events that actually take place on April Seventh are rather insignificant. Far more important are the memories evoked by Benjy's experiences on that day.

A moaning, speechless idiot, Benjy is utterly dependent upon Caddy, his only real source of affection. Benjy cannot understand any abstract concepts such as time, cause and effect, or right and wrong—he merely absorbs visual and auditory cues from the world around him. Despite his utter inability to understand or interpret the world, however, Benjy does have an acute sensitivity to order and chaos, and he can immediately sense the presence of anything bad, wrong, or out of place. He is able to sense Quentin's suicide thousands of miles away at Harvard, and senses Caddy's promiscuity and loss of virginity. In light of this ability, Benjy is one of the only characters who truly take notice of the Compson family's progressing decline. However, his disability renders Benjy unable to formulate any response other than moaning and crying. Benjy's impotence—and the impotence of all the remaining Compson men—is symbolized and embodied by his castration during his teenage years.

Exercise 34

1. *A Farewell to Arms*; Ernest Hemingway
2. George Peele
3. *A Farewell to Arms* has double meanings. One is the farewell to war. The other is the farewell to love.
4. Ernest Hemingway manages to choose words concrete, specific, more commonly found, more casual and conversational. He employs these kinds of words often in the syntax of short, simple sentences, which are orderly and patterned and sometimes ungrammatical.
5. As a writer of the Lost Generation, in addition to writing the loss of one's life, Ernest Hemingway also wrote a story *A Farewell to Arms* in 1929 about the loss of love in the war. It depicts a romance between an American army officer, Frederic Henry, and a beautiful British nurse, Catherine Barkley. Henry takes part in the war and finds it like a cruel slaughter house. He fights single-handedly against overwhelming odds, a man of action and of few words like an outsider. Lastly, he still loses his lover and faces the life solitarily. This book caught the mood of the post-war generation and brought international fame to Ernest Hemingway.

Exercise 35

1. *The Sun Also Rises*; Ernest Hemingway
2. The first quotation comes from Gertrude Stein. She was an avant-garde American poet at the center of a group of painters and expatriate writers living in Paris after World War I. Among those in her circle were the artist Pablo Picasso and the writers Sherwood Anderson and Ernest Hemingway. Stein named the generation that came of age during World War I the Lost Generation. The world

quickly adopted the phrase as the most accurate description of the generation that passed through the threshold of adulthood at this time—working, fighting, or dying in the war. This quotation also utters the theme of the novel.

By quoting a biblical passage from Ecclesiastes, it contrasts the transient nature of human generations with the eternal survival of nature: the world endures, and the sun continues to rise and set despite the inevitable passage of each human generation into death.

Ernest Hemingway's juxtaposition of the two epigraphs produces an ambivalent tone. On the one hand, there is hope, because there will be a new generation after the aimless generation that populates *The Sun Also Rises*. On the other hand, there is bitter irony, since every generation is lost, in the sense that each generation will eventually die.

3. The book, *The Sun Also Rises*, was successfully published in 1926 and took a very significant position in American literary history, especially at the beginning of the 20th century. The novel is narrated by Jake Barnes and establishes Ernest Hemingway as a representative of writers who dealt with the Lost Generation. It describes men and women caught in the war, cut off from the old value and yet unable to come to terms with the new era when civilization had gone mad. The characters in the story enjoyed things like fishing, swimming, bullfight and beauties of nature for escaping from reality. The physical impotence of the protagonist is a token of modern man's spiritual impotence. And the novel became the landmark of the revival of American novels with *The Great Gatsby* together when they were published in 1920s.

4. The theme of *The Sun Also Rises* is highly concentrated in the two quotations in the front page of the book. One is that the story paints the image of a whole generation, the Lost Generation quoting Gertrude Stein ("You are all a lost generation"). The other is tak-

en from the Ecclesiastes which was believed written by Solomon, "one generation passed away, another came to the world; the earth exists, the sun also rises." That shows that, the title of the novel, rather than pointing the character's courage to life, connotes the weakness or the feeling of the Lost Generation before the natural law. Every person is just a guest or a passing traveler of the world, but nature is continuing forever. Of course, here men and women, caught in the war, are seen wandering pointlessly and, restless and impotent, enjoying things like fishing, swimming, bullfight, and beauties of nature but aware all the while that the world is crazy and meaningless and futile. There is nothing one can do but to take care of one's own life and be tough against fate and tough with grace under pressure. This impotence not only is an impotence of modern man's spirit, but also impotence of the author himself for world after the war.

Exercise 36

1. *The Grapes of Wrath*
2. John Steinbeck
3. The title of the book is taken from *The Battle Hymn of the Republic*, a war song during the Civil War. In which there are the lines, "Mine eyes have seen the glory of the coming of the Lord, / He is tramping out the vintage where the grapes of wrath are stored." The implication is that as injustice is building up and up, something is going to explode into violence.
4. The novel covers at least the following themes:
   A. Man's inhumanity to man

   John Steinbeck consistently and woefully points to the fact that the migrants' great suffering is caused not by bad weather or mere misfortune but by their fellow human beings.

B. The saving power of family and fellowship

The Grapes of Wrath chronicles the story of two "families": the Joads and the collective body of migrant workers. In the face of adversity, the livelihood of the migrants depends upon their union. As Tom eventually realizes, "his" people are all people.

C. The dignity of wrath

The Joads stand as exemplary figures in their refusal to be broken by the circumstances that conspire against them. At every turn, John Steinbeck seems intent on showing their dignity and honor; he emphasizes the importance of maintaining self-respect in order to survive spiritually.

D. The multiplying effects of selfishness and altruism

According to John Steinbeck, many of the evils that plague the Joad family and the migrants stem from selfishness. In contrast to and in conflict with this policy of selfishness stands the migrants' behavior toward one another. Aware that their livelihood and survival depend upon their devotion to the collective good, the migrants unite—sharing their dreams as well as their burdens—in order to survive.

Exercise 37

1. *The Negro Speaks of Rivers*
2. James Mercer Langston Hughes; Harlem Renaissance
3. This is James Mercer Langston Hughes's first major poem. It was published in *The Crisis* in 1921. Langston Hughes wrote this poem on a train to Mexico in 1920 at the age of 17. When the train crossed the Mississippi River, inspired by the scene, Langston Hughes finished this poem on an envelope. It was dedicated to W. E. B. Du Bois (1868-1963), a black American writer and civil rights leader.

In the poem several rivers were mentioned. The Euphrates is a river of southwest Asia flowing about 2,735 km from central Turkey through Syria and into Iraq, a major source of the ancient civilization in Mesopotamia; The Congo is a big river of equatorial Africa, about 4,380 km long, flowing generally north and west through Congo to the Atlantic Ocean, considered as the origin of the Black culture; The Nile is the longest river in the world, flowing about 6,677 km through eastern Africa from its most remote sources in Burundi to a delta on the Mediterranean Sea in northeast Egypt, the home of the ancient Egyptian civilization; while the Mississippi is the longest river in the North American Continent, flowing from its northern source in Minnesota to the Gulf of Mexico, the symbol of the American civilization.

From the Euphrates in Asia, the Congo and the Nile in Africa to the Mississippi in America, Langston Hughes retrospects the history of African Americans with the clue of rivers. "I" represents all Black Americans. Written in free verse, it follows a loose cadence to imitate the natural rhythm of the river flow. The poem arouses pride in the African heritage of the Black people in America.

Exercise 38

1. *The Fish*
2. Elizabeth Bishop
3. It is written in free verse in a long single stanza of seventy-six lines.
4. Rainbow alludes to Genesis 9.8-17, in which rainbow is a sign of the covenant that God established with Noah—there shall never be a flood to destroy the earth and all flesh.
5. This poem is one of Elizabeth Bishop's most famous poems. It is written in objective mood as her other works will do. Elizabeth Bishop's poetry never fails to provide the cold reality as it is. It gives a true-to-life description of a caught fish, big, old and ugly,

covered with scratches. The turn happens in the end of the poem when the oil spillage of the boat makes a rainbow and the speaker, overwhelmed by the dignity of the fish, releases it. It is simple in structure, but profound in moral implications. Maybe it implies the tension and relationship between human beings and nature.

Exercise 39

1. *A Streetcar Named Desire*
2. Tennessee Williams
3. Elysian Fields is the street on which Stella and Stanley live. In Greek mythology, bad people are punished while the good and heroic are rewarded. And the Elysian Fields is the underworld place where all the heroes and the good went when they died. It is supposed to be a great place.
4. Williams is overly fond of using Freudian sexual symbols. He uses raw meat, the bowling balls and pins, and the columns of the Belle Reve plantation home as obvious phallic and sexual symbols.

   Names in the play also have symbolic meanings. Blanche DuBois means white of the woods in which white symbolizes innocence and the woods are used as another Freudian phallic symbol. Stella's name means star. The name of the plantation home is Belle Reve which means a beautiful dream. Therefore, the loss of Belle Reve implies the loss of a beautiful dream of Blanche.

   When Blanche says that she took a "streetcar named Desire, and then... one called Cemeteries," the author implies that desire leads to death which is then an escape to the Elysian Fields. But ironically, in the play, the streetcar leads her to the French Quarter which is no Elysian Fields.

Exercise 40

1. *Death of a Salesman*
2. Arthur Miller
3. Willy Loman is the tragic hero of the play *Death of a Salesman*. His dual-sided nature of a sweet husband, a driven salesman, and a protective father versus an unfaithful partner, failing salesman, and resentful father makes him a rather complex character.

    For some critics, the play presents a hero who makes some rather obvious errors. Willy makes ordinary mistakes, but he fights against his fate in an unusual way. He is sometimes full of contradictions, ambitious, and unsympathetic towards those who love him. But at other times, he is courageous, and almost a martyr to his family.

    The contradictions in Willy's character are perhaps normal in the middle of 20th century, and the inconsistency of character has almost become a milestone of literature because people are pulled in different directions by social forces.

4. *Death of a Salesman* is a play written by Arthur Miller in 1948. It was the recipient of the 1949 Pulitzer Prize for Drama and Tony Award for Best Play and it is widely considered to be one of the greatest plays of the 20th century. It created Arthur Miller's reputation and set the standard for American drama in general. Some critics even called this play the American "King Lear".

    This play tells a story of a man who comes to the conclusion that he can only save his life by losing it: Willy Loman at last has to commit suicide to redeem himself in his own eyes and achieve something for his family. The play suggests that tragedy may happen to the most ordinary people in contemporary society and it concerns with the way ordinary people live and work and their dream of happiness.

    Arthur Miller acknowledges that he wants to offer something between two dimensions—it is a study of how man and society interrelate. As Arthur Miller put it, "the assumption was that everyone knew Willy Loman".

Exercise 41

1. *Herzog*
2. Saul Bellow
3. Owing to his own experience, Saul Bellow has sensitive insight to marginal man's inner. For many years, as a Jew, a Canadian who came to the United States, and a Midwesterner dominated by the eastern part of the country, Saul Bellow regarded himself as an outsider. Thus, Saul Bellow's protagonists are often uncommon thinkers, alienated from predominant world, fighting for the certain identity, afflicted by their awareness of morality. For their marginal social position, they often are difficult or lack of equality in communications and finally get some relief from the despair by personal monologues. However, Saul Bellow thought that "no noble assumptions, man should have at least sufficient power to overcome humiliation and to complete his own life." So there are usually happy endings in his novels.
4. *Herzog* is Saul Bellow's important work, which was accomplished in 1964, revealing intensely the life and experiences of a middle-aged Jewish intellectual, showing his involvements with two wives and other women, with his children, with a friend who betrays him, and with his occupations of teaching and writing.

   Herzog depicts an intelligent and gifted man, Herzog, who finds himself in the mess of his middle years. Obviously, he is a loser, a sad impotent man and a schlemiel. His two ex-wives and his children became estranged from him, which made him feel sad. Although Herzog fully experienced the bitter failure and humiliation in the worst indignities of collapsed moral, he still seems to ask for a possible recovery. Eccentric as he seems to be, he represents a sort of 20th-century Everyman and his mind becomes the focus for some of the major conflicts of modern thought. The meaning of the book remains embedded for the most part in Herzog's memories and especially in his letters to the world, which have only a fragmentary connection to one another. The tone of the book is comic and the structure is featured by the protagonist's consciousness of life.

In *Herzog*, Saul Bellow grasps the individual intellectual, moral and emotional dilemma—of the crisis of belief that lies beneath the complex surface of Herzog's behavior. As such, the novel displays the image of a contemporary humanist, whose relations with the modern world are as unfortunate as Herzog presents them to be.

Exercise 42

1. Robert Lowell; *Armadillo*
2. *Skunk Hour*
3. The title "Skunk Hour" is interesting. It is the hour for skunks to be out eating; it is the hour when humans should realize that they have become like skunks and should behave likewise; It is the hour when the poet reaches the lowest of the low in life, when he is at the lowest circle of hell, and achieves self-realization and makes a prophetic kind of call for humankind to do the same. It is a hellish hour for him and humankind, it is true, but the way after that point can only be the way upward. Lowell's message is clear that we humans have been dehumanized, but we do not need to feel disheartened. There is yet light at the end of the tunnel. Thus, on this positive note, the poet ends.
4. The poem, at first sight, seems to offer a forthright answer. Here all around the poet is engulfed in an atmosphere of impotence: the

hermit heiress living old and purposeless, "our summer millionaire" committing suicide probably because of weariness of life or bankruptcy or both, and the fairy decorator whose existence is meaningless and without any sense of direction. All these abnormalities of life, static and hopeless, are symbols of spiritual corruption and form an objective correlative for the poet's own personal disintegration. Thus, the poem reveals the poet's loss of faith in man, in himself, and in life. His best route of escape is death. And sure enough, he knows that his mind is not right. He is going through hell. It's dark night, and he is out on "the hill's skull", looking at the lover-cars in the giant shadow of the graveyard. He feels bleak and his spirit sobs. Death becomes attractive.

Then he sees a sight of the portent which is as ambiguous as ambiguous can be. A mother skunk is dauntlessly leading her kittens out hunting for food. They are having a hearty meal and are enjoying life. At the sight of vitality and fertility, the poet suddenly realizes that he has a thing or two to learn from the animals. Life flickers up again within him. The image of the skunk is interesting. The skunk is probably the most disgusting, the most despicable, of animals, and the poet realized that he is not even as good as that. If man is reduced to such an abject animal state, there should be nothing left of his spiritual dignity. But then if there is the will to live and the courage with it, if we can forget our pettiness and stop self-deprecation, and try to pick up a lesson from our brute fellow creatures, then there should be probably still hope.

Exercise 43

1. *The Catcher in the Rye*
2. Jerome David Salinger
3. "I" in the passage refers to Holden Caulfield, the central character

of *The Catcher in the Rye*. The novel talks about the story of the rebellious teenage schoolboy, Holden, and his quixotic experiences in New York, taking place in December 1949. The story commences with Holden Caulfield describing encounters he has had with students and faculty of Pencey Prep in Agerstown, Pennsylvania. He criticizes them for being superficial, or, as he would say, "phony." After being expelled from the school for his poor academic performance, Holden packs up and leaves the school in the middle of the night after a physical altercation with his roommate. He takes a train to New York but does not want to return to his family and instead checks into the dilapidated Edmont Hotel. Holden spends a total of three days in the city, and this time is characterized largely by drunkenness and loneliness. At one point he ends up at a museum, where he contrasts his life with the statues of Eskimos on display. For as long as he can remember, the statues have been unchanging. These concerns may have stemmed largely from the death of his brother, Allie. Eventually, he sneaks into his parents' apartment while they are away, to visit his younger sister, Phoebe, who is nearly the only person with whom he seems to be able to communicate. Phoebe views Holden as a hero, and she is naively unaware that Holden's view of her is virtually identical. After leaving his parents' apartment, Holden then drops by to see a former, and much admired, English teacher, Mr. Antolini, and is offered advice on life and a place to sleep. Holden is upset when he wakes up in the night to find Mr. Antolini patting his head in a way that he perceives as "flitty." Holden leaves and spends his last afternoon wandering in the city. Holden makes the decision that he will head out west, and when he mentions these plans to his little sister, she decides she wants to go with him. Holden declines her offer and refuses to have her accompany him. This upsets Phoebe, so Holden does her a favor and decides not to leave after all. Holden tries to reverse her saddened mood by taking her to the Central Park Zoo.

He realizes his mistakes as she rides the carousel that lies within the zoo. While watching Phoebe, Holden realizes that he can't be the "catcher in the rye" and that he is in need of help.

At the conclusion of the novel, Holden decides not to mention much about the present day, finding it inconsequential. He alludes to "getting sick" and living in a mental hospital, and mentions that he'll be attending another school in September. Holden says that he has surprisingly found himself missing two of his former classmates, Stradlater and Ackley, and even Maurice the elevator operator. The last words of the novel are, "Don't ever tell anybody anything. If you do, you start missing everybody."

4. The name Holden is worth noticing. Holden sounds like "hold on". As is seen, in this book, Holden wishes to "hold on" to the protective covering that encloses the field of innocence. Holden desperately wants to remain true and innocent in a world full of "phonies."

5. *The Catcher in the Rye* was written by Jerome David Salinger. And it was this book that propelled him onto the national stage. The novel's plot is simple, detailing two days in the life of 16-year-old Holden Caulfield after he has been expelled from an elite college preparatory school. The protagonist Holden's fantasy in *The Catcher in the Rye* not only reflects his innocence, his belief in pure, uncorrupted youth, and his desire to protect that spirit, but also represents his extreme disconnection from reality and his naïve view of the world.

Exercise 44

1. *The Bluest Eye*
2. Toni Morrison
3. *The Bluest Eye* is told from the perspective of Claudia MacTeer as a child and an adult, as well as from a third-person omniscient viewpoint.

4. *The Bluest Eye* is about a year in the life of a young black girl in Lorain, Ohio, named Pecola, who develops an inferiority complex due to her eye color and skin appearance. The title "The Bluest Eye" refers to Pecola's fervent wishes to have beautiful blue eyes like the white people. She never thinks herself beautiful because she and her community base their ideal beauty on "whiteness". At the end of the novel, Pecola becomes insane and her dream of having the bluest eyes never comes true. In this book, Morrison foregrounds the demonization of Blackness in American culture, focusing on the effects of internalized racism. Through Geraldine, Polly, Pecola, and other characters, she demonstrates how even the most subtle forms of racism—especially racism from within the Black community—can negatively impact self-worth and self-esteem.

附录一
美国文学主要作家作品简录

Nathaniel Ward（纳撒尼尔·沃德，1578—1652）
　　The Body of Liberties《各类自由之主体》(1641)
　　The Simple Cobler of Aggawam in America《北美的阿格瓦姆鞋匠》(1647)

Thomas Morton（托马斯·莫顿，约1579—1647）
　　New English Canaan《新英格兰迦南》(1637)

John Smith（约翰·史密斯，1580—1631）
　　A True Relation of Virginia《关于弗吉尼亚的真实叙述》(1608)
　　The Generall Historie of Virginia《弗吉尼亚通史》(1624)

John Cotton（约翰·科顿，1584—1652）
　　A Treatise of the Covenant of Grace《恩典之约》(不详)
　　The Way of Life《生命之路》(不详)
　　The Way of the Churches of Christ in New England《新英格兰基督教会生活》(1645)
　　Milk for Babes, Drawn out of the Breasts of Both Testaments《旧约新约：幼儿奶源》(1646)
　　The Way of Congregational Churches Cleared《公理教会生活方式正名》(1648)

John Winthrop（约翰·温思罗普，1588—1649）
　　A Modell of Christian Charity《基督教慈善的典范》(1630)
　　The History of New England from 1630 to 1649《新英格兰历史：1630—

1649》(1825)

William Bradford(威廉·布雷德福,1590—1657)
History of Plymouth Plantation《普利茅斯种植园史》(1630—1651)

Edward Johnson(爱德华·约翰逊,1598—1672)
Wonder-Working Providence of Sions Savior in New England《新英格兰创造神迹的天福》(1654)

Anne Bradstreet(安妮·布拉德斯特里特,约1612—1672)
The Flesh and the Spirit《灵与肉》(1650)
The Tenth Muse Lately Sprung up in America《最近在北美出现的第十位缪斯》(1650)
Several Poems Compiled with Great Variety of Wit and Learning《一些风格各异、充满智慧的诗歌》(1678)
To My Dear and Loving Husband《献给我亲爱的丈夫》(1678)

Nathanial Morton(纳撒尼尔·莫顿,1616—1685)
New England's Memorial《新英格兰日记》(不详)

Michael Wigglesworth(迈克尔·威格尔斯沃思,1631—1705)
The Day of Doom《判决日》(1662)

Increase Mather(英克里斯·马瑟,1639—1723)
An Essay for the Recording of Illustrious Providences《上帝福佑现象录》(1684)

Edward Taylor(爱德华·泰勒,1642—1729)
Metrical History of Christianity《诗体基督教史》(不详)
God's Determinations Touching His Elect《上帝对其选民影响的决定》(1682)
Preparatory Meditations《内行录》(1682—1725)

附录一　美国文学主要作家作品简录

Cotton Mather（科顿·马瑟，1663—1728）
　　Magnalis Christi Americana《基督在北美的辉煌》（1702）

Jonathan Edwards（乔纳森·爱德华兹，1703—1758）
　　Sinners in the Hands of an Angry God《愤怒的上帝手中之罪人》（1741）

Benjamin Franklin（本杰明·富兰克林，1706—1790）
　　Poor Richard's Almanack《穷理查历书》（1732—1757）
　　The Autobiography《自传》（1794）

John Woolman（约翰·伍尔曼，1720—1772）
　　Some Considerations upon the Keeping of Negroes《关于占有黑人的几点思考》（1754）
　　The Journal of John Woolman《约翰·伍尔曼日记》（1774）

J. Hector St. John de Crèvecoeur（J. 埃克托尔·圣约翰·德克雷弗克，1735—1813）
　　Letters from an American Farmer《美国农民来信》（1782）

Ethan Allen（伊桑·艾伦，1738—1789）
　　A Narrative of Colonel Ethan Allen's Captivity《艾伦上校被俘记》（不详）

Francis Hopkinson（弗朗西斯·霍普金森，1737—1791）
　　The Prophecy《预言》（1776）
　　Political Catechism《政治教义问答》（1777）
　　Miscellaneous Essays and Occasional Writings《杂文和随笔》（1792）

Thomas Paine（托马斯·潘恩，1737—1809）
　　Common Sense《常识》（1776）
　　The American Crisis《美国的危机》（1776—1783）
　　Rights of Man《人的权利》（1791 第一部，1792 第二部）
　　The Age of Reason《理性的时代》（1794 第一部，1796 第二部）

Agrarian Justice《土地正义》(1797)

Thomas Jefferson(托马斯·杰斐逊，1743—1826)
A Summary View of the Rights of British America《英属美洲权利综论》(1774)
Declaration of Independence《独立宣言》(1776)

Timothy Dwight(蒂莫西·德怀特，1752—1817)
The Conquest of Canaan《迦南的征服》(1785)
The Triumph of Infidelity《不忠诚的胜利》(1788)
Greenfield Hill《格林菲尔德山林》(1794)

Philip Freneau(菲利普·弗瑞诺，1752—1832)
The Rising Glory of America《蒸蒸日上的美洲》(1772)
The British Prison-Ship《英国囚船》(1781)
To the Memory of the Brave Americans《纪念美国勇士》(1781)
The Wild Honeysuckle《野生的金银花》(1786)
The Indian Burying Ground《印第安人殡葬地》(1788)

Phillis Wheatley(菲莉丝·惠特利，约1753—1784)
On Messrs Hussey and Coffin《胡塞先生和科芬先生》(1767)

Joel Barlow(乔尔·巴洛，1754—1812)
The Vision of Columbus《哥伦布的远见》(1787)
The Hasty Pudding《速成布丁》(1796)

Royall Tyler(罗亚尔·泰勒，1757—1826)
The Algerine Captive《阿尔及尔俘虏》(1797)

William Hill Brown(威廉·希尔·布朗，1765—1793)
Power of Sympathy《同情的力量》(1789)

附录一　美国文学主要作家作品简录

Charles Brockden Brown（查尔斯·布罗克登·布朗，1771—1810）
 Wieland《威兰德》（1798）
 Arthur Mervyn《阿瑟·梅尔文》（1799—1800）
 Edgar Huntley《爱德加·亨特利》（1799）

Washington Irving（华盛顿·欧文，1783—1859）
 A History of New York《纽约的历史》（1809）
 Rip Van Winkle《瑞普·凡·温克尔》（1819—1820）
 The Legend of Sleepy Hollow《睡谷的传说》（1819—1820）
 The Sketch Book《见闻札记》（1819—1820）
 Bracebridge Hall《布雷斯布里奇田庄》（1822）
 Tales of a Traveler《旅客谈》（1824）
 The Alhambra《阿尔罕伯拉》（1832）

James Fenimore Cooper（詹姆斯·费尼莫尔·库珀，1789—1851）
 The Spy《间谍》（1821）
 The Pilot《领航者》（1823）
 The Pioneers《拓荒者》（1823）
 The Leatherstocking Tales《皮裹腿故事集》（1823—1841）
 The Last of Mohicans《最后的莫希干人》（1826）
 The Prairie《大草原》（1827）
 The Pathfinder《探路人》（1840）
 The Deerslayer《杀鹿者》（1841）

William Cullen Bryant（威廉·卡伦·布赖恩特，1794—1878）
 Thanatopsis《死亡随想》（1817）
 To a Waterfowl《致水鸟》（1818）
 Poems《诗选》（1821）
 The Fountain《泉》（1842）
 The White-Footed Deer《白蹄鹿》（1844）
 A Forest Hymn《森林赋》（1860）
 The Flood of Years《似水流年》（1878）

James Russell Lowell（詹姆斯·拉塞尔·洛厄尔，1801—1891）
  A Year's Life《一年的生活》（1841）
  A Fable for Critics《批评家的寓言》（1848）
  The Vision of Sir Launfal《朗佛尔爵士的幻觉》（1848）

Ralph Waldo Emerson（拉尔夫·沃尔多·爱默生，1803—1882）
  Essays: First Series《论文集：第一辑》（1841）
  Self-Reliance《论自助》（1841）
  Essays: Second Series《论文集：第二辑》（1844）
  Representative Men《代表人物》（1849）
  English Traits《英国人的性格》（1856）

Nathaniel Hawthorne（纳撒尼尔·霍桑，1804—1864）
  Twice-Told Tales《尽人皆知的故事》（1837）
  Mosses from an Old Manse《古屋青苔》（1846）
  The Scarlet Letter《红字》（1850）
  The House of the Seven Gables《有七个尖角阁的房子》（1851）
  The Blithedale Romance《福谷传奇》（1852）
  The Marble Faun《玉石雕像》（1860）

Henry Wadsworth Longfellow（亨利·沃兹沃思·朗费罗，1807—1882）
  Voices of the Night《夜吟》（1839）
  Ballads and Other Poems《民谣及其他》（1842）
  Evangeline《伊凡吉琳》（1847）
  The Song of Hiawatha《海华沙之歌》（1855）
  The Courtship of Miles Standish《迈尔斯·斯坦迪什的求婚》（1858）
  Christus: A Mystery《基督：一个神秘的故事》（1872）

John Greenleaf Whittier（约翰·格林利夫·惠蒂埃，1807—1892）
  Legends of New England in Prose and Verse《新英格兰的传说》（1831）
  Leaves from Margaret Smith's Journal《玛格丽特·史密斯日记片断》（1849）

Snow-Bound: A Winter Idyl《大雪封门》(1866)
Among the Hills《群山之中》(1869)

Edgar Allan Poe(埃德加·爱伦·坡，1809—1849)
Poems《诗集》(1831)
To Helen《致海伦》(其一)(1831)
Ligeia《莱琪儿》(1838)
Tales of the Grotesque and Arabesque《怪诞奇异故事集》(1839)
The Fall of the House of Usher《厄舍古屋的倒塌》(1839)
The Raven《乌鸦》(1845)
To Helen《致海伦》(其二)(1848)

Oliver Wendell Holmes(奥利弗·温德尔·霍姆斯，1809—1894)
The Common Law《普通法》(1881)

Fanny Fern(范妮·弗恩，1811—1872)
Ruth Hall《露丝·霍尔》(1854)

Harriet Beecher Stowe(哈丽雅特·比彻·斯托，1811—1896)
Uncle Tom's Cabin《汤姆叔叔的小屋》(1852)
A Key to Uncle Tom's Cabin《汤姆叔叔的小屋说明》(1853)
Dred: A Tale of the Great Dismal Swamp《德雷德：阴暗大沼地的故事》(1856)

Henry David Thoreau(亨利·戴维·梭罗，1817—1862)
A Week on the Concord and Merrimack River《在康考德和梅里马克河上的一周》(1849)
Resistance to Civil Government《抵制公民政府》(1849)
Walden《瓦尔登湖》(1854)

Herman Melville(赫尔曼·梅尔维尔，1819—1891)
Typee《泰比》(1846)

Omoo《奥穆》(1847)

Mardi《玛地》(1849)

Redburn《雷得本》(1849)

White Jacket《白外衣》(1850)

Moby Dick《白鲸》(1851)

Billy Budd《比利·巴德》(1924)

Walt Whitman(沃尔特·惠特曼,1819—1892)

Leaves of Grass《草叶集》(1855—1892)

Song of Myself《自我之歌》(1881)

Emily Dickinson(艾米莉·狄金森,1830—1886)

Wild Nights—Wild Nights!《暴风雨夜》(1861)

Because I Could Not Stop for Death《因为我不能停步等候死神》(1863)

The Soul Selects Her Own Society《灵魂选择自己的伴侣》(1890)

Louisa May Alcott(路易莎·梅·奥尔科特,1832—1888)

Little Women《小妇人》(1868—1869)

Mark Twain(马克·吐温,1835—1910)

The Celebrated Jumping Frog of Calaveras County《加拉维拉县有名的跳蛙》(1865)

The Innocents Abroad《傻瓜出国记》(1869)

The Gilded Age《镀金时代》(1873)

The Adventures of Tom Sawyer《汤姆·索耶历险记》(1876)

The Prince and the Pauper《王子与贫儿》(1881)

The Adventures of Huckleberry Finn《哈克贝利·费恩历险记》(1884)

A Connecticut Yankee in King Arthur's Court《亚瑟王宫廷中的美国佬》(1889)

The Tragedy of Pudd'nhead Wilson《傻瓜威尔逊》(1894)

The Man That Corrupted Hadleyburg《败坏哈德莱堡的人》(1899)

附录一　美国文学主要作家作品简录

Francis Bret Harte（弗朗西斯·布雷特·哈特，1836—1902）
  The Luck of Roaring Camp《咆哮的幸运儿》（1868）
  The Outcasts of Poker Flat《扑克海滩的流浪者》（1869）

William Dean Howells（威廉·迪安·豪威尔斯，1837—1920）
  A Modern Instance《一个现代例证》（1882）
  The Rise of Silas Lapham《塞拉斯·拉帕姆发迹》（1885）
  A Hazard of New Fortunes《新财富危机》（1890）

Sidney Lanier（悉尼·拉尼尔，1842—1881）
  Corn《谷物》（1875）
  Florida: Its Scenery, Climate, and History《佛罗里达随笔》（1875）
  The Symphony《交响乐》（1875）
  The Marshes of Glynn《格林沼泽地》（1878）
  Sunrise《日出》（1881）

Henry James（亨利·詹姆斯，1843—1916）
  Daisy Miller《黛茜·米勒》（1879）
  The Portrait of a Lady《贵妇人的画像》（1881）
  The Bostonians《波士顿人》（1886）
  The Wings of the Dove《鸽翼》（1902）
  The Ambassadors《大使们》（1903）
  The Golden Bowl《金碗》（1904）

Sarah Orne Jewett（萨拉·奥恩·朱厄特，1849—1909）
  A Country Doctor《乡村医生》（1884）
  The Country of the Pointed Firs《尖尖的枞树之乡》（1896）

Kate Chopin（凯特·肖邦，1850—1904）
  A Respectable Woman《一个体面的女人》（1894）
  Bayou Folk《支流人》（1894）
  The Story of an Hour《一小时的故事》（1894）
  A Night in Acadie《在阿卡迪的一夜》（1897）

The Storm《暴雨》（1898）
　　The Awakening《觉醒》（1899）

Harriet Monroe（哈丽雅特·门罗，1860—1936）
　　Poetry: A Magazine of Verse《诗刊：一本诗文杂志》（1912）
　　You and I《你与我》（1914）

Hannibal Hamlin Garland（汉尼巴尔·哈姆林·加兰，1860—1936）
　　Main-Traveled Roads—Six Mississippi Valley Stories《大路条条》（1891）
　　Rose of Dutcher's Cooly《荷兰人深谷的罗丝》（1895）
　　A Son of the Middle Boarder《中部边地之子》（1917）

William Sidney Porter (O. Henry)（威廉·悉尼·波特，笔名欧·亨利，1862—1910）
　　The Cop and the Anthem《警察与赞美诗》（1904）
　　The Four Million《四百万》（1906）
　　Heart of the West《西部之心》（1907）
　　The Trimmed Lamp《修剪过的灯》（1907）
　　The Gentle Grafter《温雅的贪污者》（1908）
　　The Voice of the City《城市之声》（1908）
　　Options《选择》（1909）
　　Roads of Destination《命运之路》（1909）
　　Strictly Business《仅是公事》（1910）

Edith Newbold Wharton（伊迪丝·纽博尔德·华顿，1862—1937）
　　The House of Mirth《欢乐之屋》（1905）
　　Ethan Frome《伊坦·弗洛美》（1911）
　　The Age of Innocence《天真时代》（1920）

Edwin Arlington Robinson（埃德温·阿林顿·罗宾逊，1869—1935）
　　Captain Craig《克雷格上尉》（1902）

Stephen Crane（斯蒂芬·克莱恩，1871—1900）
 Maggie: A Girl of the Street《街头女郎梅季》（1893）
 The Black Riders and Other Lines《黑骑士和其他诗篇》（1895）
 The Red Badge of Courage《红色英勇勋章》（1895）

Theodore Dreiser（西奥多·德莱塞，1871—1945）
 Sister Carrie《嘉丽妹妹》（1900）
 Jennie Gerhardt《珍妮姑娘》（1911）
 Trilogy of Desire 欲望三部曲（1912—1947）
  The Financier《金融家》（1912）
  The Titan《巨头》（1914）
  The Stoic《禁欲者》（1947）
 The "Genius"《天才》（1915）
 An American Tragedy《美国的悲剧》（1925）
 Dreiser Looks at Russia《德莱塞对俄罗斯的观感》（1928）

Robert Frost（罗伯特·弗罗斯特，1874—1963）
 A Boy's Will《少年心愿》（1913）
 North of Boston《波士顿以北》（1914）
 Mountain Interval《山间》（1916）
 New Hampshire《新罕布什尔》（1923）
 West-Running Brook《西流的溪涧》（1928）
 A Further Range《又一片牧场》（1936）
 A Witness Tree《一株作证的树》（1942）

Jack London（杰克·伦敦，1876—1916）
 The Son of the Wolf《狼之子》（1900）
 The Call of the Wild《野性的呼唤》（1903）
 The People of the Abyss《深渊中的人们》（1903）
 The Sea Wolf《海狼》（1904）
 White Fang《白獠牙》（1906）
 The Iron Heel《铁蹄》（1908）

Martin Eden《马丁·伊登》(1909)

Sherwood Anderson(舍伍德·安德森,1876—1941)
  Winesberg, Ohio《俄亥俄州的温斯堡》(1919)
  Poor White《穷白人》(1920)
  The Triumph of the Egg《鸡蛋的胜利》(1921)

Carl Sandburg(卡尔·桑德堡,1878—1967)
  Cornhuskers《碾米机》(1918)
  Smoke and Steel《烟与钢》(1920)
  The Prairie Years《草原年代》(1926)
  The American Songbag《美国歌袋》(1927)
  The People, Yes《人们,好!》(1936)
  The War Years《战争年代》(1939)

Wallace Stevens(华莱士·史蒂文斯,1879—1955)
  Harmonium《风琴》(1923)
  The Man with the Blue Guitar《弹蓝吉他的人》(1937)
  The Auroras of Autumn《秋天的晨曦》(1950)
  Collected Poems《诗集》(1954)

William Carlos Williams(威廉·卡洛斯·威廉斯,1883—1963)
  The Storm《风暴》(不详)
  The Sun Bathers《日光浴者》(1933)
  That Is Just to Say《这就是说》(1934)
  The Dance《舞蹈》(1944)
  Paterson《帕特森》(1946—1958)
  The Sparrow《麻雀》(1955)

Sinclair Lewis(辛克莱·刘易斯,1885—1951)
  Our Mr. Wrenn《我们的雷恩先生》(1914)
  Main Street《大街》(1920)

Babbit《巴比特》（1922）

It Can't Happen Here《这里不可能发生》（1935）

World So Wide《世界如此之大》（1951）

Ezra Pound（埃兹拉·庞德，1885—1972）

In a Station of the Metro《在地铁站里》（1913）

Homage to Sextus Propertius《向塞克斯特斯·普罗波蒂斯致敬》（1919）

Hugh Selwyn Mauberley《休·塞尔温·莫伯利》（1920）

Personae《人物》（1926）

The Pisan Cantos《比萨诗章》（1948）

The Cantos《诗章》（1970）

Hilda Doolittle (H. D.)（希尔达·杜丽特尔，笔名 H. D.，1886—1961）

Epigram《警言》（1913）

Hermes of the Ways《途中的赫尔姆斯》（1913）

Priapus《男性之神》（1913）

Sea Rose《海玫瑰》（1916）

Eugene O'Neill（尤金·奥尼尔，1888—1953）

Bound East for Cardiff《东航卡迪夫》（1916）

Beyond the Horizon《天边外》（1920）

The Emperor Jones《琼斯皇》（1921）

The Hairy Ape《毛猿》（1922）

All God's Chillun Got Wings《上帝的儿女都有翅膀》（1924）

Desire Under the Elms《榆树下的欲望》（1924）

The Fountain《泉》（1926）

The Great God Brown《布朗大神》（1926）

Lazarus Laughed《拉撒路笑了》（1927）

Strange Interlude《奇异的插曲》（1928）

Mourning Becomes Electra《悲悼》（1931）

Ah, Wilderness!《啊，荒原！》（1933）

Hughie《休伊》（1942）

The Iceman Cometh《送冰人来了》(1946)

A Moon for the Misbegotten《月照不幸人》(1952)

Long Day's Journey into Night《进入黑夜的漫长旅程》(1956)

A Touch of the Poet《诗人的气质》(1958)

Thomas Stearns Eliot(托马斯·斯特恩斯·艾略特,1888—1965)

Gerontion《老人》(1920)

The Sacred Wood《圣林》(1920)

The Waste Land《荒原》(1922)

The Hollow Men《空心人》(1925)

Ash Wednesday《圣灰星期三》(1930)

Murder in the Cathedral《大教堂谋杀案》(1935)

The Family Reunion《大团圆》(1939)

Four Quartets《四个四重奏》(1943)

The Cocktail Party《鸡尾酒会》(1950)

Edward Estlin Cummings(爱德华·埃斯特林·卡明斯,1894—1962)

Tulips and Chimneys《郁金香与烟囱》(1923)

&《&》(1925)

is 5《是5》(1926)

somewhere i have never traveled, gladly beyond《有个地方我从未去过》(1931)

anyone lived in a pretty how town《某人曾住在一个多美的小城镇》(1940)

1x1《1x1》(1944)

Francis Scott Key Fitzgerald(弗朗西斯·斯科特·基·菲茨杰拉德,1896—1940)

Flappers and Philosophers《姑娘们和哲学家们》(1920)

This Side of Paradise《人间天堂》(1920)

Tales of the Jazz Age《爵士时代的故事》(1922)

The Beautiful and Damned《美丽的和倒霉的》(1922)

The Great Gatsby《了不起的盖茨比》(1925)

Tender Is the Night《夜色温柔》(1934)
The Last Tycoon《最后的巨头》(1941)

William Faulkner（威廉·福克纳，1897—1962）
Sartoris《沙特里斯》(1929)
The Sound and the Fury《喧哗与骚动》(1929)
As I Lay Dying《在我弥留之际》(1930)
Sanctuary《圣殿》(1931)
Light in August《八月之光》(1932)
Absalom, Absalom!《押沙龙，押沙龙！》(1936)
Go Down, Moses《去吧，摩西》(1942)

Ernest Hemingway（欧内斯特·海明威，1899—1961）
The Sun Also Rises《太阳照样升起》(1926)
A Farewell to Arms《永别了，武器》(1929)
Death in the Afternoon《午后之死》(1932)
Green Hills of Africa《非洲的青山》(1935)
For Whom the Bell Tolls《丧钟为谁而鸣》(1940)
The Old Man and the Sea《老人与海》(1952)

Langston Hughes（兰斯顿·休斯，1902—1967）
The Weary Blues《萎靡的布鲁斯》(1926)
Dear Lovely Death《亲爱的死神》(1931)
The Ways of White Folks《白人的行径》(1934)
Shakespeare in Harlem《哈莱姆的莎士比亚》(1942)
Montage of a Dream Deferred《耽搁了的梦想蒙太奇》(1951)

John Steinbeck（约翰·斯坦贝克，1902—1968）
Cup of Gold《金杯》(1929)
Tortilla Flat《煎饼房》(1935)
In Dubious Battle《胜负未决》(1936)
Of Mice and Men《人鼠之间》(1937)

The Long Valley《长谷地》（1938）
The Grapes of Wrath《愤怒的葡萄》（1939）
The Moon Is Down《月亮下去了》（1942）
The Pearl《珍珠》（1947）
The Winter of Our Discontent《我们不安的冬天》（1961）

Nathanael West（纳撒尼尔·韦斯特，1903—1940）
The Dream Life of Balso Snell《鲍尔索·斯奈尔的梦幻生活》（1931）
Miss Lonelyhearts《孤心小姐》（1933）
A Cool Million《难圆发财梦》（1934）
The Day of the Locust《蝗灾之日》（1939）

James Thomas Farrell（詹姆斯·托马斯·法雷尔，1904—1979）
The Studs Lonigan Trilogy《斯塔兹·朗尼根》三部曲（1932—1935）
Young Lonigan《少年朗尼根》（1932）
The Young Manhood of Studs Lonigan《朗尼根的青年时代》（1934）
Judgment Day《审判日》（1935）

Lilian Hellman（莉莲·赫尔曼，1905—1984）
The Children's Hour《儿童时代》（1934）
The Little Foxes《小狐狸》（1939）
Watch on the Rhine《守望莱茵河》（1941）
The Searching Wind《彻骨的风》（1944）

Robert Penn Warren（罗伯特·佩恩·沃伦，1905—1989）
All the King's Men《国王的人马》（1946）
World Enough and Time《如此人生》（1950）
Band of Angels《天使们》（1956）

Clifford Odets（克利福德·奥德茨，1906—1963）
Awake and Sing《醒来歌唱》（1935）
Till the Day I Die《直到我死那一天》（1935）

Waiting for Lefty《等待莱弗蒂》（1935）
　　Golden Boy《天之骄子》（1937）

Wystan Hugh Auden（威斯坦·休·奥登，1907—1973）
　　Journey to a War《战地行纪》（1939）
　　In Memory of W. B. Yeats《悼叶芝》（1940）
　　The Age of Anxiety《焦虑的时代》（1947）

Richard Wright（理查德·赖特，1908—1960）
　　Uncle Tom's Children《汤姆叔叔的孩子们》（1938）
　　Native Son《土生子》（1940）
　　Black Boy《黑孩子》（1945）
　　The Outsider《局外人》（1953）
　　The Long Dream《漫长的梦》（1958）

Theodore Huebner Roethke（西奥多·许布纳·罗特克，1908—1963）
　　Open House《开着门的房屋》（1941）
　　The Lost Son《失去的儿子》（1948）
　　Praise to the End!《赞美到底》（1951）
　　The Waking《苏醒》（1953）
　　Words for the Wind《说给风听》（1957）
　　The Far Field《遥远的土地》（1964）

Eudora Alice Welty（尤多拉·爱丽丝·韦尔蒂，1909—2001）
　　Delta Wedding《三角洲婚礼》（1946）
　　The Golden Apples《金苹果》（1949）
　　The Optimist's Daughter《乐观者的女儿》（1972）

Charles Olson（查尔斯·奥尔森，1910—1970）
　　The Kingfishers《翠鸟》（1949）
　　The Maximus Poems《马克西姆斯诗抄》（1953）

Elizabeth Bishop（伊丽莎白·毕肖普，1911—1979）
  North and South《北方·南方》（1946）
  Poems《诗集》（1955）
  Questions of the Travel《旅途中的问题》（1965）
  The Complete Poems《诗歌全集》（1969）
  Geography III《地理学 III》（1976）

Tennessee Williams（田纳西·威廉斯，1911—1983）
  The Glass Menagerie《玻璃动物园》（1944）
  A Streetcar Named Desire《欲望号街车》（1947）
  The Rose Tattoo《玫瑰鲸纹》（1951）
  Cat on a Hot Tin Roof《热铁皮屋顶上的猫》（1955）
  Sweet Bird of Youth《可爱的青春鸟》（1959）

John Cheever（约翰·契弗，1912—1982）
  The Way Some People Live《某些人的生活方式》（1943）
  The Enormous Radio and Other Stories《巨大的收音机及其他故事》（1953）
  The Stories of John Cheever《约翰·契弗短篇小说集》（1978）

William Motter Inge（威廉·莫特·英奇，1913—1973）
  Come Back, Little Sheba《归来吧，小希巴》（1950）
  Picnic《野餐》（1953）
  Bus Stop《公共汽车站》（1955）
  The Dark at the Top of the Stairs《楼梯顶的黑暗》（1960）

Randall Jarrell（兰德尔·贾雷尔，1914—1965）
  Blood for a Stranger《给陌生人的血》（1942）
  Little Friend, Little Friend《小朋友，小朋友》（1945）
  Losses《损失》（1948）
  The Woman at the Washington Zoo《华盛顿动物园中的妇女》（1960）
  The Lost World《失去的世界》（1965）

John Berryman（约翰·贝里曼，1914—1972）
    The Dream Songs《梦之歌》(1969)

William Stafford（威廉·斯塔福德，1914—1993）
    West of Your City《你的城市之西》(1960)
    Traveling Through the Dark《穿越黑暗》(1962)

Ralph Ellison（拉尔夫·埃利森，1914—1994）
    Invisible Man《看不见的人》(1952)

Arthur Asher Miller（阿瑟·阿舍·米勒，1915—2005）
    All My Sons《全是我的儿子》(1947)
    Death of a Salesman《推销员之死》(1949)
    The Crucible《严峻考验》/《萨姆勒的女巫》(1953)
    A View from the Bridge《桥头瞭望》(1955)

Saul Bellow（索尔·贝娄，1915—2005）
    Dangling Man《荡来荡去的人》(1944)
    The Victim《受害者》(1947)
    The Adventures of Augie March《奥吉·玛奇历险记》(1953)
    Seize the Day《抓住这一天》(1956)
    Henderson the Rain King《雨王汉德森》(1959)
    Herzog《赫索格》(1964)
    Mr. Sammler's Planet《塞姆勒先生的行星》(1970)
    The Dean's December《院长的十二月》(1982)
    More Die of Heartbreak《更多的人死于心碎》(1987)

Walker Percy（沃克·珀西，1916—1990）
    The Last Gentleman《最后的绅士》(1966)
    Love in the Ruins《废墟里的爱情》(1971)

Carson McCullers（卡森·麦卡勒斯，1917—1967）
    The Heart Is a Lonely Hunter《心是孤独的猎手》（1940）
    Reflections in a Golden Eye《黄金眼睛的映像》（1941）
    The Ballad of the Sad Café《伤心咖啡馆之歌》（1951）

Robert Lowell（罗伯特·洛厄尔，1917—1977）
    Lord Weary's Castle《威利爵爷的城堡》（1946）
    Life Studies《人生研究》（1959）
    For the Union Dead《献给联邦死难者》（1964）

Jerome David Salinger（杰罗姆·戴维·塞林格，1919—2010）
    The Catcher in the Rye《麦田里的守望者》（1951）

Howard Nemerov（霍华德·奈莫洛夫，1920—1991）
    The Image and the Law《意象和法规》（1947）
    The Salt Garden《盐之园》（1955）
    The Blue Swallows《蓝燕》（1967）

Alex Haley（亚历克斯·哈利，1921—1992）
    Roots《根》（1976）

Richard Wilbur（理查德·威尔伯，1921—2017）
    Things of This World《世间之事》（1956）
    Advice to a Prophet《给一个先知的建议》（1961）

Jack Kerouac（杰克·凯鲁亚克，1922—1969）
    On the Road《在路上》（1957）

Kurt Vonnegut（库尔特·冯内古特，1922—2007）
    Cat's Cradle《猫的摇篮》（1963）
    Slaughterhouse-Five《第五号屠宰场》（1969）

James Dicky（詹姆斯·迪基，1923—1997）
　　Buckdancer's Choice《踢踏舞者的选择》(1965)
　　Deliverance《解救》(1970)
　　The Zodiac《黄道带》(1976)
　　The Strength of Fields《田野的力量》(1979)

Joseph Heller（约瑟夫·海勒，1923—1999）
　　Catch-22《第二十二条军规》(1961)

Norman Mailer（诺曼·梅勒，1923—2007）
　　The Naked and the Dead《裸者与死者》(1948)
　　The Armies of the Night《夜幕下的大军》(1968)
　　The Executioner's Song《刽子手之歌》(1979)

Louis Simpson（路易斯·辛普森，1923—2012）
　　At the End of the Open Road《大路尽头》(1963)

James Baldwin（詹姆斯·鲍德温，1924—1987）
　　Go Tell It on the Mountain《向苍天呼吁》(1953)

Flannery O'Connor（弗兰纳里·奥康纳，1925—1964）
　　Wise Blood《智血》(1952)
　　A Good Man Is Hard to Find《好人难寻》(1955)
　　The Violent Bear It Away《暴力夺取》(1960)

John Hawkes（约翰·霍克斯，1925—1998）
　　The Cannibal《食人者》(1949)
　　The Lime Twig《酸橙树枝》(1961)
　　Second Skin《第二层皮》(1964)

William Styron（威廉·斯泰伦，1925—2006）
　　Lie Down in Darkness《在黑暗中躺下》(1951)
　　The Confessions of Nat Turner《奈特·特纳的自白》(1967)

Sophie's Choice《苏菲的选择》(1979)

Frank O'Hara(弗兰克·奥哈拉,1926—1966)
A City Winter and Other Poems《城市之冬及其他》(1952)
Lunch Poems《午餐诗》(1964)

James Merrill(詹姆斯·梅里尔,1926—1995)
The Book of Ephraim《伊弗雷姆之书》(1976)
Mirabell《米拉贝尔》(1978)
The Higher Keys《更高的音调》(1982)

Allen Ginsberg(艾伦·金斯堡,1926—1997)
Howl《嚎叫》(1956)
Kaddish and Other Poems《〈卡迪什〉及其他诗篇》(1961)
Reality Sandwiches《现实三明治》(1963)
The Fall of America《美国的衰弱》(1972)
Mind Breaths《精神气息》(1978)
White Shroud《白色的尸衣》(1986)

Robert Creeley(罗伯特·克里利,1926—2005)
Words《言语》(1967)

Robert Bly(罗伯特·布莱,1926—2021)
Silence in the Snowy Fields《雪野里的寂静》(1962)
The Light Around the Body《身体周围的光》(1967)
Sleepers Joining Hands《手拉手入睡》(1973)

James Wright(詹姆斯·赖特,1927—1980)
The Green Wall《绿墙》(1957)
Saint Judas《圣徒犹大》(1959)
The Branch Will Not Break《树枝不会折断》(1963)

John Ashbery（约翰·阿什伯里，1927—2017）
 Self-portrait in a Convex Mirror《凸镜下的自画像》（1975）

Marvin Neil Simon（马文·尼尔·西蒙，1927—2018）
 Come Blow Your Horn《吹响你的号角》（1961）
 Barefoot in the Park《赤脚在公园》（1963）
 The Odd Couple《一对怪人》（1965）
 The Prisoner of Second Avenue《第二大街的囚徒》（1971）

Ann Sexton（安·塞克斯顿，1928—1974）
 To Bedlam and Part Way Back《去精神病院半途而返》（1960）
 Live or Die《生或死》（1966）
 The Death Notebooks《死亡笔记》（1974）

Edward Franklin Albee（爱德华·富兰克林·阿尔比，1928—2016）
 The Sandbox《沙箱》（1959）
 The Zoo Story《动物园的故事》（1959）
 The American Dream《美国梦》（1961）
 Who's Afraid of Virginia Woolf?《谁害怕弗吉尼娅·伍尔夫？》（1962）
 A Delicate Balance《微妙的平衡》（1966）

Paule Marshall（葆拉·马歇尔，1929—2019）
 Brown Girl, Brown Stones《褐肤色姑娘，褐砂石楼房》（1959）
 Praisesong for the Widow《寡妇赞歌》（1983）

John Simmons Barth（约翰·西蒙斯·巴思，1930— ）
 Giles Goat-Boy《羊孩贾尔斯》（1966）
 Lost in the Funhouse《迷失在游乐场》（1968）

Toni Morrison（托妮·莫里森，1931—2019）
 The Bluest Eye《最蓝的眼睛》（1970）
 Sula《秀拉》（1973）

    Song of Solomon《所罗门之歌》(1977)
    Tar Baby《柏油娃》(1981)
    Beloved《宠儿》(1987)
    Jazz《爵士乐》(1992)
    Paradise《乐园》(1998)

Sylvia Plath(西尔维娅·普拉思,1932—1963)
    A Winter Ship《冬之船》(1960)
    The Colossus and Other Poems《巨石像及其他》(1960)
    Winter Trees《冬天的树》(1971)

John Updike(约翰·厄普代克,1932—2009)
    Rabbit, Run《兔子,跑吧》(1960)
    Rabbit Redux《兔子归来》(1971)
    Rabbit Is Rich《兔子富了》(1981)
    Rabbit at Rest《兔子歇了》(1990)

Robert Coover(罗伯特·库弗,1932—)
    The Public Burning《公众的怒火》(1976)
    John's Wife《约翰的妻子》(1996)

Ken Kesey(肯·克西,1935—2001)
    One Flew Over the Cuckoo's Nest《飞越布谷鸟巢》(1962)

Robert Stone(罗伯特·斯通,1937—2015)
    A Hall of Mirrors《镜之厅》(1967)
    A Flag for Sunrise《日出的旗帜》(1981)

Thomas Ruggles Pynchon(托马斯·拉格尔斯·品钦,1937—)
    V《V》(1963)
    Gravity's Rainbow《万有引力之虹》(1973)
    Vineland《葡萄园》(1990)

Joyce Carol Oates（乔伊斯·卡罗尔·欧茨，1938— ）
 Them《他们》（1969）
 Wonderland《奇境》（1971）

Maxine Hong Kingston（汤亭亭，1940— ）
 The Woman Warrior: Memoirs of a Girlhood Among Ghosts《女勇士》（1976）
 China Men《中国佬》（1980）
 Tripmaster Monkey: His Fake Book《孙行者》（1989）

Sam Shepard（萨姆·谢泼德，1943—2017）
 Cowboys《牛仔》（1964）
 Icarus's Mother《伊卡鲁斯的母亲》（1965）
 The Tooth of Crime《罪恶的牙齿》（1972）

Alice Walker（爱丽丝·沃克，1944— ）
 The Color Purple《紫色》（1982）

David Alan Mamet（戴维·艾伦·马梅特，1947— ）
 Duck Variations《鸭子变奏曲》（1972）
 American Buffalo《美国野牛》（1976）

David Lehman（戴维·莱曼，1948— ）
 The Daily Mirror: A Journal in Poetry《每日镜鉴：诗的旅程》（1998）
 The Evening Sun《黄昏太阳》（2002）
 When a Woman Loves a Man《当女人爱上男人》（2005）
 Yeshiva Boys《校娃》（2009）

Amy Tan（谭恩美，1952— ）
 The Joy Luck Club《喜福会》（1989）
 The Kitchen God's Wife《灶神娘娘》（1991）
 The Hundred Secret Senses《通灵女孩》（1995）
 The Bonesetter's Daughter《正骨师的女儿》（2001）

附录二
常用文学术语

AESTHETICISM（唯美主义）

A literary and artistic tendency of the late 19th century which regards beauty as an end in itself and attempts to separate art from real life and moral, didactic or political purposes. Art for art's sake is their slogan. Walter Pater and Oscar Wilde are representatives of aestheticism in England.

ALEXANDRINE（亚历山大诗行）

An iambic hexameter line—that is, a poetic line consisting of six iambic feet. The last line of a Spenserian stanza is an alexandrine. The following alexandrine is from a stanza of John Keats's *The Eve of St. Agnes*:

$\smile$, $\smile$, $\smile$, $\smile$, $\smile$, $\smile$

She sighed for Agnes dreams, the sweetest of the year.

ALLEGORY（寓言）

A story or visual image with a symbolic meaning, distinct from and more important than, the literal meaning. An allegory often uses personifications to convey its meanings, in which abstract ideas or moral qualities are given human shape. John Bunyan's *The Pilgrim's Progress* is one of the most famous allegories in English literature.

ALLUSION（用典）

The reference to some event, person, place or artistic work. It is commonly used in poetry. The classical myths and works provide the major sources for allusions. In *To Helen*, Edgar Allan Poe alludes to the divine figures in Greek mythology to show his admiration for the lady he truly cares about:

Helen, thy beauty is to me
Like those Nicean barks of yore,
That gently, o'er a perfumed sea,
The weary, way-worn wanderer bore
To his own native shore.

Helen is a beautiful woman in Greek mythology, whose love for Paris a prince of Troy is the cause of the Trojan War. The Trojan War lasted ten years with Troy destroyed. Odysseus is one of prominent Greek leaders, who spent ten more years getting back home. The meaning of the allusion is not explained by the poet but relies on the reader's familiarity with what is thus mentioned.

ANALOGY（类比）

A comparison made between two things to show the similarities between them. Analogies are often used for illustration (to explain something unfamiliar by comparing it to something familiar) or for argument (to persuade that what holds true for one thing holds true for the thing to which it is compared). Samuel Johnson draws an analogy for the sake of argument in his *Preface to Shakespeare* when he compares a work of art to a work of nature:

> As among the works of nature no man can properly call a river deep or a mountain high, without the knowledge of many mountains and many rivers; so in the productions of genius, nothing can be styled excellent till it has been compared with other works of the same kind.

ANTAGONIST（反面人物）

A person or force opposing the protagonist in a narrative; a rival of the hero or heroine. Famous antagonists in literature include Professor Moriarty, Sherlock Holmes's antagonist in Arthur Conan Doyle's detective stories, and the monster Grendel, Beowulf's antagonist in the Anglo-Saxon epic poem *Beowulf*.

ANTITHESIS（对照）

The balancing of two contrasting ideas, words, phrases, or sentences. An antithesis is often expressed in a balanced sentence, that is, a sentence in which identical or similar grammatical structure is used to express contrasting ideas. A famous example of antithesis is this line from Alexander Pope's *An Essay on Criticism*: "To err is human, to forgive divine."

APOSTROPHE（顿呼）

A figure of speech in which an absent or a dead person, an abstract quality, or something nonhuman is addressed directly. George Gordon Byron uses apostrophe in *Childe Harold's Pilgrimage* when he addresses the ocean: "Roll on, thou deep and dark blue Ocean—roll!"

BALLAD（民谣）

A story told in song, usually in 4-line stanzas, with the 2nd and 4th lines rhymed. In many countries, the folk ballad was one of the earliest forms of literature. Folk ballads have no known authors. They were transmitted orally from generation to generation and were not set down in writing until centuries after they were first sung. The subject matter of folk ballads stems from the everyday life of the common people. The most popular subjects, often tragic, are disappointed love, jealousy, revenge, sudden disaster, and deeds of adventure and daring. Devices commonly used in ballads are the refrain, incremental repetition, and code language. A later form of ballad is the literary ballad, which imitates the style of the folk ballad. The most famous English literary ballad is Samuel Taylor Coleridge's *The Rime of the Ancient Mariner*.

BALLAD STANZA（民谣体诗节）

The usual form of the folk ballad and its literary imitations, consisting of a quatrain in which the first and third lines have four stresses while the second and fourth have three stresses. Usually only the second and fourth lines rhyme. The rhythm is basically iambic. For example, in Robert Burns's *A Red Red Rose*:

> O my Luve's like a red, red rose,
>   That's newly sprung in June;
> O my Luve's like the melodie
>   That's sweetly played in tune.

BLANK VERSE（无韵诗）

Verse written in unrhymed iambic pentameter. Blank verse is used in some of the greatest English poetry, including that of William Shakespeare and John Milton. Henry Howard wrote the first English blank verse, Marlowe first made it the principal instrument of English drama, while Milton first used it in non-dramatic works, for example *Paradise Lost*.

BYRONIC HERO（拜伦式英雄）

Characters in George Gordon Byron's works, usually men of noble birth, with fiery passions and unbending will. They rise against tyranny and injustice, express the poet's own ideal of freedom, but they are merely lone fighters striving for personal freedom and some individualistic ends. Don Juan is a typical Byronic hero.

CARPE DIEM TRADITION（只争朝夕诗歌传统，亦译及时行乐诗歌传统）

A tradition dating back to classical Greek and Latin poetry and particularly popular among English Cavalier poets. Carpe diem means, literally, "seize the day"—that is, "live for today". The carpe diem theme is epitomized in a line from Robert Herrick's *To the Virgins, to Make Much of Time*: "Gather ye rosebuds while ye may". But carpe diem is not necessarily totally passive. It is an attitude toward life.

CLASSICISM（古典主义）

A movement or tendency in art, literature, or music that reflects the principles manifested in the art of ancient Greece and Rome. Classicism emphasizes the traditional and the universal, and places value on reason, clarity, balance and order. Classicism, with its concern for reason and universal themes, is traditionally opposed to romanticism, which is concerned with emotions and personal themes. Alexander Pope is a famous representative in English classicism.

CLIMAX（层进法）

The point of greatest intensity, interest, or suspense in a narrative. The climax usually marks a story's turning point. The action leading to the climax and the simultaneous increase of tension in the plot are known as the rising action. In William Shakespeare's *Macbeth*, the climax occurs during the banquet scene in Act Three. Macbeth, overcome by guilt and nervousness over the murders of Duncan the King and Banquo, sees the ghost of Banquo in the banquet hall. This tense moment is the play's turning point. After this moment, events turn against Macbeth and lead to his final downfall. Events that occur after the climax are referred to as the falling action, or resolution. The term crisis is sometimes used interchangeably with climax.

COMEDY（喜剧）

A play typically dealing with common people and dominated by a light tone that encourages laughter (or at least amusement or entertainment), which ends happily, often with the uniting of a pair of young lovers. The comic protagonist is usually a person of ordinary character and ability. Comedies are often concerned, at least in part, with exposing human folly, and frequently depict the overthrow of rigid social fashions and customs. Wit, humor, and a sense of festivity are found in many comedies. Shakespeare wrote many comedies, such as *Twelfth Night*, *The Merchant of Venice* and *As You Like It*, etc.

CONCEIT（奇喻）

A kind of metaphor that makes a comparison between two startlingly different things. A conceit may be a brief metaphor, but it usually provides the framework for an entire poem. An especially unusual and intellectual kind of conceit is the metaphysical conceit, used by certain 17th-century poets, such as John Donne. In *A Valediction: Forbidding Mourning*, Donne compares the souls of lovers to compasses in an extended simile that begins with these lines:

If they be two, they are two so
As stiff twin compasses are two,
Thy soul the fixed foot, makes no show
To move, but doth, if th' other do.

COUPLET（双偶句）

The rhymed pair of poetic lines. The most commonly used form is Heroic Couplet, a rhymed pair of iambic pentameter lines. It was established by Chaucer as a major English verse form for narrative and other kinds of non-dramatic poetry which dominated English poetry of the 18th century notably in the poetry of Pope, before declining in importance in the early 19th century. Here is an example from *The Rape of the Lock*:

But when to mischief mortals bend their will,
How soon they find fit instruments of ill!

CRITICAL REALISM（批判现实主义）

English critical realism flourished in the 1840s and the early 1850s, which found the best expression in novel. The critical realists vividly described the English society with artistic skill. They showed hatred for the ruling classes and sympathy for the poor. Humor and satire abound in their works where they also expressed democratic and humanistic ideas. However, they were unable to find a good solution to the social problems. Charles Dickens, William Makepeace Thackeray, Brontë sisters, Elizabeth Cleghorn Gaskell, and George Eliot are all its representatives. Among them Dickens is the greatest.

DÉNOUEMENT（结局）

The outcome of a plot. The dénouement is that part of a play, short story, novel, or narrative poem in which conflicts are resolved or unraveled, and mysteries and secrets connected with the plot are explained.

DICTION（措辞）

A writer's choice of words, particularly for clarity, effectiveness, and precision. A writer's diction can be formal or informal, abstract or concrete, simple or ornate. In choosing "the right word", writers must think of their subject and their audience. Words that are appropriate in informal dialogue would not always be appropriate in a piece of formal writing.

DRAMATIC MONOLOGUE（戏剧独白）

A kind of narrative poem in which one character speaks to one or more listeners whose replies are not given in the poem. The occasion is usually a crucial one in the speaker's life, and the dramatic monologue reveals the speaker's personality as well as the incident that is the subject of the poem. Dramatic monologues occurred frequently in Renaissance poetry, especially in metaphysical poetry. But people often consider the best example of dramatic monologue is *My Last Duchess* written by Robert Browning.

ELEGY（挽诗）

A poem of mourning, usually over the death of an individual. It may also be a lament over the passing of life and beauty or a meditation on the nature of death. An elegy is a type of lyric poem, usually formal in language and structure, and solemn or even melancholy in tone. Among the best are Thomas Gray's *Elegy Written in the Country Churchyard* and John Milton's *Lycidas*. But John Donne wrote some elegies which were actually love poems.

EPIC（史诗）

A long narrative poem of great scale and grand style telling about the deeds of a great hero and reflecting the values of the society from which it originated. Many epics were drawn from an oral tradition and were transmitted by song and recitation before they were written down. Two of the most famous epics of Western civilization are Homer's *Iliad* and *Odyssey*. The great epic of the Middle Ages is the *Divine Comedy* by the Italian poet Dante. The Anglo-Saxon poem *Beowulf* is the oldest surviving national epic poem.

EPIGRAM（隽语）

A short, witty, pointed statement often in the form of a poem. Here is an example from Alexander Pope's *Essay on Criticism*:

Be not the first by whom the new are tried,
Nor yet the last to lay the old aside.

EPIGRAPH（题词）

A quotation or motto at the beginning of a chapter, book, short story, or poem that makes the point about the work. One of the epigraphs preceding Thomas Sterns Eliot's *The Hollow Men* is a reference to Guy Fawkes Day, when English children carry stuffed effigies, or likenesses, of the traitor Fawkes. The epigraph serves as a motif throughout the poem for the ineffectuality Eliot identifies with his generation of "stuffed men."

EPILOGUE（后记）

A short addition or conclusion at the end of a literary work. In the epilogue to *Pygmalion*, George Bernard Shaw tells his readers what happened to his characters after the conclusion of the play.

EPIPHANY（顿悟）

A moment of illumination, usually occurring at or near the end of a work. In James Joyce's story *Araby*, the epiphany occurs when the narrator realizes, with sudden clarity, that his dream of visiting the splendid bazaar has resulted only in frustration and disillusion.

EPITAPH（碑文）

An inscription on a gravestone or a short poem written in memory of someone who has died. Many epitaphs are actually epigrams, or short witty sayings, and are not intended for serious use as monument inscriptions.

Here is an example:

Life is a jest, and all things show it.
I thought so once; but now I know it.
  —John Gay, *My Own Epitaph*

ESSAY（随笔）

A piece of prose writing, usually short, that deals with a subject in a limited way and expresses a particular point of view. An essay is never a comprehensive treatment of a subject (the word comes from a French word, essai, meaning "attempt" or "try"). An essay may be serious or humorous, tightly organized or rambling, restrained or emotional.

The two general classifications of essay are the informal essay (also called the familiar or personal essay) and the formal essay. An informal essay is usually brief and is written as if the writer is talking informally to the reader about some topic, using a conversational style and a personal or humorous tone. In an informal essay, the writer might digress from the topic at hand, or express some amusing, startling, or absurd opinions. In general, an informal essay reveals as much about the personality of its author as it does about its subject. By contrast, a formal essay is tightly organized, dignified in style, and serious in tone. Francis Bacon's *Of Studies* is an example of a formal essay and must be learned by heart.

FABLE（寓言）

A brief story that is told to present a moral, or practical lesson. The characters of fables are often animals that speak and act like human beings.

FARCE（滑稽剧）

A type of comedy based on a ridiculous situation, often with stereotyped characters. The humor in a farce is largely slapstick—that is, it often involves crude physical action. The characters in a farce are often the butts of practical jokes: flying cream-pies hit them in the face and beds cave in on them.

FLASHBACK（倒叙）

A scene in a short story, novel, play, or narrative poem that interrupts the action to show an event that happened earlier. Most narratives present events in chronological order—that is, as they occur in time. Sometimes, however, a writer interrupts this natural sequence of events and "flashes back" to tell the reader what happened earlier in the story or in a character's life. Often a flashback takes the form of a character's recollection. Katherine Mansfield, in *A Dill Pickle*, and Elizabeth Bowen, in *Tears, Idle Tears*, both use this technique.

FORESHADOWING（伏笔）

The use of hints or clues in a narrative to suggest what will happen later. Writers use foreshadowing to create interest and to build suspense. Sometimes foreshadowing also prepares the reader for the ending of the story. In Graham Greene's *Across the Bridge*, the ending of the story is foreshadowed in the fifth paragraph when the narrator refers to Mr. Calloway's story as a tragedy.

FREE VERSE（自由诗）

Verse that has either no metrical pattern or an irregular pattern. Although most free verses belong to the nineteenth and twentieth centuries, it can be found in earlier literature, particularly in the Psalms of the Bible. But do not totally believe that free verses have no rhythm and rhyme—they are merely different from traditional poems.

HYPERBOLE（夸张）

A figure of speech using exaggeration, or overstatement, for special effect. In Robert Burns's *A Red, Red Rose*, the speaker expresses his constant love for his beloved girl:

> Till a' the seas gang dry, my Dear,
> And the rocks melt wi' the sun;
> O I will love thee still, my Dear,
> While the sands o' life shall run.

Surely the exaggerated statement is not meant to be taken literally, but we are deeply moved by the passion between the lines.

IMAGERY（意象）

Words or phrases that create pictures, or images, in the reader's mind. Images are primarily visual, as in these lines from William Wordsworth's *Lines Composed a Few Miles Above Tintern Abbey*:

> Once again I see
> These hedgerows, hardly hedgerows, little lines
> Of sportive wood run wild: these pastoral farms,
> Green to the very door; and wreaths of smoke
> Sent up, in silence, from among the trees!

Images can appeal to other senses as well: touch, taste, smell, and hearing.

IMAGISM（意象主义）

An Anglo-American poetic movement flourishing in the 1910s. Led at first by Ezra Pound, the Imagists shake off the conventional meters and emphasize the use of common speech, new rhythms and clear images. Hilda Doolittle is one of the representative writers.

IRONY（反讽）

A contrast or an incongruity between what is stated and what is really meant, or between what is expected to happen and what actually happens. Three kinds of irony are (1) verbal irony, in which a writer or speaker says one thing and means something entirely different; (2) dramatic irony, in which a reader or an audience perceives something that a character in the story or play does not know; (3) irony of situation, in which the writer shows a discrepancy between the expected results of some action or situation and its actual results.

An example of verbal irony occurs in this speech from *Macbeth*. Lennox, a Scottish nobleman, tells another Lord how Macbeth responded to Duncan's murder by killing the two grooms:

How it did grieve Macbeth! Did he not straight
In pious rage the two delinquents tear,
That were the slaves of drink and thralls of sleep?
Was not that nobly done?
　　(III, 6,11-14)

The real meaning of this speech, of course, is that Macbeth acted to cover his own crimes.

An example of dramatic irony can be found in Scene 6 of Act 1. We know that Macbeth and Lady Macbeth are plotting to murder Duncan, but Duncan does not know that he is walking into a trap. The irony is intensified by the opening lines of the scene in which Duncan and Banquo remark on the serenity and loveliness of the setting.

In Thomas Hardy's *The Three Strangers*, an irony of situation occurs when the two strangers at the chimney corner turn out to be the hangman and his intended victim.

KENNING（复合比喻）

In Old English poetry, an elaborate phrase that describes persons, things, or events in a metaphorical and indirect way. The Anglo-Saxon poem *The Seafarer* contains kennings, such as "whales' home" for the sea.

LYRIC（抒情诗）

A poem, usually a short one that expresses a speaker's personal thoughts or feelings. Elegy, ode and sonnet are all forms of lyric poetry. As its Greek name indicates, a lyric was originally a poem sung to the accompaniment of a lyre, and lyrics to this day have retained a melodic quality. Lyrics may express a range of emotions and reflections: Robert Herrick's *To the Virgins, to Make Much of Time* reflects on the brevity of life and the need to live for the moment, while Thomas Stearns Eliot's *Preludes* observes the sordidness and depression of modern life.

MASQUE（假面剧）

An elaborate and spectacular dramatic entertainment that was popular among the English aristocracy in the late sixteenth and early seventeenth centuries. Masques were written as dramatic poems and made use of songs, dances, colorful costumes, and startling stage effects.

MELODRAMA（情节剧）

A drama that has stereotyped characters, exaggerated emotions, and a conflict that pits an all-good hero or heroine against an all-evil villain. The good characters always win and the evil ones are always punished. Originally, melodramas were so called because melodies accompanied certain actions (*melos* means "song" in Greek). Also, each character in a melodrama had a theme melody, which was played each time he or she made an appearance on stage.

METAPHOR（隐喻）

A figure of speech that makes a comparison between two things that are basically dissimilar. "Life is a dream", "Life is a vale of tears", and "Life is a hard road" are all examples of metaphor. Unlike a simile, a metaphor does not use a connective word such as "like", "as", or "resemble" in making the comparison. Many metaphors are implied, or suggested. An implied metaphor does not directly state that one thing is another, different thing. Alfred Tennyson uses an implied metaphor in these lines from *Crossing the Bar*:

> I hope to see my Pilot face to face
> When I have crossed the bar.

By capitalizing the word Pilot, the poet implies a comparison between the maker and the pilot of his ship.

An extended metaphor is a metaphor that is extended throughout a poem. In *Crossing the Bar*, Tennyson compares death to a voyage at sea, at the end of which he will meet the "Pilot".

A dead metaphor is a metaphor that has become so commonplace that it seems literal rather than figurative. Some examples are the foot of a hill, the head of the class, a point in time, and the leg of a chair.

A mixed metaphor is the use of two or more inconsistent metaphors in one expression. When they are examined, mixed metaphors make no sense. Mixed metaphors are often unintentionally humorous: "The storm of protest was nipped in the bud" or "To hold the fort, he'd have to shake a leg."

METAPHYSICAL POETRY（玄学派诗歌）

The poetry of a group of 17th-century English poets including John Donne, Andrew Marvell, George Herbert, Henry Vaughan and Richard Crashaw with John Donne the leader. Metaphysical poetry is notable for surprising conceits, strange paradoxes and far-fetched imagery. But none of the above-mentioned poets knew they were metaphysical poets.

METER（格律）

A generally regular pattern of stressed and unstressed syllables in poetry. Meter is the rhythm and essential feature of poetry. There are various types of meter. The four popular types in English are illustrated as follows.

(1) Iamb（iambic, *adj*., 抑扬格 ˇ ´）

For example,

She walks in beauty, like the night

(2) Trochee（trochaic, *adj*., 扬抑格 ´ ˇ）

For example,

Tell me not, in mournful numbers,

(3) Anapest（anapestic, *adj*., 抑抑扬格 ˇ ˇ ´）

For example,

And a sound of a voice that is still!

(4) Dactyl（dactylic, *adj*., 扬抑抑格 ´ˇˇ）

For example,

　　´ ˇ ˇ ´ ˇ ˇ
　　Gently and Humanly

Except the four major types of meter, there are also other variations:

(5) Spondee（扬扬格 ´ ´）

For example,

　　　´　´
　　Rough winds do shake the darling buds of May,

(6) Pyrrhic（抑抑格 ˇ ˇ）

For example,

　　　　　ˇ ˇ
　　Thou art more lovely and more temperate.

METONYMY（转喻）

A figure of speech in which something very closely associated with a thing is used to stand for or suggest the thing itself. "Three sails came into the harbor" is an example of metonymy; the word "sails" stands for the ships themselves. Other common examples of metonymy are crown to mean a king, hardhat to mean a construction worker, and White House to mean the President. William Shakespeare uses metonymy in the following lines from his play *Cymbeline*:

　　The scepter, learning, and physic, must
　　All follow this, and come to dust.

The words "scepter", "learning", and "physic" stand for the king, the scholar, and the doctor.

MIRACLE PLAY（奇迹剧）

A popular religious drama of medieval England. Miracle plays are based on stories of the saints or on sacred history.

MODERNISM（现代主义）

A movement of experiments in new technique in writing, which in English literature prevailed during the 1920s and 1930s. The major landmarks are James Joyce's *Ulysses* and Thomas Stearns Eliot's *The Waste Land*.

MORALITY PLAY（道德剧）

An outgrowth of miracle plays. Morality plays were popular in the fifteenth and sixteenth centuries. In them, virtues and vices are personified.

MOTIF（主旨）

A recurring feature (such as a name, an image, or a phrase) in a work of literature. A motif generally contributes in some way to the theme of a short story, novel, poem, or play. For example, a motif used by David Herbert Lawrence in his story *The Rocking-Horse Winner* is the word luck. The main character of the story, a boy named Paul, discovers that he has the power to predict the winner in a horse race. However, this becomes an ironic kind of luck, for Paul grows obsessed with his power and is finally destroyed by it.

At times, motif is used to refer to some commonly used plot or character type in literature. The "ugly duckling motif" refers to a plot that involves the transformation of a plain-looking person into a beauty. Two other commonly used motifs are the "Romeo and Juliet motif" (about doomed lovers) and the "Horatio Alger motif" (about the office clerk who becomes the corporation president).

MYTH（神话）

A story, often about immortals and sometimes connected with religious rituals, that is intended to give meaning to the mysteries of the world. In myths, gods and goddesses are usually identified with the immense powers of the universe: in the Greek myths, Zeus is associated with the sky, Hades with the underworld, Poseidon with the sea, Apollo with the sun, Athena with wisdom, Ares with war. But the gods are also given the forms and feelings of human beings. Thus, myths make it possible for people to understand and deal with things that they cannot control and often cannot see.

A body of related myths that is accepted by a people is known as its mythology. A mythology tells a people what it is most concerned about: where it came from, who its gods are, what its most sacred rituals are, and what its destiny is.

NARRATIVE POEM（叙事诗）

A poem that tells a story. It is always told by a narrator. Narrative poetry is written with the poet standing outside his or her material, representing human experiences by what is often called the "objective" method. It aims primarily at telling a story in a sequence of events. Epic, ballad and metrical romance are three main categories of narrative poetry.

NARRATOR（叙事者）

One who narrates, or tells, a story. A story may be told by a first-person narrator, someone who is either a major or minor character in the story. Or a story may be told by a third-person narrator, someone who is not in the story at all.

The word narrator can also refer to a character in a drama who guides the audience through the play, often commenting on the action and sometimes participating in it. In Thornton Wilder's play *Our Town*, the Stage Manager serves as the narrator.

NATURALISM（自然主义）

A literary trend prevailing in Europe in the second half of the 19th century which focuses on the "true to life" description and exact reproduction of real life, including all its details without any selection. Naturalist writers usually write the lives of the poor and oppressed, but they can only represent the external appearance instead of the inner essence of real life. It can be taken as an extreme form of realism. George Gissing's *New Grub Street* is an example in English.

NEO-CLASSICISM（新古典主义）

A revival in the seventeenth and eighteenth centuries of classical standards of order, balance, and harmony in literature. John Dryden and Alexander Pope were major exponents of the neoclassical school.

NEO-ROMANTICISM（新浪漫主义）

A literary trend prevailing at the end of the 19th century which lays emphasis upon the invention of exciting adventures and fascinating stories to entertain the reading public instead of dealing with the social reality. Robert Louis Stevenson's *Treasure Island* is an example.

NOVEL（小说）

A book-length fictional prose narrative, having many characters and often a complex plot. Some important English novels are *Tom Jones* by Henry Fielding, *Pride and Prejudice* by Jane Austen, *Great Expectations* by Charles Dickens, and *Ulysses* by James Joyce.

ODE（颂诗）

A complex lyric poem of some length, dealing with a noble theme in a dignified manner and originally intended to be sung. Odes are often written for a special occasion, to honor a person or a season or to commemorate an event. John Keats is famous for his odes such as *Ode to a Nightingale*, *Ode on a Grecian Urn* and *To Autumn*.

ONOMATOPOEIA（拟声）

The use of a word whose sound in some degree imitates or suggests its meaning. The names of some birds are onomatopoetic, imitating the cry of the bird named: cuckoo, whippoorwill, owl, crow, towhee, bobwhite. Some onomatopoetic words are hiss, clang, rustle, and snap. In these lines from *The Rime of the Ancient Mariner*, Coleridge reproduces the fearful sounds of the land of ice:

It cracked and growled, and roared and howled
Like noises in a swound!
  (lines 61-62)

OTTAVA RIME（八行体诗节）

A form of eight-line stanza. The rhyme scheme is abababcc. *Don Juan* by George Gordon Byron is written in this form.

OXYMORON（矛盾修饰）

A figure of speech that combines opposite or contradictory ideas or terms. An oxymoron suggests a paradox, but it does so very briefly, usually in two or three words, such as "living death," "dear enemy," "sweet sorrow," and "wise fool."

PARADOX（似非而是）

A statement that reveals a kind of truth, although it seems at first to be self-contradictory and untrue. One of the best examples appears in John Milton's *On His Deceased Wife*.

But O, as to embrace me she inclined,
I waked, she fled, and day brought back my night.

By the famous paradox in the last line, Milton shows his great happiness in seeing his wife in his dream and his deep sorrow when he has lost her in reality.

PARALLELISM（排比）

The use of phrases, clauses, or sentences that are similar or complementary in structure or in meaning. Parallelism is a form of repetition. In Alfred Tennyson's poem *Sweet and Low*, the first and third lines of the first stanza are parallel in structure:

Sweet and low, sweet and low
Wind of the western sea,

Low, low, breathe and blow,
Wind of the western sea.

PARODY（戏仿）

The humorous imitation of a work of literature, art, or music. A parody often achieves its humorous effect through the use of exaggeration or mockery. In literature, parody can be made of a plot, a character, a writing style, a sentiment or theme. The poet Algernon Charles Swinburne parodies his own verse in a humorous poem called *Nephelidia*. In these lines, Swinburne is mocking a kind of lush verse that makes excessive use of alliteration:

Pallid and pink as the palm of the flag flower that
flickers with fear of the flies as they float,

PASTORAL（牧歌）

A type of poem that deals in an idealized way with shepherds and rustic life. It describes the loves and sorrows of shepherds, and the rustic innocence and idleness. A popular pastoral is Christopher Marlowe's *The Passionate Shepherd to His Love*.

PATHOS（悲情）

The quality in a work of literature or art that arouses the reader's feelings of pity, sorrow, or compassion for a character. The term is usually used to refer to situations in which innocent characters suffer through no fault of their own. An example of a scene with pathos is Scene 2 in Act 4 of *Macbeth* in which Lady Macduff and her son are ruthlessly murdered by Macbeth's assassins.

PERSONIFICATION（拟人）

A figure of speech in which something nonhuman is given human qualities. Percy Bysshe Shelley, in his *Ode to the West Wind*, says that "O wild West Wind, thou breath of Autumn's being", as if Autumn were a human that had breath. In this famous ode, he further compares the west wind to both destroyer and preserver, as if the west wind were a powerful man that could destroy all the old and decayed, and preserve the new and fresh. The west wind represents the great power of the revolutionary people. The comparison makes this concept vivid and alive.

PLOT（情节）

The sequence of events or actions in a short story, novel, play, or narrative poem. Plots may be simple or complicated, loosely constructed or close-knit. But every plot is made up of a series of incidents that are related to one another.

Conflict, a struggle of some kind, is the most important element of plot. Conflict may be external or internal, and there may be more than one form of conflict in a work. As the plot advances, we learn how the conflict is resolved, either through the action or through major changes in the attitudes or personalities of the characters.

Action is generally introduced by the exposition, information essential to understand the situation. The action rises to a crisis, or climax. This movement is called the rising action. The falling action, which follows the crisis, shows a reversal of fortune for the protagonist. In a tragedy this reversal leads to disaster; in a comedy, it leads to a happy ending.

The denouement or resolution is the moment when the conflict ends and the outcome of the action is clear.

POINT OF VIEW（视角）

The vantage point from which a narrative is told. There are two basic points of view: first-person and third-person. In the first-person point of view, the story is told by one of the characters in his or her own words. The first-person point of view is limited, since the reader is told only what this character knows and observes. Here is an example of first-person point of view from Jonathan Swift's *Gulliver's Travels*: "The King was struck with horror at the description I had given of those terrible engines, and the proposal I had made. He was amazed how so impotent and groveling an insect as I (these were his expressions) could entertain such inhuman ideas..."

In the third-person point of view, the narrator is not a character in the story. The narrator may be an omniscient, or "all-knowing", observer who can describe and comment on all the characters and actions in the story. Thomas Hardy's *The Three Strangers* is written from a third-person omniscient point of view: "Shepherdess Fennel fell back upon the intermediate plan of mingling short dances with short periods of talk and singing, so as to hinder any ungovernable rage in either."

On the other hand, the third-person narrator might tell a story from the point of view of only one character in the story, as Virginia Woolf does in *The New Dress*. All the action in that story is told by the third-person narrator, from the limited point of view of Mable Waring.

PROTAGONIST（主要人物）

The central character of a drama, novel, short story, or narrative poem. The protagonist is the character on whom the action centers and with whom the reader sympathizes most. Usually the protagonist strives against an opposing force, or antagonist, to accomplish something. The protagonist can be either heroic or ordinary, good or bad. For example, Beowulf is brave and good. Macbeth is noble and honorable at first, but becomes increasingly hateful.

PSALM（赞美诗）

A song or lyric poem in praise of God. The term usually refers to the one hundred and fifty sacred lyrics in the Book of Psalms in the Bible. Now any praise of anything may be named "psalm", for example, *A Psalm of Life* written by Henry Wadsworth Longfellow.

PUN（双关）

The use of a word or phrase to suggest two or more meanings at the same time. Puns are generally humorous. In Act 2, Scene 3 of *Macbeth*, the Porter plays on the two meanings of the word "goose" in this line: "Come in tailor, here you may roast your goose." The goose was a tailor's pressing iron.

REALISM（现实主义）

The attempt in literature and art to represent life as it really is, without sentimentalizing or idealizing it. Realistic writing often depicts the everyday life and speech of ordinary people. The rise and growth of the realistic novel is the most prominent achievement in the 18th-century English literature. Daniel Defoe, Jonathan Swift and Henry Fielding are its representatives.

REFRAIN（叠句）

A word, phrase, line, or group of lines repeated regularly in a poem, usually at the end of each stanza. Refrains are often used in ballads and narrative poems to create a songlike rhythm and to help build suspense. Refrains can also serve to emphasize a particular idea. A familiar example is *Auld Lang Syne* written by Robert Burns. Here the second stanza is the refrain that is repeated in the poem and song.

> Should auld acquaintance be forgot,
> And never brought to mind?
> Should auld acquaintance be forgot,
> And days o'lang syne?
>
> For auld lang syne, my dear,
> For auld lang syne,
> We'll tak'a cup o' kindness yet,
> For auld lang syne.

A modern example of the use of refrain appears in Dylan Thomas's *Do Not Go Gentle into That Good Night*.

RENAISSANCE（文艺复兴）

The "rebirth" of literature, art and learning that progressively transformed European culture from the mid-14th century in Italy to the mid-17th century in England and other countries, strongly influenced by the rediscovery of classical

Greek and Latin literature, and promoted by the development of printing. In the Renaissance period, man began to live for his own sake more than for God and for the future world. The Renaissance is commonly held to mark the close of the Middle Ages and the beginning of the modern Western world.

RHYME（韵）

The repetition of certain sounds in words that appear close to each other in a poem, usually at the end of poetic lines. For example: river/shiver, song/long, leap/deep. Approximate rhyme is rhyme in which only the final consonant sounds of the words are identical (as opposed to exact rhyme). Cook/look is an exact rhyme; cook/lack is an approximate rhyme. To poetry composition, rhyme, wherever it may exist, is quite important, though we cannot say rhyme is the soul of poetry.

A. Types of rhyme according to its position
(1) End rhyme（尾韵）

The repetition of the last stressed vowel in a line and all the following syllables. End rhyme is the commonest type of rhyme in English poetry after the medieval period. Here is an example from William Blake's *The Tyger*:

> In what distant deeps or skies
> Burnt the fire of thine eyes?
> On what wings dare he aspire?
>   What the hand, dare seize the fire?

(2) Internal rhyme（行内韵）

If the rhyme occurs within a line, it is called internal rhyme. Here is an example from *The Rime of the Ancient Mariner*: "The guests are *met*, the feast is *set*".

B. Types of rhyme according to its structure
(1) Masculine rhyme（阳韵）

The repetition of one syllable at the end of respective lines. For example,

Under the green wood tr*ee*
Who loves to lie with m*e*.

(2) Feminine rhyme（阴韵）

A rhyme that matches two or more syllables, usually at the end of respective lines, in which the final syllable or syllables are unstressed. Feminine rhyme is relatively rare in English poetry and usually appears as a special effect.

C. Other types of rhyme

Besides the above rhymes, there are other types of rhyme frequently used in English poetry as follows.

(1) Alliteration（also called head rhyme or initial rhyme, 头韵）

The repetition of the same sounds—usually initial consonants of words or of stressed syllables—in any sequence of neighboring words. Although alliteration sometimes appears in prose, it is mainly a poetic device. For example, in Shelley's *Ode to the West Wind*: "O *w*ild *W*est *W*ind, thou *b*reath of Autumn's *b*eing."

(2) Assonance（腹韵，亦称元音韵）

The repetition of vowel sounds within a noticeable range. Assonance occurs in words as fight/bike; fat/map; morning/falling. In poetry, it goes as follows in George Gordon Byron's *She Walks in Beauty*:

She walks in beauty, l*i*ke the n*i*ght
Of cloudless cl*i*mes and starry sk*i*es.

(3) Consonance（辅音韵）

The repetition of consonant sounds before and after different vowels. Consonance occurs in words as *bl*ock/*bl*ack; *cr*eak/*cr*oak.

(4) Eye rhyme or sight rhyme（眼韵）

Eye rhyme occurs when the spelling of the rhyming element match, but the sound does not. For example,

Come live with me and be my L*ove*,
And we will all the pleasures pr*ove*.

D. Rhyme scheme（押韵格式，亦称韵式或韵制）

The pattern of rhymes in a poem. English poetry has various rhyme schemes. Here we take the 4-line stanza as an example to illustrate its diverse patterns.

(1) abab（crossed rhyme / alternating rhyme, 隔行押韵 / 交叉韵）

For example,

Gather ye rosebuds while ye may,
Old time is still a-flying;
And this same flower that smiles today,
Tomorrow will be dying.

(2) aabb（双偶四行）

For example,

Come live with me and be my Love,
And we will all the pleasures prove
That valleys, groves, hills and fields,
Woods, or steepy mountain yields.

(3) aaaa（通韵，一韵到底）

For example,

The woods are lovely, dark, and deep,
But I have promises to keep,
And miles to go before I sleep.
And miles to go before I sleep.

(4) abba（enclosed rhyme, 抱韵）

For example,

I envy not in any moods
The captive void of noble rage,
The linnet born within the cage,
That never knew the summer woods;

(5) aaba（Tang poetry rhyme, 唐诗韵）

For example, the first three stanzas of *Stopping by Woods on a Snowy Evening* written by Robert Frost:

Whose woods these are I think I know.
His house is in the village, though;
He will not see me stopping here
To watch his woods fill up with snow.

My little horse must think it queer
To stop without a farmhouse near
Between the woods and frozen lake
The darkest evening of the year.

He gives his harness bells a shake
To ask if there is some mistake.
The only other sound's the sweep
Of easy wind and downy flake.

ROMANCE（骑士文学；传奇文学）

Any imaginative literature in verse or prose that deals with idealized characters' heroic adventures in some remote setting. Originally, the term referred to a medieval tale dealing with the loves and adventures of kings, queens, knights, and ladies, and including unlikely or supernatural happenings. *Sir Gawain and the Green Knight* is the best of the medieval romances. John Keats's *The Eve of St. Agnes* is one of the greatest metrical romances ever written.

ROMANTICISM（浪漫主义）

A movement that flourished in literature, philosophy, music, and art in Western culture during most of the 19th century, beginning as a revolt against classicism. There have been many varieties of romanticism in many different times and places. It prevailed in England during the period 1798-1832. Many of the ideas of English romanticism were first expressed by the poets William Wordsworth and Samuel Taylor Coleridge. But before William Wordsworth stated his manifesto of Romantic poetry, William Blake and Robert Burns had already broken with classicism and begun to write Romantic poems. Walter Scott is also a great Romantic poet.

SATIRE（讽刺）

A kind of writing that holds up to ridicule or contempt the weaknesses and wrongdoings of individuals, groups, institutions, or humanity in general. The aim of satirists is to set a moral standard for society, and they attempt to persuade the reader to see their point of view through the force of laughter. The most famous satirical work in English literature is Jonathan Swift's *Gulliver's Travels*. In the distant land of Brobdingnag, where people are twelve times as tall as a normal human being, Gulliver is brought before the King to describe the English people. Swift satirizes the English people through the King's response:

> He was perfectly astonished with the historical account I gave him of our affairs during the last century, protesting it was only a heap of conspiracies, rebellions, murders, massacres, revolutions, banishments; the very worst effects that avarice, faction, hypocrisy, perfidiousness, cruelty, rage, madness, hatred, envy, lust, malice, and ambition could produce.

SENTIMENTALISM（感伤主义）

A movement popular in the poetry and novels in the latter part of the 18th century. The writers regarded sentiment as a sort of relief for the social evils and a mild protest against the social injustice. They advocated that sentiment should take the place of reason. Sentimental poetry is represented by Edward Young's *Night Thoughts* and Thomas Gray's *Elegy Written in a Country Churchyard*. Samuel Richardson's *Pamela* and *Clarissa*, Oliver Goldsmith's *The Vicar of Wakefield*; and Laurence Sterne's *Tristram Shandy* are all sentimental novels.

SETTING（背景）

The time and place in which the events in a short story, novel, play or narrative poem occur. A setting may serve simply as the physical background of a story, or a skillful writer may use setting to establish a particular atmosphere, which in turn contributes to the plot and theme of the story.

SIMILE（明喻）

A comparison made between two things through the use of a specific word of comparison, such as "like", "as", "than", or "resembles". The comparison must be between two essentially unlike things. To say "Susan is like her grandmother" is not to use a simile, but to say "Susan is like a golden flower" is to use a simile. In *To a Skylark*, Percy Bysshe Shelley uses a simile to describe the flight of the bird:

> Higher still and higher
> From the earth thou springest
> Like a cloud of fire...

SOLILOQUY（独白）

In drama, an extended speech delivered by a character alone on the stage. The character reveals his or her innermost thoughts and feelings directly to the audience, as if thinking aloud. One of the most famous soliloquies in literature occurs at the end of Shakespeare's *Macbeth*, when Macbeth, near defeat, expresses a bleak and bitter vision of life:

> Tomorrow, and tomorrow, and tomorrow,
> Creeps in this petty pace from day to day

To the last syllable of recorded time
And all our yesterdays have lighted fools
The way to dusty death. Out, out, brief candle!
Life's but a walking shadow, a poor player
That struts and frets his hour upon the stage
And then is heard no more. It is a tale
Told by an idiot, full of sound and fury,
Signifying nothing.

SONG（歌）

A short lyric poem with distinct musical qualities, normally written to be set to music. It expresses a simple but intense emotion. *She Walks in Beauty* by George Gordon Byron is a song. Robert Burns wrote over 300 songs. Percy Bysshe Shelley's *A Song* is a very good example:

A widow bird sat mourning for her love
Upon a wintry bough;
The frozen wind crept on above;
The freezing stream below.

There was no leaf upon the forest bare,
No flower upon the ground,
And little motion in the air
Except the mill-wheel's sound.

SONNET（十四行诗）

A lyric poem consisting of a single stanza of fourteen iambic pentameter lines linked by an intricate rhyme scheme. There are mainly two major patterns of rhyme scheme in sonnets written in English. The Italian or Petrarchan sonnet comprises an octave (eight lines) rhyming abbaabba and a sestet (six lines) rhyming cdecde or cdccdc. The transition from octave to sestet usually coincides with a "turn" in the argument or mood of the poem, usually in line 9. The

English or Shakespearean sonnet comprises three quatrains and a final couplet, rhyming abab cdcd efef gg. The "turn" comes with the final couplet, which may sometimes achieve an epigram. Yet, one can still find the influence of the Italian form, that is, in some sonnets the turn comes in line 9. There was one notable variant, the Spenserian sonnet, in which Spenser linked each quatrain to the next by a continuing rhyme: abab bcbc cdcd ee. There are three famous sonnet sequences in the Elizabethan Age in England: Spenser's *Amoretti*, Shakespeare's sonnets and Sidney's *Astrophel and Stella*. Sonnet later was used to describe other feelings rather than love alone.

SPENSERIAN STANZA（斯宾塞诗节）

The 9-line stanza form rhymed ababbcbcc, in which the first eight lines are in iambic pentameter while the ninth in iambic hexameter. It was invented by Edmund Spenser who first used it in his masterpiece *The Faerie Queene*.

SPRUNG RHYTHM（跳韵）

A term created by the poet Gerard Manley Hopkins to designate a variable kind of poetic meter in which a stressed syllable may be combined with any number of unstressed syllables. Poems with sprung rhythm have an irregular meter and are meant to sound like natural speech.

STEREOTYPE（类型人物）

A commonplace type or character that appears so often in literature that his or her nature is immediately familiar to the reader. Stereotypes, also called stock characters, always look and act the same way and reveal the same traits of character. Examples of stereotypes are the temperamental movie star, the talkative cab driver, the mad scientist, the villain with a waxed mustache, and the wisecracking, hard-boiled private detective.

STREAM OF CONSCIOUSNESS（意识流）

The style of writing that attempts to imitate the natural flow of the characters' mental and emotional reactions to external events rather than the events themselves. The school of "stream of consciousness" refers to a group of novelists in the 20th century who followed this style. James Joyce and Virginia Woolf are the two best-known novelists of this school.

SUSPENSE（悬念）

The quality of a story, novel, or drama that makes the reader or audience uncertain or tense about the outcome of events. Suspense makes readers ask, "What will happen next?" or "How will this work out?" and impels them to read on. Suspense is greatest when it focuses attention on a sympathetic character. Thus, the most familiar kind of suspense involves a character in mortal danger: hanging from the ledge of a tall building; tied to railroad tracks as a train approaches; or alone in an old house, ascending a staircase to open the attic door. But suspense may simply arise from curiosity, as when a character must make a decision, or seek an explanation for something.

SYMBOL（象征）

Any object, person, place, or action that means not only what it is, but something else as well, especially something larger than itself, such as a quality, an attitude, a belief, or a value. A symbol can be universal or unique. For example, as is known to all, a dove suggests peace and a rose signifies love. But in Donne's poetry, a flea, which is a common, ugly insect to others, can be the symbol of love.

SYMBOLISM（象征主义）

A literary movement that arose in France in the last half of the 19th century and that greatly influenced many English writers, particularly poets, of the 20th century. To Symbolist poets, an emotion is indefinite and therefore difficult to communicate. Symbolist poets tend to avoid any direct statement of meaning. Instead, they work through emotionally powerful symbols that suggest meaning and mood.

SYNECDOCHE（提喻）

A figure of speech that substitutes a part for a whole. An example is Thomas Stearns Eliot's use of "feet" and "hands" to stand for "people" in the poem *Preludes*.

TERZA RIMA（三行体诗节）

An Italian verse form consisting of a series of three-line stanzas in which the middle line of each stanza rhymes with the first and third lines of the following stanza, as follows: aba bcb cdc, etc. Percy Bysshe Shelley's *Ode to the West Wind* is written in *terza rima*. Here are the first two stanzas:

O wild West Wind, thou breath of Autumn's being,	a
Thou, from whose unseen presence the leaves dead,	b
Are driven, like ghosts from an enchanter fleeing,	a
Yellow, and black, and pale, and hectic red,	b
Pestilence-stricken multitudes: O thou,	c
Who chariotest to their dark wintry bed...	b

THEME（主题）

The general idea or insight about life that a writer wishes to express in a literary work. All the elements of a literary work—plot, setting, characterization, and figurative language—contribute to the development of its theme. A simple theme can often be stated in a single sentence. But sometimes a literary work is rich and complex, and a paragraph or even an essay is needed to state the theme. Not all literary works have a controlling theme. For example, the purpose of some simple ghost stories is to frighten the reader, and some detective stories seek only to thrill.

TONE（基调）

The attitude a writer takes toward his or her subject, characters, or audience. It could be happy or sad, gloomy or light, serious or satiric, calm or excited, etc. Tone is found in every kind of writing. It is created through the choice of words and details. In writing about his childhood in his poem *Fern Hill*, Dylan Thomas's tone is nostalgic. In *Preface to Shakespeare*, Samuel Johnson's tone is serious and admiring.

TRAGEDY（悲剧）

Traditionally, a play dominated by a serious tone, concerns characters of noble birth, perhaps a king like Oedipus or a prince like Hamlet, deals with profound issues, and usually concludes with the death of the leading character. Shakespeare is famous for his four great tragedies *Hamlet*, *Othello*, *King Lear* and *Macbeth*.

UNDERSTATEMENT（低调陈述）

An expression with less strength than what would be expected. This is not to be confused with euphemism, where a polite phrase is used in place of a harsher or more offensive expression. No strong feeling is shown in words when William Wordsworth says in his *She Dwelt Among the Untrodden Ways*: "But she is in her grave, and, oh, / The difference to me!" But everyone knows how mournful the speaker is and what great changes has happened after the death of Lucy.

VILLANELLE（维拉内拉诗）

An intricate verse form of French origin, consisting of several three-line stanzas and a concluding four-line stanza. The first and third lines of the first stanza are used as refrains in the succeeding stanzas and as the last two lines of the concluding stanza. Only two rhymes are allowed in a villanelle. A famous modern villanelle is Dylan Thomas's *Do Not Go Gentle into That Good Night*.

WIT（巧智）

A brilliance and quickness of perception combined with a cleverness of expression. In the 18th century, wit and nature were related-nature provided the rules of the universe; wit allowed these rules to be interpreted and expressed.

附录三

常用美国文学术语

AMERICAN ENLIGHTENMENT（美国启蒙运动）

The Age of Enlightenment (or simply the Enlightenment or Age of Reason) was a cultural movement of intellectuals beginning in late 17th-century Europe emphasizing reason and individualism rather than tradition. Its purpose was to reform society using reason, to challenge ideas grounded in tradition and faith, and to advance knowledge through the scientific method. It promoted scientific thought, skepticism and intellectual interchange. The Enlightenment was a revolution in human thought. The ideas of the Enlightenment continue to exert significant influence on the culture, politics and governments of the Western world. It was also very successful in America, where its influence was manifested in the works of Benjamin Franklin and Thomas Jefferson, among others. It played a major role in the American Revolution. The political ideals of the Enlightenment influenced the *Declaration of Independence* and the *Bill of Rights*.

AMERICAN NATURALISM（美国自然主义）

A new and harsher realism or pessimistic realism. Naturalism also came from Europe. Nature here means to put a man into a mechanized world, and the man is the victim of several forces hard to control in the world, including environment, heredity, serene and indifferent nature. Man is a weak, incompetent animal. He cannot control his fate. He is not free. This ideology of "framing up man" is the core of naturalistic literature. The milestones in the development of American naturalism were the publication of Emile Zola's novels in the 1870s and 1880s, the success of Stephen Crane's *The Red Badge of Courage* in the 1890s, and the continual appearance of Theodore Dreiser's *Sister Carrie* (1900),

The Financier (1912), and *An American Tragedy* (1925). In poetry, it was represented by Edgar Lee Masters's *Spoon River Anthology* (1915), etc.

AMERICAN PURITANISM（美国清教主义）

The beliefs and practices characteristic of Puritans (most of whom were Calvinists who wished to purify the Church of England of its Catholic aspects). The American Puritans accepted the doctrine and practice of predestination, original sin, total depravity, and limited atonement through a special infusion of grace from God. Strictness and austerity in conduct and religion are characteristic of American puritans. But due to the grim struggle for living in the new continent, they became more and more practical. American Puritanism was one of the most enduring shaping influences in American thought and American literature. It has become, to some extent, so much a state of mind, rather than a set of tenets, so much a part of the national cultural atmosphere that the Americans breathe. Without some understanding of Puritanism, there can be no real understanding of American culture and literature.

AMERICAN REALISM（美国现实主义）

In American literature, the Civil War brought the Romantic Period to an end. The Age of Realism came into existence. It came as a reaction against romanticism and sentimentalism. Realism turned from an emphasis on the strange toward a faithful rendering of the ordinary, a slice of life as it is really lived. It expresses the concern for commonplace and the low, and it offered an objective rather than an idealistic view of human nature and human experience. The arbiter of 19th-century realism in America was William Dean Howells. He defined realism as "nothing more and nothing less than the truthful treatment of material". The greatest of America's realists are Henry James and Mark Twain. They moved beyond a superficial portrayal of social reality. Henry James probed deeply at the individual psychology of his characters, writing in a rich and intricate style that supported his intense scrutiny of complex human experience. Mark Twain, breaking out of the narrow limits of local color fiction, described the breadth of American experience.

AMERICAN ROMANTICISM（美国浪漫主义）

The Romantic Period covers the first half of the 19th century. A rising America with its ideals of democracy and equality, its industrialization, its westward expansion, and a variety of foreign influences such as Sir Walter Scott were among the important factors which made literary expansion and expression not only possible but also inevitable in the period immediately following the nation's political independence. Yet, Romantics frequently shared certain general characteristics: moral enthusiasm, faith in value of individualism and intuitive perception, and a presumption that the natural world was a source of goodness and man's societies a source of corruption. Romantic values were prominent in American politics, art and philosophy until the Civil War. The Romantic exaltation of the individual suited the nation's revolutionary heritage and its frontier egalitarianism.

Washington Irving deserves credit for the part he played in inspiring the American Romantic imagination. His fascinating *The Sketch Book* with two of his most famous stories, "Rip Van Winkle" and "The Legend of Sleepy Hollow" will be placed at the top of any reading list for course on American literature. The importance of the frontier and the wilderness in American literature was for the first time well-illustrated in James Fenimore Cooper's *The Leatherstocking Tales* and was to remain a major concern for many later authors.

American romanticism culminated around the 1840s in what has come to be known as "New England transcendentalism" or "American Renaissance". One of the major literary figures in this period is Ralph Waldo Emerson. Ralph Waldo Emerson's *Nature* has been called "the manifesto of American transcendentalism". Henry David Thoreau, the author of *Walden* was a faithful follower of Ralph Waldo Emerson.

Shaping an American poetry out of the native elements of the New World, Walt Whitman and Emily Dickinson were the two major American poets of the 19th century. Walt Whitman tried to write poetry describing the native American experience, and Emily Dickinson wrote about the life of her time in her completely original way.

Nathaniel Hawthorne and Herman Melville belonged to another type of romanticists. Nathaniel Hawthorne did not feel comfortable with Ralph Waldo Emerson's buoyant sense of optimism about man and his nature. Herman Melville was critical of Ralph Waldo Emerson's optimistic view of life, as is shown in his famous work *Moby Dick*. Such Romantic writers placed increasing value on the free expression of emotion and displayed increasing attention to the psychic states of their characters. Heroes and heroines exhibited extremes of sensitivity and excitement. The novel of terror became the profitable literary staple. A preoccupation with the demonic and the mystery of evil marked the works of Edgar Allan Poe, Nathaniel Hawthorne, Herman Melville, and a host of minor writers.

The New England poets, such as Henry Wadsworth Longfellow and William Cullen Bryant formed a different school from Ralph Waldo Emerson, Henry David Thoreau, Walt Whitman, Emily Dickinson and Edgar Allan Poe.

AMERICAN TRANSCENDENTALISM（美国先验主义）

In New England, an intellectual movement known as transcendentalism developed as an American version of romanticism. The movement began among an influential set of authors based in Concord, Massachusetts and was led by Ralph Waldo Emerson. Like romanticism, transcendentalism rejected both the 18th-century rationalism and established religion, which for the transcendentalists meant the Puritan tradition in particular. The transcendentalists celebrated the power of the human imagination to commune with the universe and transcend the limitations of the material world. They found their chief source of inspiration in nature. Ralph Waldo Emerson's essay *Nature* was the major document of the transcendental school and stated the ideas that were to remain central to it.

BOHEMIANISM（波西米亚主义）

Bohemianism refers to the living style which is unconventional or abnormal. Many idealistic young Americans who had volunteered to take part in the "war to end wars", discovered that modern warfare was not glorious or heroic. Disillusioned by slogans of patriotism and glory, disgusted by the new frivolous, greedy, heedless way of life in America, and alarmed by the low level of culture, many young Americans adopted such a "bohemian", that is, unconventional living style. They lived among writers, artists and actors in a cheap section of New York City called Greenwich Village.

DEISM（自然神论）

Deism is derived from *deus*, the Latin word for god. Deism is not a specific religion but rather a particular perspective on the nature of God. Deists believe that a creator god does exist, but that after the motions of the universe were set in place, he retreated, having no further interaction with the created universe or the beings within it. Deism gained prominence in the 17th and 18th centuries during the Age of Enlightenment. Deistic ideas influenced several leaders of the American and French Revolutions.

HARLEM RENAISSANCE（哈莱姆文艺复兴）

Harlem Renaissance, also known as the "New Negro Movement", was a burst of literary achievement in the 1920s by Negro playwrights, poets, and novelists who presented new insights into the American experience and prepared the way for the emergence of numerous Black writers after mid-20th century. (Black Arts Movement—the mid 1960s to the mid 1970s) Harlem Renaissance was more than just a literary movement: It included racial consciousness, "the back to Africa" movement led by Marcus Garvey, racial integration, the explosion of music, particularly jazz, spirituals and blues, painting, dramatic revues, and others.

HEMINGWAY HEROES（海明威式英雄）

The Hemingway heroes refers to some protagonists in Ernest Hemingway's works. Such a hero usually is an average man of decidedly masculine tastes, sensitive and intelligent. And usually he is a man of action and of few words. He is such an individualist, alone even when with other people, somewhat an outsider, keeping emotions under control, stoic and self-disciplined in a dreadful place where one cannot get happiness. Frederic Henry in *A Farewell to Arms* is completely disillusioned. He has been to the war, but has seen nothing sacred and glorious. Like Jake Barnes in *The Sun Also Rises* who hates to talk about the war, Henry is shocked into the realization that "abstract words such as glory, honor, courage, or hallow were obscene", and feels "always embarrassed by words such as glory, sacred and sacrifice." The Hemingway heroes stand for a whole generation. In a world which is essentially chaotic and meaningless, a Hemingway hero fights a solitary struggle against a force he does not even understand. The awareness that it must end in defeat, no matter how hard he strives, engenders a sense of despair. But Hemingway heroes possess a kind of "despairing courage" as Bertrand Russell terms. It is this courage that enables a man to behave like a man, to assert his dignity in face of adversity. This is the essence of a code of honor in which all of Ernest Hemingway's heroes believe, whether he is Nick Adams, Jake Barnes, Frederic Henry, Robert Jordan, Santiago or the undefeated bullfighter. But surely they differ, some from others, in their view of the world. The difference which comes gradually in view is an index to the subtle change which Ernest Hemingway's outlook had undergone.

IMAGISM(意象主义)

A movement in early 20th-century Anglo-American poetry that favored precision of imagery and clear, sharp language. It came into being as a reaction to the traditional English poetry to express the sense of fragmentation and dislocation. Imagism called for a return to what were seen as more classical values, such as directness of presentation and economy of language, as well as a willingness to experiment with non-traditional verse forms. Imagists use free verse. Imagist publications appearing between 1914 and 1917 featured works by many of the most prominent modernist figures, both in poetry and in other fields. The Imagist group was centered in London, with members from Great Britain, Ireland and the United States. A characteristic feature of Imagism is its attempt to isolate a single image to reveal its essence. The poem of Ezra Pound entitled *In a Station of the Metro* is the most outstanding representative poem of this movement.

INTERNATIONAL THEME（国际主题）

International theme refers to the meeting of America and Europe, American innocence in contrast with European decadence and the moral and psychological complications arising therefore. The typical pattern of the conflict between the two cultures could be that of a young American man or girl who goes to Europe and affronts his or her destiny. Marriage and love are used by Henry James as the focal point of the confrontation between the two value systems, and the protagonist usually goes through a painful process of spiritual growth, gaining knowledge of good and evil from the conflict.

LOCAL COLORISM（地方色彩主义）

Hamlin Garland defined local colorism as having "such quality of texture and background that it could not have been written in any other place or by anyone else than a native." Local color fiction had a brief vogue when realism first emerged in the United States. It mixed Romantic plots with realistic descriptions of things which were readily observed, i.e., with the customs, dialects, sights, smell, sounds of regional America. Local colorism or regionalism as a trend first made its presence felt in the late 1860s and early 1870s in America. The movement once was so much widespread that it became contagious. The list of names of the local colorists is a long one among which Mark Twain is the most remarkable. They presented some ingenious and authentic regional stories of the life of the common people. Local color fiction reached its culmination in the 1880s, but by the turn of the century it had lost its vogue and began to decline since its subject matter was more and more limited and its most popular writers were caught in its set practices or turned to adopt other artistic forms. Mark Twain was the one who broke out of the narrow limits of local color fiction, described the breadth of American experience as no one had ever done before.

MEDITATIVE POETRY（冥想诗）

Meditative poetry combines the religious practice of meditation with verse. It occurs in many cultures. Especially Buddhist and Hindu writers have developed extensive theories and phase models for meditation. In Christianity, meditation became a major devotional practice during the Middle Ages. During the Protestant Reformation and Counter-Reformation, Jesuits like Ignatius of Loyola formalized the process of meditation, as a channeling of memory, understanding and will. Puritan meditation emphasized self-examination, applying Bible verses to contemporary, everyday life. Ralph Waldo Emerson's essay *Nature* (1836) freed the meditation from its theological underpinnings and its reliance on the Bible. He encouraged poets to view nature as a storehouse of symbols that they could use simply relying on their imagination. Walt Whitman and Emily Dickinson took meditation into this direction and paved the way for modernist and postmodernist practices in poetry. The method of the three main steps (composition of place, examination of points, colloquies) had survived into the 20th century in many poems, as had the devotional practice of verse meditation. Leading modernist poets like Thomas Stearns Eliot and Wallace Stevens began to fragmentarize the process, blending thoughts and sense perceptions in a sort of spiritual diary. Postmodernist poets like John Ashbery deconstruct the contemplative aspect, the reference of the poem to an object outside itself, dissolving narrative or episodic structures of the spiritual diary in an ironic and open association, and thereby turning the poem itself into the object the reader can use for contemplation or meditation.

Meditative poetry has often been correlated to relaxation through poetry, which is simply using poetry to relax or relieve stress whenever someone is in need. It can also be seen in group visualization sessions where a speaker tries to get the audience to forget all about their stress by the use of calm and relaxing poetry.

MODERNISM（现代主义）

Modernism is a general term applied retrospectively to the wide range of experimental and avant-garde trends in literature of the early 20th century, including symbolism, futurism, Expressionism, Imagism, Vorticism, Dadaism, and surrealism, along with the innovations of the unaffiliated writers. Modernist literature is characterized chiefly by a rejection of the 19th-century traditions and of their consensus between author and reader: the conventions of realism, for instance, were abandoned by Franz Kafka and other novelists, and by expressionist drama, while several poets rejected traditional meters in favor of free verse. Modernist writers tended to see themselves as an avant-garde disengaged from bourgeois values, and disturbed their readers by adopting complex and difficult new forms and styles.

MULTIPLE POINTS OF VIEW（多重叙事视角）

The modern American writer William Faulkner used a remarkable range of techniques, themes and tones in his fiction. He successfully advanced two modern literary techniques, one was stream of consciousness, and the other was multiple points of view. William Faulkner was a master at presenting multiple points of view, showing within the same story how the characters reacted differently to the same person or the same situation. The use of this technique gave the story a circular form wherein one event was the center, with various points of view radiating from it. The multiple points of view technique makes the reader recognize the difficulty of arriving at a true judgment.

NEW CRITICISM（新批评）

A dominant trend in English and American literary criticism of the mid-20th century, from the 1920s to the early 1960s. Its adherents were emphatic in their advocacy of close reading and attention to texts themselves, and their rejection of criticism based on extra-textual sources, especially biography. They insisted on treating the poem as a self-sufficient verbal object; warned against the critical practices that distract the reader from the poem itself; and avoided readings that relied upon biographical, psychological or historical context. New criticism had its advantages in guiding people's new way of reading and commenting, but its limitations also abound.

PSYCHOLOGICAL REALISM（心理分析现实主义）

The realistic writing that probes deeply into the complexities of characters' thoughts and motivations. Henry James's novel *The Ambassadors* is considered to be a masterpiece of psychological realism. And Henry James is considered the founder of psychological realism. He believes that reality lies in the impressions made by life on the spectator, and not in any facts of which the spectator is unaware. Such realism is therefore merely the obligation that the artist assumes to represent life as he sees it, which may not be the same life as it "really" is.

SCHOOL-ROOM POETS（校园诗人）

School-room poets, also called "New England poets" or "Fireside poets", refer to Henry Wadsworth Longfellow, Oliver Wendell Holmes, Sr., James Russell Lowell and John Greenleaf Whittier. They began writing during the time of Ralph Waldo Emerson, Nathaniel Hawthorne and Herman Melville. Their visions, however, were neither strictly transcendental nor difficult or bleak. They did not form an organized group, but history has linked them for what they had in common. They were often concerned with ordinary American people and values. Their poems were inspiring and easy to read; they made the reading of poetry immensely popular. But they were likely conservative and imitative. The names suggest their honored place in American schools and homes during the 1800s. Their contribution to the development of American poetry deserves appreciation and recognition.

SEPARATISTS（英国教会分离派）

The Puritans in the colonial period who had gone to extremes. Unlike the majority of Puritans, they saw no hope of reforming the Church of England from within. They felt that the influences of politics and the court had led to corruptions within the church. They wished to break away from the Church of England. Among them is the Plymouth Plantation group. They wished to follow Calvin's model, and to set up "particular" churches.

SHORT STORY（短篇小说）

A brief prose fiction, usually one that can be read in a single sitting. It generally contains the six major elements of fiction—characterization, setting, theme, plot, point of view, and style. Characterization refers to the way an author develops the personalities of the characters. In a short story there is usually only one character whose personality is fully developed; there are rarely more than two or three. The main character is often called the protagonist. The setting is the time and place in which the events occur. Most short stories have only one setting that is described in detail and rarely more than two or three settings. The theme is the main idea that the writer communicates to the reader. In a short story there is usually one theme. The plot is the series of events that takes us from a beginning to an end. Each event in the plot is related to the conflict, the struggle that the main character undergoes. Traditionally, a short story opens with exposition, background information vital to our understanding of what will follow. The events in the story follow a rising action until they reach a climax—the point of highest dramatic tension or excitement. After the climax a falling action leads to a resolution—a conclusion in which the conflict is resolved and the "knot" of the plot is untied. The resolution of the story is sometimes called the denouement, a French word meaning "untying".

SOUTHERN RENAISSANCE（南方文艺复兴）

Southern Renaissance refers to the reinvigoration of American Southern literature that began in the 1920s and 1930s with the appearance of writers such as William Faulkner and others. For writers in the South, the questions often involved a desire to protect tradition and myth from being destroyed by the influx of new ways of thinking and living. Southern Renaissance explores some of the ways writers who either lived in, wrote about, or were otherwise associated with the South between 1920 and 1950 responded to the many changes during the period. Among the writers of the Southern Renaissance, William Faulkner is arguably the most influential and famous, having won the Nobel Prize in Literature in 1949 (for his anti-racist *Intruder in the Dust*).

STREAM OF CONSCIOUSNESS（意识流）or "INTERIOR MONOLOGUE"（内心独白）

Stream of consciousness is one of the modern literary techniques. It was first used in 1922 by the Irish novelist James Joyce. This modernistic trend in 1920s, deeply influenced by the psycho analytic theories of Sigmund Freud, adopted the psycho-analytic approach in literary creation to explore the existence of sub-conscious and unconscious elements in the mind. In English fiction, the novels of stream of consciousness were represented by James Joyce and Virginia Woolf. Those novels broke through the bounds of time and space, and depicted vividly and skillfully the unconscious activity of the mind fast changing and flowing incessantly, particularly the hesitant, misted, distracted and illusory psychology people had when they faced reality. Britain was the center of the novels of stream of consciousness. The modern American writer William Faulkner successfully advanced this technique. In his stories, action and plots are less important than the reactions and inner musings of the narrators. Time sequences are often dislocated. The reader feels himself to be a participant in the stories, rather than an observer. A high degree of emotion can be achieved by this technique. But it also makes the stories hard to understand.

SURREALISM（超现实主义）

Surrealism was launched as a concerted artistic movement in France by Andre Breton's *Surrealist Manifesto* (1924). It was a successor to the brief movement known as Dadaism, which emerged in 1916 out of disgust with the brutality and destructiveness of the First World War, and set out, according to its manifestos, to engender a negative art and literature that would destroy the false values of modern bourgeois society, including its rationality and the art and literature it had fostered. Among the exponents of Dadaism were, for a time, artists and poets such as Tristan Tzara, Marcel Duchamp, Man Ray, and Max Ernst.

The expressed aim of surrealism was a revolt against all restraints on free creativity, including logical reason, standard morality, social and artistic conventions and norms, and all control over the artistic process by forethought and intention. To ensure the unhampered operation of the "deep mind", which they regarded as the only source of valid knowledge as well as art, surrealists turned to automatic writing (writing delivered over to the promptings of the unconscious mind), and to exploiting the material of dreams, of states of mind between sleep and waking, and of natural or artificially induced hallucinations.

Surrealism is a revolutionary movement in painting, sculpture, and the other arts, as well as literature; and it often joins forces, although briefly, with one or another revolutionary movement in the political and social realm. The effects of surrealism extended far beyond the small group of its professed adherents such as Andre Breton, Louise Aragon, and the painter Salvador Dali. The influence, direct or indirect, of surrealist innovations can be found in many modern writers of prose and verse who have broken with conventional modes of artistic organization to experiment with free association, a broken syntax, nonlogical order, dreamlike and nightmarish sequences, and juxtaposition of bizarre, shocking, or seemingly unrelated images. In England and America such effects can be found in a wide range of writings, from the poetry of Dylan Thomas to the flights of fantasy, hallucinative writing, starling inconsequences, and black humor in the novels of Henry Miller, William Burroughs, and Thomas Pynchon.

SYMBOLISM（象征主义）

Symbolism is the writing technique of using symbols. A symbol is something that conveys two kinds of meaning; it is simply itself, and it stands for something other than itself. In other words, a symbol is both literal and figurative. People, places, things and even events can be used symbolically. A symbol is a way of telling a story and a way of conveying meaning. The best symbols are those that are believable in the lives of the characters and also convincing as they convey a meaning beyond the literal level of the story. Nathaniel Hawthorne and Herman Melville were the two masters of symbolism. For example, the scarlet letter "A" on Hester's breast can give you symbolic meanings. If the symbol is obscure or ambiguous, then the very obscurity and the ambiguity may also be part of the meaning of the story.

THE BEAT GENERATION（垮掉的一代）

The Beat Generation is a term used to describe a group of American writers who came to prominence in the late 1950s and early 1960s, and the cultural phenomena that they wrote about and inspired: a rejection of mainstream American values, experimentation with drugs and alternate forms of sexuality, and an interest in Eastern spirituality. The major works of Beat writing are Allen Ginsberg's *Howl* (1956), William Seward Burroughs II's *Naked Lunch* (1959) and Jack Kerouac's *On the Road* (1957). During the 1960s, the rapidly expanding Beat culture underwent a transformation: the Beat Generation gave way to the 1960s counterculture, which was accompanied by a shift in public terminology from "beatnik" to "hippie".

THE BLACK MOUNTAIN POETS（黑山派诗人）

Sometimes called projectivist poets, were a group of mid-20th century American avant-garde or postmodern poets centered on Black Mountain College. In 1950, Charles Olson published his seminal essay *Projective Verse*. In this, he called for the poetry of "open field" composition to replace traditional closed poetic forms with an improvised form that should reflect exactly the content of the poem. This form is to be based on the line, and each line is to be a unit of breath and of utterance. The content is to consist of "one perception immediately and directly (leading) to a further perception". This essay was to become a kind of *de facto* manifesto for the Black Mountain poets. One of the effects of narrowing the unit of structure in the poem down to what could fit within an utterance was that the Black Mountain poets developed a distinctive style of poetic diction (e.g. "yr" for "your"). In addition to Charles Olson, the poets most closely associated with Black Mountain include Larry Eigner, Robert Duncan, Ed Dorn, Paul Blackburn, Hilda Morley, John Wieners, Joel Oppenheimer, Denise Levertov, Jonathan Williams and Robert Creeley.

THE CONFESSIONAL SCHOOL（自白派）

Confessional poetry or "confessionalism" is a style of poetry that emerged in the United States during the 1950s. It has been described as poetry "of the personal", focusing on extreme moments of individual experience, the psyche, and personal trauma, including previously taboo matter such as mental illness, sexuality, and suicide, often set in relation to broader social themes. It is sometimes also classified as postmodernism. The school of confessional poetry is associated with several poets who redefined American poetry in 1950s and 1960s, including Robert Lowell, Sylvia Plath, John Berryman, Anne Sexton, Allen

Ginsberg, and William De Witt Snodgrass.

THE JAZZ AGE（爵士时代）

The Jazz Age refers to the 1920s in America characterized by frivolity and carelessness. It was brought vividly to life in Francis Scott Key Fitzgerald's *The Great Gatsby*. To many, World War I was a tragic failure of old values, old politics and old ideas. The social mood was one of confusion and despair. Yet, on the surface the mood in America did not seem desperate. It entered a decade of prosperity and exhibitionism. Fashions were extravagant; more and more automobiles crowded the roads; advertising flourished. This was the Jazz Age, when New Orleans musicians moved "up the river" to Chicago and the theater of New York's Harlem pulsed with the music that had become a symbol of the time. These were the roaring twenties. It served to mask a quiet pain, the sense of loss.

THE LOST GENERATION（迷惘的一代）

The Lost Generation is also termed as the Sad Young Men, which was created by Francis Scott Key Fitzgerald in his book *All the Sad Young Men*. The term in general refers to the post-World War I generation, but specifically a group of US writers who came of age during the war and established their reputation in the 1920s. It stems from a remark made by Gertrude Stein to Ernest Hemingway, "You are all a lost generation." Ernest Hemingway used it as an epigraph to *The Sun Also Rises*, a novel that captures the attitudes of a hard-drinking, fast living set of disillusioned young expatriates in postwar Paris. The generation was "lost" in the sense that its inherited values were no longer relevant in the postwar world and because of its spiritual alienation from US, they seemed hopelessly provincial, materialistic, and emotionally barren. The term embraces Ernest Hemingway, Francis Scott Key Fitzgerald, John Dos Passos, Edward Estlin Cummings and so on.

THE NEW YORK SCHOOL（纽约派）

The New York School (synonymous with abstract expressionist painting) was an informal group of American poets, painters, dancers, and musicians active in the 1950s and 1960s in New York City. The poets, painters, composers, dancers, and musicians often drew inspiration from surrealism and the contemporary avant-garde art movements, in particular action painting, abstract Expressionism, Jazz, improvisational theater, experimental music, and the interaction of friends in the New York City art world's vanguard circle. Concerning the New York School poets, critics argue that their works are a reaction to the Confessionalist Movement in contemporary poetry. Their poetic subject matter is often light, violent, or observational, while their writing style is often described as cosmopolitan and world-traveled. The poets often wrote in an immediate and spontaneous manner reminiscent of stream of consciousness writing, often using vivid imagery. Poets most often associated with the New York School are John Ashbery, Frank O'Hara, Kenneth Koch, James Schuyler, Barbara Guest, Ted Berrigan, Bernadette Mayer, Alice Notley, Kenward Elmslie, Ron Padgett, Lewis Warsh, and Joseph Ceravolo.

THE WASTE LAND PAINTERS（荒原派画家）

It refers to Francis Scott Key Fitzgerald, Ernest Hemingway, Thomas Stearns Eliot, William Faulkner. They all painted the post-war western world as a waste land, lifeless, and hopeless. Thomas Stearns Eliot's *The Waste Land* depicts a picture of modern social crisis, in which modern civilized society turns into a waste land due to ethnical degradation and disillusionment with dreams. *The Hollow Men* is no less depressing. Francis Scott Key Fitzgerald's *The Great Gatsby* is about the frustration and despair from the failure of the American dream. Ernest Hemingway's *The Sun Also Rises* and *A Farewell to Arms* portray the dilemma of modern man utterly thrown upon himself for survival in an indifferent world, revealing man's impotence and his despairing courage to assert himself against overwhelming odds.

TRANSCENDENTAL CLUB（先验俱乐部）

In 1842, many outstanding people, headed by Ralph Waldo Emerson, began to meet informally in Concord, home of American transcendentalism, for the purpose of discussing the new outlook on life. Their meeting, however, at a place called the Transcendental Club, tended to advertise the movement, and added prominence to it. Margaret Fuller edited a new magazine which served to stimulate interest in transcendentalism for several years. It was called *The Dial*, and served as a kind of unofficial organ for the new ideas.

UNITARIANISM（唯一神教派）

A new religious sect that grew up within the Puritan church and eventually separated from it. It emphasized the religious aspects of transcendentalism. Its principles, being more logical and rational, occupying a sort of middle ground between extremes, include the fatherhood of God, the brotherhood of men, the leadership of Jesus, salvation by character, and continual progress of mankind. It once had obvious influence on American transcendental writers, such as Ralph Waldo Emerson and Henry David Thoreau.

参考文献

Abrams, M. H. A Glossary of Literature Terms [M]. Beijing: Foreign Language Teaching and Research Press, 2004.

Booz, Elisabeth B. A Brief Introduction to Modern American Literature [M]. Shanghai: Shanghai Foreign Language Education Press, 1982.

Chace, William & Collie, Peter. An Introduction to Literature [M]. New York: Harcourt Brace Jovanovich, Inc., 1985.

Chang Yaoxin. A Survey of American Literature [M]. Tianjin: Nankai University Press, 1990.

Chang Yaoxin. Selected Readings in American Literature [M]. Tianjin: Nankai University Press, 1991.

Kearns, George. American Literature [M]. New York: Macmillan Publishing Company, 1984.

Mednick, Fred. An Introduction to American Literature [M]. Kaifeng: Henan University Press, 1985.

Wang Shouren. History of American Literature[M]. Shanghai: Shanghai Foreign Language Education Press, 2002.

Yang Qishen. Selected Readings in American Literature[M]. Shanghai: Shanghai Translation Press, 1989.

桂扬清，吴翔林. 英美文学选读 [M]. 北京：中国对外翻译出版公司，1991.

胡家峦. 英美诗歌名篇详注 [M]. 北京：中国人民大学出版社，2008.

李正栓. 美国文学简史与选读 [M]. 北京：清华大学出版社，2015.

李正栓. 英美诗歌欣赏 [M]. 北京：清华大学出版社，2021.

李正栓，白凤欣. 英语诗歌教程 [M]. 北京：高等教育出版社，2009.

李正栓，陈岩. 美国诗歌研究 [M]. 北京：北京大学出版社，2007.

李正栓，申玉革. 美国诗歌欣赏教程 [M]. 上海：复旦大学出版社，2022.

李正栓，申玉革. 英美诗歌欣赏教程 [M]. 北京：北京师范大学出版社，2014.

李正栓，吴伟仁，李圣轩. 美国文学史及选读：第一册 [M]. 第三版. 北京：外语教学与研究出版社，2022.

李正栓，吴伟仁，李圣轩. 美国文学史及选读：第二册 [M]. 第三版. 北京：外语教学与研究出版社，2022.

陶洁. 美国文学选读 [M]. 北京：北京大学出版社，2012.